SIXTEENTH STREET NW

Other Titles of Interest from Georgetown University Press

Between Freedom and Equality: The History of an African American Family in Washington, DC
Barbara Boyle Torrey and Clara Myrick Green

DC Jazz: Stories of Jazz Music in Washington, DC
Maurice Jackson and Blair A. Ruble, Editors

A Georgetown Life: The Reminiscences of Britannia Wellington Peter Kennon of Tudor Place
Grant S. Quertermous, Editor

*Georgetown's Second Founder: Fr. Giovanni Grassi's News on the Present Condition
of the Republic of the United States of North America*
Antonio Grassi, Translated and Introduced by Roberto Severino

George Washington's Final Battle: The Epic Struggle to Build a Capital City and a Nation
Robert P. Watson

Spy Sites of Washington, DC: A Guide to the Capital Region's Secret History
Robert Wallace and H. Keith Melton with Henry R. Schlesinger

SIXTEENTH STREET NW

WASHINGTON, DC'S AVENUE *of* AMBITIONS

John DeFerrari and Douglas Peter Sefton

GEORGETOWN UNIVERSITY PRESS / WASHINGTON, DC

Library of Congress Cataloging-in-Publication Data

Names: DeFerrari, John, author. | Sefton, Douglas Peter, author.
Title: Sixteenth Street NW : Washington, DC's avenue of ambitions /
John DeFerrari and Douglas Peter Sefton.
Description: Washington, DC : Georgetown University Press, [2022] |
Includes bibliographical references and index.
Identifiers: LCCN 2021005684 (print) | LCCN 2021005685 (ebook) |
ISBN 9781647121563 (hardcover) | ISBN 9781647121570 (ebook)
Subjects: LCSH: Architecture—Washington (D.C.)—History. | Sixteenth
Street (Washington, D.C.)—History. | Washington (D.C.)—History. |
Washington (D.C.)—Social life and customs.
Classification: LCC F203.7.S6 D44 2022 (print) |
LCC F203.7.s6 (ebook) | DDC 975.3—dc23
LC record available at https://lccn.loc.gov/2021005684
LC ebook record available at https://lccn.loc.gov/2021005685

♾ This paper meets the requirements of
ANSI/NISO Z39.48-1992 (Permanence of Paper).

23 22   9 8 7 6 5 4 3 2 First printing

Printed in the United States of America

Cover and interior design by Erin Kirk

Contents

Acknowledgments

THE WRITING OF THIS BOOK would not have been possible without the gracious assistance of many people. The authors are extremely grateful for all the assistance and encouragement we have received from many quarters. Jessica Smith and Anne McDonough of the Historical Society of Washington, DC, provided valuable assistance in locating and examining key historical photographs. The entire staff of the Washingtoniana Division of the DC Public Library—especially Mark Greek, Jerry McCoy, Derek Gray, and Michele Casto—provided critical assistance, as they always do, in accessing a variety of important source materials, including photographs from the *Washington Star* collection and the library's historical image collection. Others who helped with locating hard-to-find photographs included Katie Crabb, librarian, DC Department of Transportation; Sonja N. Woods, archivist, Howard University Moorland-Spingarn Research Center; Susan Raposa, US Commission of Fine Arts; and Tracie Logan, senior curator, United States Naval Academy Museum. Malcolm C. Peck and Elfa Halloway of the Church of the Holy City shared their time and archival information and provided an excellent tour of the church. Dr. Vicken Y. Totten shared her photographs and information about architect George Oakley Totten Jr. Others who helped track down elusive information and Sixteenth Street–related artifacts included Barbara D. Bates, Bill Rice, Ryan Shepard, and Wendy Turman, Jewish Historical Society. Sally Berk shared her encyclopedic knowledge of developer Harry Wardman. Hans Bruland, vice president and general manager of the Hay-Adams Hotel, graciously gave us access to the roof of the hotel to take photographs. Several people with experience living on and around Sixteenth Street, including Gloria Pineda, Denise Champion, Charles Robertson, and Anne Sellin, graciously shared their stories. The authors wish they had had an opportunity to meet with and hear from more former Sixteenth Street residents, but the onset of the pandemic in early 2020 cut those opportunities short.

The book is illustrated with a custom set of detailed maps that the authors hope will help orient the reader and show how different sites are spatially related. Charlie Lefrak prepared the map for the first chapter, and Matthew Gilmore created the maps for the rest of the book, seven in all. We deeply appreciate the time and energy that Charlie and Matthew spent developing these maps; they are a beautiful addition to the book. The project as a whole would not have come to fruition without the support and encouragement of Don Jacobs, senior acquisitions editor at the Georgetown University Press. We appreciate all of the help we have received from the Georgetown University Press staff in bringing this book to publication.

Perhaps most essential in helping us ensure the quality, completeness, and readability of the information contained herein was the assistance of our reviewers, Jane Levey, Frances White, and Kim Williams, who took the time to read the text and provided many useful and incisive comments. The book is far better as a result of their gracious and generous assistance. That said, the book remains the work of the authors—any omissions or inaccuracies are solely our responsibility.

INTRODUCTION

A Multiplicity of Ambitions

I n may 2020 one of the most significant events in the history of Sixteenth Street NW unfolded dramatically.[1] A massive popular uprising against police brutality took shape across the country following the death of George Floyd in Minneapolis. While some looting occurred in the first few days of demonstrations, the vast majority of protesters were peaceful. National news was made when police used violent tactics, including pepper spray, to clear demonstrators from Lafayette Square on June 1. The protesters were pushed a block up Sixteenth Street so that the president could hold up a Bible in front of historic Saint John's Episcopal Church at the corner of Sixteenth and H Streets NW, a move denounced by Right Reverend Mariann Budde, bishop of the Episcopal Diocese of Washington.

Sixteenth Street subsequently gained special significance when Mayor Muriel Bowser rechristened the two blocks between K Street and Lafayette Square as Black Lives Matter Plaza. DC government workers and volunteers painted a giant yellow "BLACK LIVES MATTER" mural on the street, large enough to be visible to satellites in space. It became one of the most memorable symbols of the grassroots movement and was copied in other cities, including New York City.

The hopes and convictions displayed on Sixteenth Street in 2020 are among the most vocal, but they are not the first social ambitions to find expression on this uniquely situated boulevard. Sixteenth Street is broad and ceremonial by design, extending ramrod straight from the White House to the Maryland line seven miles north. It offers cultural as well as architectural diversity. The lofty social ambitions and conspicuous consumption of late nineteenth- and early twentieth-century residents are still on display, but the aspirations of ordinary Washingtonians are witnessed here as well. This book charts Washington history in both the buildings that have lined this avenue and the lives that have been lived within them.

The street's rich history, from its dirt-path beginnings through to the imposing churches, office buildings, apartments, and rowhouses built in the mid-twentieth

Painted shortly before the designation of the blocks north of Lafayette Square as Black Lives Matter Plaza in June 2020, the Black Lives Matter street mural is partially visible in this view from the Hay-Adams Hotel. *Authors' collection.*

century, is recounted here, with discussions of sites along the full length of the street rather than just the downtown segment. The street's great Beaux-Arts mansions and other early twentieth-century architectural landmarks have been previously studied in an excellent two-volume architectural history prepared by the US Commission of Fine Arts in the 1980s.[2] While some of the same buildings appear in these pages, our emphasis is different. This book aims for a broader cultural chronicle, albeit with less detail about any given landmark.

In terms of prestige, Sixteenth Street has seen plenty of competition, especially from two of the city's other grand boulevards: Massachusetts Avenue NW and Connecticut Avenue NW. In some regards, it has lost to both. While the ambitious and powerful Mary Foote Henderson, the doyenne of Sixteenth Street's development (see chapter 3), worked hard to lure diplomatic missions to Sixteenth Street, Massachusetts Avenue between Dupont Circle and Wisconsin Avenue NW remains the capital's key diplomatic precinct to this day. Dozens of major embassies line the avenue and adjoining streets, whereas only a few remain in Henderson's Meridian Hill enclave.[3] Massachusetts Avenue benefited from the tireless support of Henderson's contemporary Charles C. Glover (1846–1936), a banker and philanthropist who wooed diplomats and donated land and money toward establishing parkland around Massachusetts Avenue, including Glover-Archbold Park and parts of Rock Creek Park.

Sixteenth Street's rivalry with Connecticut Avenue, on the other hand, was for apartment houses, a different sort of residential prestige. Connecticut Avenue had gained prominence in the 1870s and 1880s when posh private residences—including a few embassies—were built in the blocks between Farragut Square and Dupont Circle. Then, in 1890, Senator Francis G. Newlands (1846–1917), along with several other wealthy investors, extended the avenue to the Maryland line, equipping it with streetcar service and establishing the suburb of Chevy Chase, Maryland, near its terminus. The resulting residential corridor, originally pristine and bucolic, would attract luxurious apartment houses from Kalorama to Chevy Chase for decades to come. As a rival commuter artery, Sixteenth Street also drew extensive apartment house development (chapter 4). If zoning hadn't effectively banned apartment buildings north of Piney Branch, Sixteenth Street might well have hosted as many apartment houses as Connecticut Avenue.

Rather than the most famous, the most prestigious, or the most opulent, Sixteenth Street has had a mix of everything. While the emphasis has always been on residential living—there have been only a handful of retail stores on the street and almost no industrial facilities or government offices—Sixteenth Street abodes have ranged from modest frame houses to imposing mansions. In 1900 visionary urban planner Franklin W. Smith deplored the "shanties" and tumble-down stables on Sixteenth Street between L and M Streets, urging they be torn down (chapter 2). Mary Foote Henderson and her husband, Senator John B. Henderson, likewise had no use for the humble frame dwellings inhabited primarily by African Americans on Meridian Hill, across Sixteenth Street from their extravagant castle (chapter 3). While Smith and the Hendersons got what they wanted in the near term, their visions ultimately would not determine what was built on Sixteenth Street or who would live there. In fact, this may be what makes Sixteenth Street's story most interesting: the push and pull of the diverse forces, democratic and otherwise, that have influenced the street's development.

Sixteenth Street stands as a microcosm of the District's urban planning history. The first part of the street to be laid out and eventually paved—from Lafayette Square to what would become Florida Avenue NW—closely followed Peter L'Enfant's plan for the capital, as refined by Andrew Ellicott. A planned street from the start, the ceremonial expanse of Sixteenth Street was imposed on a marshy scrubland. With Lafayette Square, one of the city's earliest residential enclaves, at its southern end, Sixteenth Street attracted some of the city's earliest restrictions on real estate development at the end of the nineteenth century. The looming Cairo apartment building at 1615 Q Street NW, only half a block from Sixteenth Street, spurred the city's first height restrictions on new development when it was completed in 1894.

Meanwhile, the wealthy were busy building mansions from Lafayette Square to Scott Circle and beyond. When the DC commissioners surveyed property owners about restricting development on Sixteenth Street in 1905, the results were overwhelmingly in favor of limiting the street to residential use. Streetcars—noisy, bustling, and associated with the city's major commercial corridors—never plied Sixteenth Street. DC established its first zoning rules in 1920, limiting the entire length of Sixteenth Street to residential use (chapter 4). It was only in 1947 that a special, limited modification allowed office buildings below Scott Circle (chapter 6). Finally, beginning in the 1980s, designations under the city's 1979 historic preservation statute set limits on how historic structures can be modified (epilogue). Within this carefully curated environment, a rich assortment of individual homesteads, apartment complexes, institutional headquarters buildings, religious congregations, and parks have taken root.

Roughly speaking, Sixteenth Street has four major segments. From Lafayette Park to Scott Circle is the downtown part. It has probably seen the greatest change of any portion of the street. It began as hardly much of a street at all, a dirt road with one beautiful church (Saint John's) and not much else. It certainly wasn't at the center of the city, socially or commercially. Pennsylvania Avenue, between the Capitol and the White House, attracted early business development, while Georgetown was an earlier residential center. Sixteenth Street was on the outskirts—the boondocks of the nascent town in the early 1800s. Now it is a prestigious address for fine hotels, national associations, legal firms, and expensive office buildings.

The second section of Sixteenth extends from Scott Circle to Florida Avenue, the boundary of the original Washington City and the foot of Meridian Hill. There are a variety of buildings along this stretch, but most are residential. Early twentieth-century apartment buildings and a few churches are scattered throughout, as well as a few modern insertions, but this section is dominated by Victorian rowhouses. It shows off the rowhouse style of Washington living to great advantage. Most of the houses are a bit fancier and more varied than the more uniform rowhouses that line many other DC streets.

The third section stretches from Florida Avenue up Meridian Hill to the bridge over Piney Branch, sometimes called the Tiger Bridge for its statuary. This is the street's most varied section. Beyond the formally landscaped park, alternately known as Meridian Hill Park and Malcom X Park, stand impressive early twentieth-century mansions interspersed with tall apartment buildings built from the 1920s through the 1960s. This is where Mary Foote Henderson had her greatest influence, reflected in the stunning mansions that were once homes to top Washington diplomats. Among the many apartment buildings, some elegant and some mundane, rise many of Sixteenth Street's most impressive religious structures. Since the 1920s, Sixteenth Street has been known as the Avenue of Churches or Church Row, with dozens lining its route. The ceremonial character of the route, its centrality and proximity to the White House, and its noncommercial character have combined to form a strong draw for religious groups.

The final section of the street is the long stretch from the Piney Branch Bridge to the Maryland border. Serenely residential, it features mostly detached single-family houses, with churches, synagogues, and a few schools peppered in along its long border with Rock Creek Park. Opened up in the early twentieth century, when shrewd property owners donated hundreds of acres of land to extend the wide boulevard to the edge of the District, this part of Sixteenth saw suburban-style house development begin around 1910 and continue through much of the twentieth century. In the late nineteenth century some well-to-do African Americans chose Sixteenth Street between K and M Streets to build their homes; beginning in the mid-twentieth century, they would increasingly choose the long, restful corridor north of the Piney Branch Bridge.

Sixteenth Street ultimately is a triumph—a triumph of Washingtonians living their lives in diversity and prosperity. It isn't as ceremonial as L'Enfant may have expected it to become. It isn't the boulevard of elites that Mary Henderson envisioned. It isn't any one person's vision of what it should have been. From the

White House to the office buildings full of lawyers and lobbyists, the Victorian townhouses, the drum groups in Malcom X Park, the apartment homes of Hispanic immigrants in Columbia Heights, the churches of every denomination, the tennis courts in Rock Creek Park, the fancy houses of the Gold and Platinum Coasts—there are slices of the best parts of the whole city here. As its slow evolution continues—changes to commuter patterns and downtown office buildings seem inevitable in the wake of the coronavirus pandemic—it remains an avenue to be proud of, an avenue that shows the best of what Washington can be, both as the nation's capital and as a great city for people to live in and call home.

ONE

Planning a Grand Avenue

T HE STORY OF Sixteenth Street NW begins with the original plans for the nation's capital on a site chosen as a result of a famous compromise. After much wrangling over where the national capital should be located, northerners agreed to put it in the south in exchange for southerners' acquiescence to northern wishes that the federal government assume states' debts from the Revolutionary War. George Washington selected the site, straddling Maryland and Virginia on the Potomac River, not far from his Mount Vernon home. The capital city would be located roughly at the center of the new diamond-shaped district—the District of Columbia—which would include the existing port towns of Georgetown in Maryland and Alexandria in Virginia, as well as the rural and undeveloped land surrounding them.

In 1791 George Washington chose Peter Charles L'Enfant (1754–1825) to draw up plans for the proposed new capital city. Born a French aristocrat, L'Enfant enthusiastically took up the cause of American independence and served as an engineer on Washington's staff. After the war, he designed Federal Hall in New York City, an early meeting space for the US Congress. L'Enfant quickly devised his plan for the new capital, but his quirky personality just as quickly proved too difficult for Washington and the city's newly appointed commissioners to work with. In 1792 Washington dismissed L'Enfant from the project. Development of the capital then proceeded according to a plan drawn up by Andrew Ellicott (1754–1820), the official surveyor for the new city, who largely followed L'Enfant's plan with a variety of minor revisions.[1]

As planned by L'Enfant and laid out by Ellicott, Sixteenth Street was to be one of the capital city's most prominent thoroughfares. Of the "grand avenues" designed to be wide enough to allow for "foot ways, walks of trees, and a carriage way," Sixteenth Street was one of only three that ran on a north-south axis, the other two being North and South Capitol Streets.[2] Ellicott's map shows Sixteenth Street heading north from the spacious open area, later known as Lafayette Square, in front of the president's house. Two blocks to the north Sixteenth intersects K Street, a broad east-west thoroughfare, then continues three blocks further to the future Scott Circle, another open space where Massachusetts and Rhode Island Avenues crisscross Sixteenth. The street proceeds through eight more blocks, finally ending at the original northern boundary of Washington City. Though not on Ellicott's map, Sixteenth intersected the path of the boundary here, a winding country road linking Georgetown on the western side with the village of Bladensburg, Maryland, to the east. Called Boundary Street in the nineteenth century, this route would be renamed Florida Avenue in 1890.[3]

The planned Sixteenth Street was just one piece in an elegant mosaic of interlaced avenues, public squares, and residential blocks that reflected the planners' lofty ambitions. Historians have argued that the plan devised by L'Enfant and enthusiastically embraced by George Washington was meant to celebrate American democracy, with the executive branch (President's House) and legislative branch (Capitol) in separate camps, as it were, linked by Pennsylvania Avenue. Diagonal avenues named after the states would energetically interconnect the gridded expanse of the new city, as if to map out the young nation's democratic ideals and economic ambitions.[4] L'Enfant wrote that the grand avenues of the city "will serve as does the main artery in the animal body, which diffuses life throughout the smaller vessels, and inspires vigor, and activity throughout the whole frame."[5]

Critics, on the other hand, have pointed out that L'Enfant's grand avenues had their roots in the baroque plan for Versailles, which was certainly far from democratic in its conception. In Europe, such wide, straight thoroughfares were built—at great expense—to speed the carriages and horses of the aristocracy, freeing them from the chaotic bustle of mere commoners, and were also ideal for ostentatious parades of military power—goals that George Washington and Thomas Jefferson clearly did not embrace. Another downside of wide streets is that they limit real estate development. L'Enfant's streets swallowed up 3,606 acres of the new 6,111-acre town, more than all of the other public and residential space.[6] Nevertheless, L'Enfant was convinced that nothing should get in the way of the grand scale of the federal city and that the nation would one day live up to it. Of the anticipated design for the new capital, he wrote to George Washington in 1789, "Although the means now within the power of the Country are not such as to pursue the design to any great extent, it will be obvious that the plan should be drawn on such a scale as to leave room for that aggrandizement and embellishment which the increase of wealth of the nation will permit it to pursue at any period however remote."[7]

According to L'Enfant's plan, Sixteenth Street and two other grand avenues—Connecticut Avenue and Vermont Avenue—all were to radiate from a semicircular forecourt in front of a palatial executive mansion. George Washington discreetly

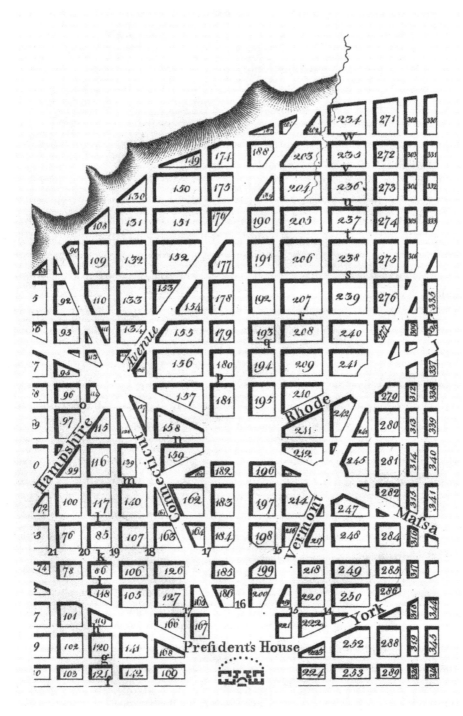

Excerpt from Andrew Ellicott's 1792 plan for the City of Washington, based on Peter L'Enfant's design. Sixteenth Street runs straight to the north from the center of the President's House. *Library of Congress.*

toned down the scale of the President's House. No forecourt was constructed, and the precise southern terminus of each of the three radiating avenues was left undefined. All three dissolved into the seven-acre open space that would later become Lafayette Square. It wasn't until James Madison was president that the decision was made to officially terminate the three avenues at H Street, a block away from the grounds of the executive mansion. Madison's successor, James Monroe, had the open space graded and turned into something resembling a park. In 1824 he named it Lafayette, after the French hero of the American Revolution who was making a grand tour of America at the time.[8]

George Washington and other early leaders confidently but naïvely believed they could plan a capital city from scratch and have it pay for its own development through the dynamo of American capitalism. Private lots would be sold for development, and the proceeds would pay for the city's infrastructure and public buildings. This scheme proved disastrous; few people were interested in investing in land uncertain to appreciate in a city that might never grow. The fledgling federal government inspired little economic confidence. Who was to say whether it would even survive, let alone stay in this spot? As a result, construction of new houses in the first few decades of the nineteenth century took place slowly, in fits and starts.

The impressive street grid, likewise, was slow to materialize—especially in the case of Sixteenth Street. With nowhere to go, this "grand avenue" simply petered out when it reached the Georgetown-Bladensburg Road at the city's boundary. For most of the nineteenth century, it was little more than a muddy path through a scrubland, much of it covered by marshes. Early on, trees were cleared as far as Massachusetts Avenue, but there was nothing prestigious about this route. A few wood-frame dwellings, brick kilns, and storage sheds dotted the blocks closest to Lafayette Square. New arrivals to the city had no reason to choose Sixteenth Street as a place to live or work.

The city's development in the early 1800s, limited as it was, was to the southeast of Sixteenth Street, mostly along or near Pennsylvania Avenue from the White House to the half-built Capitol one and a half miles away. After Abigail Adams moved into the unfinished President's House in November 1800, she wrote to her sister that the city was like "a new country, with houses scattered over a space of ten miles, and trees and stumps in plenty. . . . The country around is romantic, but a wild, a wilderness at present." Such would have been her view of the future Sixteenth Street from her front windows.[9]

Others were even more pessimistic. Sitting in his new federal office near the White House on July 4, 1800, treasury secretary Oliver Wolcott heaped scorn on life in the capital as he wrote a letter to his wife back in Connecticut. "I have made every exertion to secure good lodgings near the office, but shall be compelled to take them at the distance of more than half a mile," he wrote. "There are, in fact,

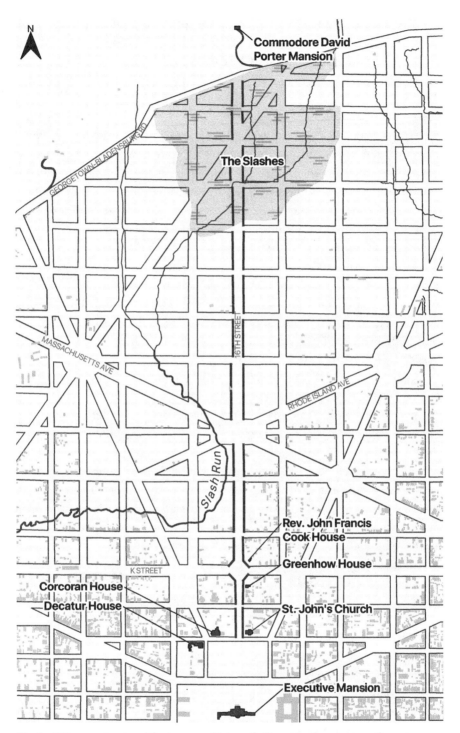

Key buildings and natural features on Sixteenth Street in the nineteenth century. Shown in gray are the footprints of all existing buildings in 1857; note that few stood on Sixteenth Street above L Street. © *Charlie Lefrak. Used by permission.*

but few houses at any one place, and most of them small miserable huts, which present an awful contrast to the public buildings. The people are poor, and, as far as I can judge, they live like fishes, by eating each other."[10]

Saint John's Church: Grandeur and Simplicity

Wolcott, of course, was exaggerating; no reports of cannibalism in early Washington have surfaced. Many early residents, like him, were newly arrived government employees seeking residences near the White House and the four handsome executive-branch office buildings, designed by English architect George Hadfield, that flanked it. As the bureaucrats and clerks that Wolcott disdained moved into the neighborhood, one of the things they needed was a place of worship.

The result was the first structure of any note to be constructed on Sixteenth Street: Saint John's Episcopal Church, designed by Benjamin Henry Latrobe (1764–1820) and completed in 1816, which remains to this day one of the city's most distinguished landmarks. Located across H Street from Lafayette Square, the church is known as the Church of the Presidents and has been attended by every one of them since James Madison. The Episcopal church in Washington had two earlier parishes, one in Georgetown (also called Saint John's) and one on Capitol Hill (Christ Church). The new edifice would supersede them as the flagship of the Episcopal church in the nation's capital.

Church records indicate that contracts were let to a master carpenter, Richard Skinner, and a brick mason, Peter Morte, to build the church. While there is no direct evidence that any enslaved people worked on the construction, it is certainly possible that at least a few were involved. It was a common practice in the early nineteenth century Washington to employ slave labor for tasks such as brick-making and sawing lumber, with the owners being paid for the work.[11] While it is not known whether Skinner and Morte made such arrangements, Skinner's work seems to have impressed the Saint John's building committee, which subsequently hired him to be the permanent church sexton.[12]

When it opened, the *Daily National Intelligencer*, owned by two of the parish's most prominent members, expressed "peculiar satisfaction" in announcing the church's completion. In understated terms typical of its era, the paper observed that "the beauty of its external, and elegance of the internal arrangements, combining grandeur and simplicity, are well calculated to make impressions favorable to . . . the public spirit of the citizens of Washington."[13]

"Grandeur" and "simplicity" are watchwords for the work of Latrobe, the nation's first professional architect and a master who tastefully embodied the orderliness of the Age of Reason. Born and raised in England, Latrobe was the son of a Moravian bishop and was imbued as much with the passion of the Protestant Reformation as with neoclassical ideology. He ultimately rebelled against the strict

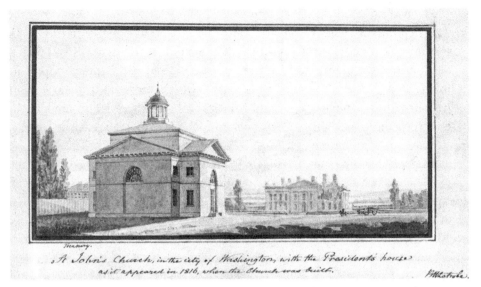

Sketch of Saint John's Church and the White House in 1816 by Benjamin Latrobe. The White House still shows damage from being burned by the British in August 1814. *Library of Congress.*

isolation of the Moravian sect but benefited from the rich and broad education he had received. A voracious learner, as a young man Latrobe mastered the architectural profession as an apprentice to the well-known London architect Samuel Pepys Cockerell before moving to America.[14]

Like L'Enfant, whom he considered an amateur, Latrobe was passionate about his work and deeply committed to rational, practical architecture.[15] He devoted some twenty years to architectural and engineering projects in Washington, the most important being his adaptations and improvements to William Thornton's design for the US Capitol. Thornton, who had no experience as an architect, produced a design with unrealistic spacing of columns on the façade, inadequate lighting and ventilation in many rooms, cramped stairwells, and many other flaws, all of which Latrobe expertly addressed. Latrobe also embellished James Hoban's design for the President's House, adding the grand prostyle portico on its north side facing Sixteenth Street across Lafayette Square. And on the west side of that square he designed a fashionable home for Commodore Stephen Decatur, which was completed just three years after Saint John's Church in 1819 and remains a noted historical landmark today.

For ecclesiastical architecture, Protestant English architects of Latrobe's era frowned on iconography and ornamentation, which were seen as the trappings of the Roman Catholic Church. Thus Saint John's originally had no statues or stained-glass windows and few decorative frills. Latrobe's design—for which he refused any compensation—is a masterwork. Despite its many alterations over the years, its core is an elegant circular auditorium nestled like a jewel in the center of a symmetrical Greek-cross floor plan. The main meeting space is completely open. Four sturdy columns originally stood at the corners of the room, supporting a broad, domed ceiling crowned with a cupola (or lantern, as it is more properly termed) that brought in daylight from above. The four shallow arms of the Greek cross emphasized the close-knit communal space; their large, clear windows bathed the space in natural light.

Elegant as the design may have been, the building was constructed on a budget; the walls are of brick, stuccoed in a common technique at the time to create an inexpensive stone-like appearance, and the floors were also originally brick rather than stone. The original layout of box pews within a circular aisle could seat just eighty-six.[16] Here was a serene meeting space where believers could congregate and contemplate the words of their pastor, spoken from a wineglass-shaped pulpit visible to all. Late in 1816, Latrobe boasted to his son that the church was "a pretty thing" that "has made people religious who were never before at church."[17]

The church was well attended from the start, but it was also woefully small. As early as 1818, church leaders began looking for ways to expand the building, both to accommodate more worshipers and to generate more income from the sale and rental of pews.[18] Church elders solicited a design for expanding the church from Charles Bulfinch (1763–1844), America's first great native-born architect, who was already busy designing the city's first Unitarian church, at Sixth and D Streets NW. What ultimately became of Bulfinch's proposal is unclear. The architect of the Saint John's expansion, completed in 1822, is not documented. The expansion lengthened the western arm of the Greek cross, bringing the front of the church up to the building line on Sixteenth Street. A new columned portico was added, as well as a bell tower. The church remains elegant and distinguished—perhaps the new façade was based on Bulfinch's proposal—but in any event Latrobe's design was seriously compromised. Latrobe's son John later commented that "my father designed St. John's Church, Washington, which was really a beautiful little thing in its day, before some dull fellow made a Roman Cross out of a Greek one, and stuck on a stupid, nondescript portico and an abominable pretext for a tower."[19]

Another celebrated architect, James Renwick (1818–95), the designer of the Smithsonian Castle, worked on an expansion of the church in the early 1880s. His additions were mainly to the chancel on the eastern end of the building. By this time, the earlier Protestant disdain for Gothic design elements had been forgotten, and stained-glass windows were now enthusiastically added to Saint John's, congregants fighting among themselves for the honor of sponsoring the most prominent windows. The interior took on a dark, Victorian look for a while before extensive renovations in 1919 removed these heavy decorative additions. Further

View of Saint John's Church from Lafayette Square, 1858, showing the 1822
extension of the church that added the columned portico and bell tower. The statue
of Andrew Jackson was erected in 1853 as Washington's first equestrian statue in a
public space. *Library of Congress.*

midcentury renovations strengthened the aging structure and restored some elements of the auditorium's original Latrobe design.[20]

In the 1810s Latrobe's church and the house he designed for Stephen Decatur
were among the few permanent buildings facing the large open area in front of
the President's House. However, by the time James Monroe named the square in
honor of the Marquis de Lafayette in 1824, it was beginning to attract the young
city's most prestigious residents. The minister of France, Jean-Guillaume, Baron
Hyde de Neuville, rented the Decatur house in the 1820s. He would be followed
by the minister of Russia and two secretaries of state: Henry Clay, while John
Quincy Adams was president, and Martin van Buren, who served under Andrew
Jackson. Doctors, lawyers, and other well-to-do Washingtonians built impressive
townhouses along all three sides of the square, which President Monroe had ordered to be graded and turned into a proper park. By the 1850s Lafayette Square
was the most fashionable place to live in Washington.

The grandest private residence of any note stood on H Street on the north side
of Lafayette Square, a block to the west of Sixteenth Street. This was the mansion
of William Wilson Corcoran (1798–1888), the fabulously wealthy banker who supported many of Washington's civic institutions and would endow its first public art
gallery.

Corcoran was born in Georgetown, the son of Thomas Corcoran, a prominent
Irish-born leather merchant who served as the town's elected mayor. The son's

Home of William W. Corcoran on H Street facing Lafayette Square, photographed in 1919. The US Chamber of Commerce building, completed in 1925, now stands on this site. *Authors' collection.*

first independent venture, in the dry goods business at age twenty-five, was a disaster, but Corcoran quickly regrouped and went into banking. His timing was impeccable; banking in Washington was in its infancy, leaving him few competitors. Corcoran used his personal connections to gain the trust of major clients, including the US government. With his partner, George Washington Riggs, the Corcoran & Riggs bank became enormously successful in the 1840s, allowing Corcoran to retire from banking in 1854, at age fifty-six, to devote his attention to other, mostly philanthropic, pursuits.[21]

In 1848 Corcoran bought the former home of his friend Daniel Webster on Lafayette Square. He then hired James Renwick to transform the simple three-story brick Federal-style house into a palatial mansion. The result was one of the city's first great Victorian houses, a sprawling Italianate complex with two wings extending broadly along H Street and a great, high-walled garden in back that reached all the way to I Street. Completed in 1852, the mansion's richly decorated parlors were filled with ornate furnishings, artworks, statuary, and ancient armor. When lit up at night for a party, the palatial residence would draw envious spectators in carriages and on foot to admire its unparalleled elegance.[22]

Other than Saint John's, Sixteenth Street saw few improvements in the first half of the nineteenth century. However, several important developments foreshadowed its future extension outside the city limits. Everything to the north of the existing road ending at Boundary Street was rugged countryside, a vast area of rolling hills covered with a mix of dense virgin woods, scattered small-scale farms, and rustic country estates. Though part of the District of Columbia, this land was a separate legal jurisdiction at the time called Washington County. L'Enfant's plan did not specify how Sixteenth or any other street would be extended into this rural landscape, and the steep hills at the edge of the city would remain a physical barrier to systematic residential development for much of the nineteenth century.

This doesn't mean, however, that Washington County was a desolate place. The farms and estates—the larger ones often relying in part on slave labor—cultivated a wide variety of crops, including wheat, corn, and rye that were ground into flour and meal at gristmills along Rock Creek and other streams. Farmers would fill their wagons with produce and bring it down to the Center Market at Seventh and Pennsylvania Avenue, a sprawling open-air bazaar, completed in 1801, that bustled with activity on market days.[23]

The estate houses, built by successful businessmen, landowners, and politicians, were often perched atop hills that offered commanding views of the city below and the Potomac River in the distance. One of the best spots for such a mansion was a steep outcropping that rose just beyond the Georgetown-Bladensburg Road in the line of Sixteenth Street. This was the spot Commodore David Porter (1780–1843) chose to build his estate.

Porter was one of three prominent senior naval officers who were called to Washington in 1815 to form the Board of Naval Commissioners, a committee charged with administering materiel support for the growing navy. In addition to Porter, Stephen Decatur, the country's most celebrated naval hero from the Barbary Wars and the War of 1812, was also nominated to the board, as was John Rodgers, famous for leading the successful defense of Baltimore from British attack in 1814. As was the custom in those days, each of these naval heroes had earned prize money from the US government for the ships and materiel they had seized in combat from the enemy, and each sought to reflect his wealth and prestige by building or moving into a suitably grand residence. As noted above, Stephen Decatur hired Benjamin Latrobe to design his elegant mansion on the northwest corner of the future Lafayette Square. Rodgers first settled into an existing house on the heights above Georgetown and later also lived on Lafayette Square before moving to a large house that he built on Greenleaf Point, near present-day Fort McNair.

Portrait of Commodore David Porter. *Courtesy of United States Naval Academy Museum.*

David Porter did the most extensive construction, building not only a grand estate house but a complete farm with barns, stables, slave quarters, and other structures on the promontory overlooking Sixteenth Street. Porter was one of the most colorful exemplars of the swashbuckling early days of the US Navy. Like many naval officers, he lived by a precarious code of honor, valuing rank and privilege above everything else. He was full of daring and initiative, but he was also plagued by insecurity, forever craving respect and advancement and resenting the accomplishments of his peers. Short of stature and not particularly dashing, he quarreled easily and often alienated his superiors.

In 1806 Porter married Evalina Anderson, daughter of a tavernkeeper in Chester, Pennsylvania. The couple had ten children.[24] One of their sons, David Dixon Porter, would rise to the rank of admiral during the Civil War and become widely celebrated. In addition, Porter's foster son, David Glasgow Farragut, would serve as the navy's first admiral, outshining both of the Porters.

While the elder Porter had earned his share of prize money from conquests during the War of 1812, he never collected as much as he believed he deserved. During the war, he commanded two ships that rounded Cape Horn and single-handedly wreaked havoc on the British whaling trade in the Pacific, capturing fifteen British whaling ships. However, none of those prize ships made it back to the

States; all were destroyed or recaptured by the British. In addition, Porter's own ship, the *Essex*, ultimately became trapped in the port of Valparaiso, Chile, where it fought and lost a bloody battle against a better-armed British frigate.[25] Porter thus came to Washington a hero with a mixed record.

Nevertheless, he was determined to live the life of a wealthy and prosperous war hero. Borrowing as much as he could, he spent thirteen thousand dollars—a fortune at the time—to purchase 110 acres of land just beyond Boundary Street in 1816 as the site for a large estate house and farm. The original property extended northwest to what is now Columbia Road and east to Fourteenth Street. Porter was the one who gave this estate the name Meridian Hill. The name derived from a marker that Thomas Jefferson had placed here in 1804 for a new American prime meridian that was supposed to run north from the White House through the marker. The prime meridian stands as a common reference point on the globe for measuring time and position. This American prime meridian was never widely adopted, however. It caused too much confusion for sailors accustomed to the English prime meridian, which ran through Greenwich. The Greenwich meridian would later be established as an international standard; the American version lives on only in the name Commodore Porter chose for this hill.[26]

Easily visible from the White House, Porter's mansion, completed in 1817, was designed by architect George Hadfield (1763–1826).[27] Born and trained in England, Hadfield's genius as an architect was recognized early, and he received many honors from the Royal Academy of Arts. American artist John Trumbull recommended him to George Washington, who recruited him from England to work on the US Capitol. Though rivals soon had him removed from the Capitol project, he remained in Washington as an architect for the rest of his life and designed many of the city's finest early buildings, including the original DC City Hall, the four executive office buildings that originally flanked the White House, and the Arlington House mansion, which overlooks the city from a steep hilltop across the Potomac and now stands at the center of Arlington National Cemetery.

Like Arlington House, Meridian Hill featured Neoclassical design elements, including a large central block with wings on either side. A majestic projecting portico supported by four classical columns looked down on Sixteenth Street below. No definitive drawings or photos of the house are known to have survived, but at the time the house was said to be "the finest in Washington."[28]

The beautifully sited Porter mansion became the scene for many elegant dinner parties. Porter's son, Admiral David Dixon Porter, later recalled that both his father and fellow navy commissioner Stephen Decatur were lavish spenders: "Although their entertainments materially affected their financial resources, yet they were the means of bringing the naval officers in contact with the men who held the public purse strings, and who were not always inclined to be liberal where the Navy was concerned."[29]

Part of the prestige came from the fact that Meridian Hill was not just a rural retreat but also a working farm. Porter had many servants performing a wide variety of jobs on his farm, including nursemaids, kitchen maids, dairymaids, boys to cut wood, and stable boys to groom horses and keep the mud off of Porter's carriage. As was typical of the larger estates in Washington County, these tasks were performed by a mix of enslaved and free servants. The 1820 US census lists six male and three female enslaved individuals in Porter's household, as well as one free Black.[30] These individuals were doubtless called upon to perform much of the tedious, backbreaking work required to keep a farm like Porter's in operation.

Porter's aim was to show that he could be just as successful as a farmer as he had been as a ship's captain. Unfortunately, the hill's gravelly soil was not well suited to this role. Admiral Porter commented vividly about his father's lack of success as a farmer:

> He had a kitchen garden of five acres, and had to buy vegetables for winter; he had a hundred acres in corn, oats, wheat, &c., and was obliged to purchase grain for his stock. He imported English bulls, at twelve hundred dollars apiece, people would not patronize them. He had the finest piggery in the country, but alas, it did not pay. Thousands of cart loads of manure were hauled upon the farm, only to be washed away by the spring rains; the place was in beautiful order, highly satisfactory to the casual observer, but it yielded absolutely nothing.[31]

Porter continued as a naval commissioner until 1822, when he grew restless and sought a fresh assignment at sea. He was charged with policing the Caribbean for pirates, who posed a serious threat to travel and trade. At one point, Porter "invaded" the island of Cuba, briefly landing with a small party of sailors to investigate stolen goods in the small town of Fajardo. Even though the Spanish did not protest the incursion, the administration of John Quincy Adams saw fit to court-martial Porter for this violation of Spain's sovereignty. Porter was found guilty and sentenced to a six-month suspension with pay.

Light as his sentence was, Porter could never accept the humiliation of being convicted. After resigning from the navy in 1826, he sought new adventures as head of the Mexican Navy, a three-year stint that proved frustrating and unrewarding. Porter wrote to his wife in late 1826 that he wished he could be at Meridian Hill, "that most beloved of all spots on the earth."[32] He would never get the chance to return. Two years later and virtually penniless, he was forced to put the estate up for sale. While his wife moved back to Chester, Pennsylvania, Porter was appointed envoy to Turkey by the new president, Andrew Jackson, a position he would retain until the end of his life.

At the time of his court-martial, Porter had profoundly alienated John Quincy Adams, and thus it is surprising that in 1829 Porter briefly rented Meridian Hill to Adams when Adams's presidential term expired. On March 3, 1829, the day before

Andrew Jackson took office, Adams walked out to Meridian Hill to take up his new residence, avoiding the raucous celebrations for the man who had thwarted his reelection bid.[33] Adams was said to have enjoyed his respite at Meridian Hill, pleasantly removed from the nasty partisan politics of Washington City, but his stay was brief. In August Porter sold the mansion (reportedly for only a third of what he had paid for it), and Adams was forced to clear out.[34]

Across Meridian Hill and Beyond

The Porter estate was not the only development on Meridian Hill. Just to the northeast lay the Washington Jockey Club's National Course racetrack, one of the most popular of the city's few entertainment venues of the early 1800s. It was constructed in about 1802 by wealthy Virginia landowner Colonel John Tayloe, who also owned the Octagon House at Eighteenth Street and New York Avenue NW, just west of the White House. Horse races were a semiannual event, usually taking place over several days in the spring and the fall, and they drew large crowds. Congressmen and ordinary Washingtonians alike flocked to the National Course track. Regarding the November 1803 race days, Reverend Manasseh Cutler, a representative from Massachusetts, wrote in his diary that attendees comprised "three and four thousand, black, white, and yellow; of all conditions from the President of the United States to the beggar in his rags, of all ages and of both sexes, for I should judge one-third were females."[35] Both houses of Congress adjourned so their members could attend.

Andrew Jackson, a sports enthusiast, often made heavy wagers at the National Course. In 1836 he entered one of his own horses and was sorely disappointed when it lost to an imported Irish colt owned by a navy captain. Jackson is said to have lost nearly a thousand dollars on bets he had made on his prized filly. Horse racing continued at this track until the 1840s, when the track closed and the property was subdivided for country estates.

Another adjoining neighbor on Meridian Hill was Columbian College, the second-oldest institution of higher learning in the District (Georgetown College was the first). George Washington had hoped to establish a national university, and L'Enfant's plan located it on the Mall, but nothing came of the idea until several Baptist bishops proposed establishing such a university in 1819. In 1821 they received a charter from Congress to establish Columbian College. The new institution purchased about forty-seven acres next to the extension of Fourteenth Street that climbed the eastern side of Meridian Hill. The college's main building was a sizable five-story brick structure, completed in time for the opening of the college in 1822. Its fifty-eight rooms were designed to accommodate both housing and classrooms for up to one hundred students. Three other nearby houses were built for the college president, faculty, and ground superintendent. The college stayed

Portrait of Count Alexander
de Bodisco, early landowner
in Washington County, DC.
General Portrait Collection,
DC History Center.

at this location until 1884, when it moved downtown to Fifteenth and H Streets
NW. It later moved to Foggy Bottom and changed its name to George Washington
University.[36]

Beyond Meridian Hill lay more hills and valleys, most of which were still wooded.
One of the deepest crosswise cuts in the terrain was the valley of the Piney Branch
creek, which flowed southwest from what is now Brightwood near the Maryland
border to join Rock Creek at a spot near modern-day Mount Pleasant. Just north
of where the Piney Branch valley crosses the path of Sixteenth Street rose another
formidable hill, and it was on land here, known as the Argyle tract, that Count
Alexander de Bodisco (1786–1854), the Russian envoy to the United States,
staked out a restful country retreat in 1845. Bodisco built a "large, old-fashioned
mansion" on this estate, as well as a conservatory, barns, and numerous other
outbuildings.[37]

Bodisco was by all accounts a gracious and sophisticated—if perhaps a bit
pompous—diplomat. He came to Washington as Russia's representative in 1838,
taking up primary residence in a townhouse that still stands at 3322 O Street NW
in Georgetown. In his fifties when he arrived in the capital, Bodisco began wooing
Harriet Beall Williams, a sixteen-year-old schoolgirl, in 1840. The May-September
romance and the elaborate wedding ceremony that ensued became the fodder of
gossip in the press for years to come, though by all accounts the marriage was a
happy one. Nicknamed "Uncle Sasha," Bodisco was very popular, in part due to

the lavish dinners and parties he hosted at this Georgetown residence. He always dressed to the nines in the most elaborate of courtly attire, and he and Madame de Bodisco would turn heads when they rode through the streets of Washington in their elegant coach drawn by four milk-white steeds imported from Russia and attended by liveried outriders.[38]

Bodisco's Argyle house was gutted by fire in January 1849.[39] The family was safely at the Georgetown house at the time. The house was rebuilt, however, and, shortly before his death in 1854, Bodisco sold the estate to Thomas Blagden (1803–70), a wealthy lumber merchant who had owned a large farm on the east side of the Anacostia River that he sold to the US government for the establishment of Saint Elizabeths Hospital. Blagden settled in at the Argyle estate as a farmer, expanding livestock and agricultural production on the estate and revitalizing a pair of mills along Rock Creek that came to bear his name. Census records indicate that he, like Commodore Porter and other landowners in Washington County, relied on both enslaved and free Blacks to help run his estate and farm. In 1860 six African Americans were living on the Blagden estate, working as gardeners and domestic servants. Among them, two teenage brothers, John and Walter Boyd, were recorded in the census as "bound," indicating they were enslaved. They would be freed two years later, under the District of Columbia Compensated Emancipation Act, and Walter Boyd would join the navy in 1864.[40]

Blagden's son, also named Thomas (1853–1938), continued to live on the estate after his father died and would later be influential in persuading government officials to extend Sixteenth Street past Piney Branch and in promoting development of the surrounding lands as residential neighborhoods. Gradually surrounded by residential development in the early twentieth century, the abandoned Blagden estate house was demolished in 1934 after being wrecked by vandals.[41]

Sixteenth Street during the Civil War

The Civil War brought enormous change to Washington and to Sixteenth Street. The vast influx of new residents created pressure for new housing in undeveloped parts of the city. In addition to whites from the North, many enslaved African Americans sought refuge in Washington, particularly after the early emancipation of DC enslaved people in 1862. Overall, the population of the District more than doubled during the war, from 75,000 in 1860 to approximately 155,000 in 1864.[42]

These figures do not account for the soldiers bivouacked around the city, a number totaling as many as 125,000 by the end of 1862. In many ways, the whole District became an armed camp. Ringed with a network of sixty-eight forts and batteries, Washington was the most heavily fortified city in the world. "Horsemen were galloping in every direction; long trains of army wagons rattled over the pavements at every turn of the eye; squads of soldiers marched here and there;

all was hurry, bustle and confusion," observed one soldier as his regiment arrived in December 1861.[43]

The wartime traffic played havoc with Washington's fragile roads, which, contrary to the soldier's account, were largely unpaved. Bumpy and rutted from the army wagons, many roads grew nearly impassable when rains turned them to a sea of mud. Sixteenth Street's marshy stretches north of N Street limited their usability, either for living space or for traveling. In contrast, Fourteenth Street, two blocks to the east, offered a hardier parallel route that continued out into Washington County and connected with turnpikes to the north and west. Serving as one of the city's few north-south arteries, it became the focus of commercial development. When the exigencies of the war finally propelled Congress in 1862 to approve the first streetcar routes in Washington, one was along Fourteenth Street. (The other was to the east on Seventh Street—a commercial thoroughfare that also extended into Maryland.) Sixteenth Street would never be in contention for this kind of development until its marshy areas were drained and a way was found to extend it up and over Meridian Hill, something that would not happen until late in the century.

On Lafayette Square, the army closed up or took over the homes of Southern sympathizers for use by officers. Most native white Washingtonians considered themselves Southerners, and many were sympathetic to the Confederacy. Corcoran, an avowed Confederate supporter, fled to Europe when the Civil War began, renting his mansion to the French diplomatic delegation to keep it from being seized by the government. Nearby on Pennsylvania Avenue, his new art gallery, begun in 1858 and also designed by James Renwick, was seized and used as the Union quartermaster's headquarters for the duration of the war.[44]

Several three-story brick townhouses stood on the east side of Sixteenth Street just two blocks north at K Street. One of these, 398 Sixteenth Street, was the home of celebrated Confederate spy Rose O'Neale Greenhow. Like Corcoran, Greenhow was an uncompromising supporter of the Southern cause, and she had been well connected in Washington's antebellum society. President James Buchanan was a longtime friend. Widowed in 1854, she remained a prominent socialite and hosted many soirees in the parlors of her Sixteenth Street house, gathering vital information about the Union war effort along the way. Historians believe Greenhow gave the Confederates advance notice of troop movements before the First Battle of Manassas, contributing to the Confederate victory. One of Allan Pinkerton's first assignments as head of the newly formed US Secret Service in 1861 was to spy on Greenhow at her Sixteenth Street home. One story has it that he stood on the shoulders of an assistant to peer into her window as she was entertaining a prominent government official.

On August 23, 1861, Pinkerton arrested Greenhow as she was walking up Sixteenth toward her home from Lafayette Park. The Secret Service kept her

Portrait of Rose Greenhow,
socialite and Confederate spy.
Library of Congress.

under house arrest at her home for five months, during which time other women Confederate spies were brought in and held there as well, earning the house the nickname "Fort Greenhow." It seems very possible that Greenhow continued to relay signals to Confederate couriers from the house's upper-story windows. A news correspondent wrote in early 1862, "Before the windows of the upper stories were 'blinded,' the prisoners often appeared at these points, and were viewed by pedestrians on the other side of the way; but since the 'cake affair' of New-Year's Day, the prisoners have been forbidden to appear at the windows, and the excitement, instead of having been allayed, has been still further increased."[45] Finally, in January 1862, Greenhow and her fellow prisoners were transferred to the Old Capitol Prison on Capitol Hill, where she was held for several more months before being turned over to the Confederates in Virginia. One condition of her release was that she stay within the Confederacy, where she presumably could do no further harm to the Union war effort.

Greenhow could not be contained, however, traveling as a celebrated Confederate emissary to Europe. In 1864 she was aboard a British blockade-running ship off the coast of North Carolina when the ship ran aground while being pursued by a Union gunboat. Greenhow tried to escape in a rowboat, but it capsized, and she drowned, weighed down by two thousand dollars in gold that she had sewn into her clothes.[46]

Meanwhile, the hills on the outskirts of Washington became a massive staging ground for the Union Army as it prepared to clash with Confederate troops on

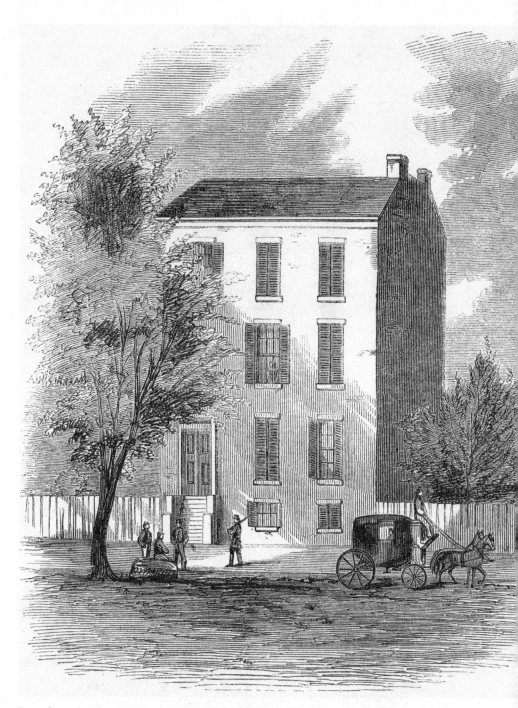

Rose Greenhow's townhouse at 398 Sixteenth Street while she was imprisoned there behind barred shutters in 1861. Federal guards keep watch at the entrance. The townhouse was replaced by the Nicholas Anderson House (see chapter 2) in 1883. *Engraving from* Frank Leslie's Illustrated Magazine, *Sep. 14, 1861.*

New York volunteers on Meridian Hill, 1861. Note the African American boy seated in front, most likely brought with the troops from New York to serve them in the field. *Library of Congress.*

battlefields in nearby Virginia. Meridian Hill, which stretched from what is now Adams Morgan on the west to beyond Fourteenth Street on the east, was the site of one of the city's largest group of encampments. Regiments from New York, New Jersey, Maine, and Connecticut all camped on this hill in 1861 and 1862.

The first to arrive was the Seventh New York State Militia, nicknamed the "Silk Stocking" regiment for the many socially elite New Yorkers within its ranks. The Seventh sported distinctive gray and black uniforms. The regiment was the first to protect the capital after war broke out in April 1861, and it chose arguably the best location of all potential spots around the city for its encampment. Dubbed Camp Cameron in honor of Secretary of War Simon Cameron, the bivouac was located just east of the Fourteenth Street Road on Meridian Hill from April to May 1861, before any fighting took place. The site was the estate and farm of William Stone (1798–1865), a prominent Washington businessman who had engraved a copy of the Declaration of Independence for the State Department in 1823.[47]

Other encampments soon spread over the rest of the hill's open space, including the farmland around the former Porter mansion. The Seventy-Seventh New

York Volunteers arrived in December 1861. George T. Stevens, a surgeon in the Seventy-Seventh, recalled that other regiments arrived and departed from the hill "almost daily," and he felt that his encampment was one of the nicest: "The grounds had been elegantly laid out with box and juniper, while the rich groves of oak and chestnut surrounding lent additional charms to the locality. The hill was dotted with the white tents of a dozen regiments, but none were so pleasantly located as our own, under the shadow of those grand old trees." Stevens noted that the house, which the regiment used as a hospital and headquarters, "still bore the name of 'the Porter Mansion.'"[48] All the large structures on the hill, including the Porter and Stone mansions and the massive Columbian College building, were used as hospitals, and when these filled up, long rows of tents were erected for additional space.

The views from the hill were said to be spectacular, stretching to the Potomac and beyond, but the army was everywhere. Matthew Baird of the Sixth Michigan Cavalry wrote to his girlfriend Maggie Bowker in December 1862, "There is scarcely a direction that you may look, but your eye meets an encampment. Scarcely a hillside that is not dotted with tents. The whole country here is one grand military encampment. Washington abounds with hospitals. There is nothing to be heard around but the rattling of army wagons, the rolling of drums, and the sounding of bugles; with now and then the heavy booming of cannon in the far distance."[49] There was so much activity on Meridian Hill that in March 1862, George M. Miller started daily stagecoach service from in front of the Willard Hotel on Pennsylvania Avenue to Meridian Hill, via Fourteenth Street. One-way fare was ten cents.[50]

Though it is hard to imagine now, troops on Meridian Hill could observe activities in the city many blocks away. When a certain Private Michael Lanahan was hanged in January 1862 for killing his sergeant, the troops quartered on snowy Meridian Hill gathered in groups to observe the proceedings, which took place almost half a mile away in a clearing near what is now Logan Circle.[51]

After 1862 soldiers left fewer accounts of idling away their time on Meridian Hill; the war kept most of them in the field. Washington became a primary destination for receiving and caring for those wounded in combat on the front lines in Virginia. As large wood-frame hospital complexes were constructed, including Carver Hospital on Meridian Hill, the mansions, churches, hotels, and other private structures that had been commandeered early on to shelter the wounded were given back to their owners. The old Porter mansion, owned since 1858 by Oliver Pettit of New York, may have been reoccupied by Pettit's tenants later in the war. In 1866, a year after the war ended, the house caught fire due to a chimney defect. Tenants were able to save some of their furniture, but with the nearest water source being Rock Creek more than a mile away, firefighters were unable to quench the flames, and the house was reported to be "entirely consumed."[52]

A classified advertisement appearing in the *Evening Star* in 1871 suggests that the house may have been repaired or rebuilt and occupied at that time,[53] but it disappeared completely by the end of the century.

The Crystal Spring Resort and Brightwood Race Track

Well beyond the military encampments lay a "resort" and racetrack where soldiers and civilian residents alike could go to get away from the chaos of the war. The track was originally known as the Piney Branch or Crystal Spring course, after several natural springs that bubbled up nearby. It was located just north of the present-day intersection of Sixteenth Street and Colorado Avenue NW. It was reportedly laid out in 1859. A summer resort hotel was constructed adjacent to it shortly thereafter.[54]

During the war, the Piney Branch Hotel's owner would organize picnics on the hotel grounds.[55] The wooded, rural site graced by natural springs was a great spot for a summer retreat. Access to the hotel and racecourse was via the three-and-a-half-mile Piney Branch Road, a dirt path that extended Fourteenth Street outside the city. For part of its length, Piney Branch Road meandered close to the path of the future extension of Sixteenth Street. An 1863 advertisement for the "new and handsome hotel" at Crystal Spring claimed that the rugged Piney Branch Road was "unsurpassed for the quiet beauty of the scenery: the road itself, during the summer, being the very best in this vicinity." It concluded that "to those of our citizens desiring a pleasant ride, free from the dust and turmoil of the city, this place offers inducements superior to any other."[56] Roundtrip stagecoach service was available from points downtown for seventy-five cents, putting an escape to Crystal Spring within reach of middle-class Washingtonians.[57]

The same advertisement noted, "There is also on the premises a large and well furnished bar, stocked with an extensive and well selected variety of the choicest wines and liquors," which, along with gambling at the racetrack, facilitated a broader array of recreational activities than just picnics on Sunday afternoons. In August 1862 military police temporarily shut down the restaurant and bar "as a result of the disorderly conduct of persons, civilians as well as soldiers, who visited there recently."[58] Such episodes would plague the resort throughout its history.

After the war, the racetrack gained patronage and prestige. A formal racing club took control in 1873.[59] By 1876 Brightwood Park, as it was then known, drew national attention, including coverage in the *New York Times*.[60] Horses would typically run races of five-mile-long heats, a challenge of endurance as much as speed. Purses were generally pegged at a few hundred dollars but could run higher if well-known horses were trotting.

The horse racing season was limited—a few races in spring and then again in the fall—but other amusements drew spectators as well. An 1878 competition, for

View in the 1890s of the rustic Piney Branch Hotel, also known as the Crystal Spring Hotel, located near the present-day intersection of Sixteenth Street and Colorado Avenue NW. *General Photograph Collection, DC History Center.*

example, featured a "professional pedestrian" who attempted to walk a quarter mile while a horse trotted a half-mile (outcome of the race unknown).[61] Local amateurs could enter their horses in races, vying for a nominal purse of perhaps five dollars. In one humorous event in 1884, three local bakers named Hoge, Blair, and Mehan ran their delivery wagon horses against each other. None of the horses cooperated, all of them showing "a decided preference for the outside of the track and a great animosity for the outside gate." Finally, Baker Hoge's horse "by a noble effort managed to walk in about a hundred yards ahead of the others. Blair's came in a few hours later, while Mehan's is yet to be heard from."[62]

Life in and around "the Slashes"

From K to Boundary Street, Sixteenth Street remained little developed through the Civil War, and north of P, it ran directly through a broad wasteland known as "the Slashes." This mini wilderness comprised hundreds of acres of marshy ground on both sides of Slash Run, a stream that snaked its way south and west from Meridian Hill, veering close to Sixteenth Street in the blocks between Scott Circle and L Street and then turning west to eventually empty into Rock Creek.

Dense underbrush covered much of this land—hence the need to "slash" one's way through. Some spots were nearly impenetrable. Near Boundary Street, wild blackberry bushes grew, attracting large numbers of pickers when they were in season. Small game animals lived among the underbrush, and "the man with dog and gun often enjoyed a day's hunting in that portion of the city," according to a 1906 newspaper reminiscence. "Boys were wont to spend hours in exploring the mysteries of the section, fishing for suckers and other small fish; catching frogs and 'bludnouns' [bullfrogs], or hunting birds and snakes."[63]

Scattered small-scale industry—chiefly brick kilns and slaughterhouses—dotted the landscape, accessible only by winding paths through the thick brush. Slaughter-houses, due to their noxious odors, were not welcome in the more developed parts of the city. Their owners sought locations by streams, both as a source of water and as a convenient drain to dispose of offal. The offal, of course, polluted the stream and could at times create a powerful stench. Parts of Slash Run functioned as an open sewer, and only a few of the poorest residents, who could find nowhere else to live, lived in shacks in the Slashes. Marshy pools of stagnant water were used as a general dumping ground. In August 1861 a soldier stationed just upwind, on Meridian Hill, wrote to the *Daily National Republican* to complain about "the existence of numerous carcasses on the northern limit of this city, in the immediate neighborhood of Meridian Hill, which are constantly emanating noxious effluvia. . . . At morn and eve, the stench that arises from the decaying bodies of horses, &c., deposited there, is almost insupportable."[64]

As demand for housing grew after the Civil War, the Slashes were gradually eliminated. The street had been graveled from I Street to Boundary Street as early as 1845, but it remained rutted and muddy as it traversed the Slashes.[65] Throughout this period, streets in Washington periodically received this treatment, whereby ruts and pits were smoothed out and the surfaced coated with a layer of gravel to suppress dust and mud. Such improvements never lasted very long.[66] In 1866 Sixteenth was graded and re-graveled again, and in 1867 a contract was awarded to pave a "footway" (sidewalk) and set curbstones along the west side of the street from K to Boundary. Three years later the same work was authorized for the east side. The whole street, from I to Boundary, was graded and graveled yet again in 1868. Drinking water from the Potomac first came to Sixteenth Street after a water main, from K to Boundary Street, was authorized in 1870.[67]

The 1870s ushered in more substantial infrastructure improvements throughout the city as part of the concerted effort by Alexander Shepherd, first as director of the Board of Public Works and subsequently as governor of the District of Columbia, to turn the capital into a clean and modern city. In addition to paving streets and planting trees, the board laid many miles of new sewer lines. One of the board's projects was to bury Slash Run by enclosing it in a sewer. This not only removed the smell and the health hazard but also drained the surrounding marshland to allow for new development. The area to the west of Sixteenth, particularly along Massachusetts Avenue to Dupont Circle, was transformed from a backwater of small industrial shops and frame shanties inhabited by impoverished shop workers to a fashionable residential neighborhood.

In 1872 Sixteenth Street was paved for the first time with wooden blocks as part of a citywide effort to overcome the endless dust and mud associated with graveled roads.[68] Pennsylvania Avenue had been the first street in the city to be so paved in 1870, and many other streets from the West End to the Capitol, received similar treatment by 1873. However, the wood pavement did not hold up as well as it was expected to, and after the 1870s more durable paving materials, like macadam, were gradually substituted.

Emma Prall Knorr, a sixth-generation resident of Sixteenth Street, recalled in 1926 that even after all this work, the street still seemed primitive: "Sixteenth street was paved with wooden blocks, worn by the elements into steep hills and dales impassable save to a venturesome coal cart. The brick [sidewalk] pavements [below Scott Circle] were richly carpeted with moss and illuminated by one feeble gas lamp for each block." She further observed that "Scott Circle at that date was the end of civilization! Beyond lay a wilderness of vacant lots, with a sprinkling of negro cabins, tin cans and stray cats."[69]

Marshy, unhealthful conditions persisted in isolated parts of the former Slashes until the 1880s. A letter to the editor of the *Evening Star* in 1886 seems to indicate that the problem identified by the Civil War soldier in 1861 still hadn't been corrected twenty-five years later. The 1886 writer complained that just west of Sixteenth Street, between S and T, "there is a large pond of stagnant water covering half an acre or more. In it are the carcasses of numerous dogs and cats which, a pest while living, are thus become a vastly more intolerable nuisance when dead. The effect of the warm sun is to pollute and poison the whole air in the neighborhood."[70]

Noxious as the marshy land may have been, it was not bad enough to keep sports fans from heading out to this part of Sixteenth Street to watch their favorite baseball teams play on a pair of diamonds that were laid out here in the 1860s and 1870s. Even before the Civil War, amateur baseball teams had played at various spots around the city, including the famous White Lot (now the Ellipse) behind the White House, where President Andrew Johnson attended games.[71] In 1859 a group of players, many of whom had day jobs as government clerks, formed a club called the Nationals, which after the war began traveling around the country to play match games against other cities' semiprofessional teams.

By 1867 the Nationals were hosting games at National Grounds on the west side of Sixteenth north of R Street.[72] Their success soon led to the formation of a rival semiprofessional team, the Olympics, whose games against the Nationals in 1868 drew as many as three thousand spectators.[73] In 1870 the Olympics opened their own park, with seating for one thousand, on the east side of Sixteenth Street roughly opposite the National Grounds. Team officials invited newspaper reporters out to the field for a grand opening in April. "The fences are colored with a wash of a bluish tint, which answers the purpose much better than the ordinary white," observed the *Daily National Republican*, which also approved of the stands set up specifically for the press, noting that "the grounds are so drained that no water can remain upon the field."[74]

The Nationals and Olympics graduated to professional status after playing against the Cincinnati Red Stockings, the first professional baseball team, in the 1869–70 season.[75] In 1871 the Olympics joined the National Association of Professional Baseball Players, an ancestor of the National League, compiling a record of 15–15. This, unfortunately, would be the high-water mark for Washington baseball for forty seasons. In 1872 the Olympics finished at a poor 2–7, but the Nationals were even worse, losing all eleven of their games. In 1873 the teams reformed as the Washington Blue Legs, who finished 8–31. A National Association team called the Nationals took to the field in 1875, but it soon folded with a 5–23 record.[76] The Sixteenth Street diamonds were thereafter home to amateur contests such as "Bankers versus Lawyers" and inter-departmental club play until 1879–80, when a new Washington Nationals team played at National Grounds.[77] A few more professional games may have been played on Sixteenth Street when yet another edition of the Nationals joined the Union Association in 1884, but by this time the area was beginning to redevelop as a residential neighborhood.

Besides giving Washington fans the opportunity to see the top stars of such talented teams as the Brooklyn Eckfords, Troy Haymakers, Philadelphia Athletics, and Boston Red Stockings, the Sixteenth Street grounds were a place to cheer on hometown heroes like outfielder Paul Hines, a native Washingtonian who won a batting championship and triple crown during his seventeen-year National League career, as well as Hall of Fame shortstop George Wright, dapper cricketeer-turned-pitcher Asa Brainerd, and bat magician Fred Waterman, all later members of the 1869–70 Cincinnati Red Stockings team that played an incredible ninety-five games without a defeat.[78] Although the Nationals and Olympics had only white players, the Olympics played at least one game against the African American Alert team in 1869, and African American teams met separately on the Sixteenth Street diamonds for their own games.[79]

Free African Americans had been living in every part of the city, side by side with whites, throughout the first half of the nineteenth century. "These early Negro inhabitants of pre–Civil War days lived in the little huts, hovels, and shacks which were stuck here and there among the shadows of the finer and more pretentious homes of the white population," according to William Henry Jones, an African American sociologist working in the 1920s.[80] It was only after the Civil War that exclusively African American enclaves began to emerge as whites began pushing Blacks out of desirable neighborhoods.

One area that grew to be a center of African American cultural life spanned the blocks on either side of Sixteenth Street between K and M. While not far from the President's House and the wealthy residents of Lafayette Square, these blocks were also close to the Slashes—Slash Run flowed through two of the three blocks on the west side of Sixteenth—and thus had drawn little interest from moneyed whites.[81]

During and after the Civil War, formerly enslaved African Americans streamed in from the surrounding area and points farther south, forming new local communities here and elsewhere in the District. Even before Congress emancipated the District's enslaved in 1862, thousands fleeing slavery in Maryland and Virginia had sought refuge in the nation's capital. By 1863 ten thousand formerly enslaved people had arrived, and as many as forty thousand by 1865.[82] The newcomers packed into a city already bursting at the seams from the war effort.

Among the wartime arrivals to this neighborhood were former members of the Shiloh Baptist Church of Fredericksburg, Virginia, who had fled their homes when the war came to town in 1862. "The army had scattered these brethren; some had been driven South, some were in the Confederate army, and about four hundred had sought shelter in the District for personal safety," the church's deacon explained to the DC Council of Baptist Churches in 1863.[83] The council approved the establishment of a new church by twenty-three members of the old congregation. It acquired a tiny frame structure just west of Sixteenth Street on L Street.[84] The congregation thrived and grew, rapidly attracting former members as well as new ones. It moved across the street to a bigger building in 1868 and then replaced it with a sizable red brick Victorian meeting house in 1883.[85]

A pattern began to emerge where whites (and some Blacks) with the means to do so built substantial houses on streets like Sixteenth amid a motley assortment of previously constructed "shanties" and other small frame structures that the newcomers assumed would soon be torn down and replaced by fine homes. This pattern created striking juxtapositions. "One's attention is frequently arrested by the sight of an ordinary-looking house, occupied by Negroes, attached to an imposing mansion of a white millionaire, or the presence of two or three small shacks—Negro homes—in the very center of an aristocratic block," scholar William Henry Jones observed.[86]

The alleys located behind Sixteenth between the K and M blocks were where the neediest African Americans—largely the formerly enslaved war refugees—ended up. Alley dwellings had sprung up beginning in the 1850s as large lots with houses facing the streets were subdivided to create smaller lots facing the service alleys in back. Property owners built and rented out flimsy frame structures on these alley lots at as high a price as they could obtain. Everyone who lived in the K and M Street alley dwellings was Black, including twenty-eight residents who jammed into two frame dwellings in the alley just to the east of Sixteenth and K. A dozen frame dwellings, similarly packed, faced the adjoining Union Alley.

During and after the war, African American and white civic leaders and officials expressed serious concerns about the squalid living conditions among the formerly enslaved. In April 1886, William F. Spurgin, the local superintendent of the Freedmen's Bureau, reported on efforts to prevent cholera by cleaning up spots inhabited by the newcomers, including "the square lying between L and M north [now NW] and Fifteenth and Sixteenth Streets west." Spurgin reported, "The sanitary condition of this square . . . is deplorable. The vacant lots and alleys are filled with filth. There are several springs, the waters of which, flowing through this filth, produce quagmires, from which emanate sickening odors, and which, if not remediated, will most certainly engender disease." Spurgin recommended that the square be cleaned up immediately but noted that "even after this is done great evils remain, and can only be removed by *tearing down* the miserable tenements occupied by many of the freedmen, and by scattering the occupants."[87] His views would be widely shared among whites and would lead to persistent efforts to "scatter" Blacks from areas that were close to well-to-do white areas and that whites wanted to occupy for themselves.

Lower Sixteenth Street in those days was a workingman's neighborhood, not nearly as squalid as Spurgin would have us believe. By 1874 the block between L and M Streets was lined with clusters of small gabled and flat-roofed houses punctuated by vacant lots. Other than a few Irish immigrant householders like coachman Thomas O'Connell and grocer Mary Donovan, the block was African American. The three dwellings between H and I Streets on the east side of the street also housed Blacks, including Lloyd Harper, sexton at Saint John's Church. Reflecting lower Sixteenth Street's proximity to downtown hotels and restaurants, its residents included cooks, confectioners, coachmen, barbers, domestic servants, and fifteen waiters. School teachers, a postal clerk, and a "helper at the Supreme Court," represented the emerging African American middle class. Sophia Thomas, who lived just north of K Street, was a government messenger, holding one of the few federal positions available to African American women. In general, Black women were offered few work opportunities outside of charwoman duties.

Reverend John Francis Cook (circa 1810–55), scion of one of the most prominent of Washington's nineteenth-century African American families, settled on
the northeast corner of Sixteenth and K some time before 1850.[88] "Cook Corner,"
as it would come to be known, was a large tract with roughly one hundred feet of
frontage on both Sixteenth and K Streets where Cook's extended family occupied
a two-story frame house angled to face the broad intersection. Cook was among
twenty-three relatives bought out of slavery in 1826 with money his aunt, Alethia
Browning Tanner, earned by selling produce near Lafayette Square.[89] Trained as a
shoemaker, Cook dislocated his shoulder as a teenager and had to find less physical work. This turned out to be a godsend; he studied at John W. Prout's free
school for African American children at Fourteenth and H Streets and proved a
precocious learner. Soon landing a job as an assistant messenger for a government
office, he astonished his supervisor with his aptitude. Based on his writing abilities,
he was promoted to clerk, but after three years he quit to devote his life to im-
proving the lives of his fellow African Americans through education. He took over
Prout's school in 1834, renaming it the Union Seminary.[90]

Cook was forced to temporarily abandon the school in August 1835, after an
ominous incident occurred late one night on nearby F Street. Arthur Bowen, an
enslaved servant, became inebriated and entered the bedchamber of his owner,
Anna Thornton, carrying an ax. He didn't strike her, but she was terrified. News
of the incident sparked hysteria among many whites, whose fears about being at-
tacked by slaves had been heightened by the Nat Turner Rebellion in Virginia,
which had occurred only four years earlier and had resulted in more than fifty
whites being murdered. In response to the Bowen incident, a throng of angry
young white "mechanics" (skilled laborers) gathered and vandalized several Black-
owned properties. It was known that Bowen had been a student at John Cook's
school and had participated in debates led by Cook on the subject of abolition.
Incensed that Black children were being educated and encouraged to think about
freedom, the rioters vandalized and partially destroyed Cook's school. Cook was
warned to get out of town before the angry mob could get their hands on him, and
he fled to Pennsylvania.[91]

Ultimately undeterred, Cook returned to the District a year later and reopened
the Union Seminary at Fourteenth and H Streets. He also began studying for the
ministry, and in 1843 he was ordained and elected the first pastor of the newly
organized First Colored Presbyterian Church of Washington. Reverend Cook originally preached from the Union Seminary building, until a new church building
was constructed on Fifteenth Street in 1853. The church, located just two blocks
east of Cook Corner, was then renamed the Fifteenth Street Presbyterian Church,

Reverend John Francis Cook
lived at Cook Corner, the
northeast corner of Sixteenth
and K Streets NW. *Courtesy
of Moorland-Spingarn Research
Center, Howard University.*

and it would endure as a center of civil rights activism. Today the church stands on the northeast corner of Fifteenth and R Streets NW.

By the time of Cook's untimely death at age forty-five in 1855, he was a widely admired advocate for civil rights and a determined proponent of education for African Americans. "A feeling of sincere regret is experienced in this community for the death of Rev. John F. Cook, a man of color and the founder and pastor of the Fifteenth street Presbyterian Church," the *Daily National Intelligencer,* Washington's foremost newspaper, reported. "He died in this city yesterday morning. His walk and conversation were such as to command general respect of white and black."[92]

Cook's sons George and John Jr. continued his work after his death and remained associated with property on Sixteenth Street. Both had been educated at Oberlin College in Ohio and returned to Washington to become teachers at Union Seminary after their father passed away. Next to Frederick Douglass, John F. Cook Jr. (1833–1910) was perhaps the best known and most influential of the "elite" African American Washingtonians in the Reconstruction era. He was active in local politics, serving as an alderman, clerk in the District Tax Office, and justice of the peace.[93] In 1865, as founder of the Colored Citizens' District Equal Rights Association, he presented a petition, signed by 2,500 Black Washingtonians, demanding suffrage in the District of Columbia.[94] The question of suffrage for

African American men in the District was a tumultuous one that inspired bitter opposition from many whites. Nevertheless, under the leadership of the so-called Radical Republicans, Congress overrode a veto by President Andrew Johnson to grant that right in January 1867, ushering in a brief period of political power for Black men in Washington. In 1874 President Ulysses S. Grant appointed Cook District registrar of taxes, a position that extended his power and influence in local government. Ever interested as his father had been in education and the advancement of his race, Cook served as a trustee of Howard University. Cook, his wife, their five children, and an African American servant lived in a substantial, two-story brick house erected during or just after the Civil War next to the old family homestead on Cook Corner.

"An Air of Refinement" for African American Churches

The strength of the African American community in this neighborhood is reflected in the influential churches that took root here, including Cook's Fifteenth Street Presbyterian Church, the Union Bethel African Methodist Episcopal (AME) Church, and the previously discussed Shiloh Baptist Church. African Americans and whites of Protestant faiths had worshiped together in the same churches in the early nineteenth century, but they had never been on equal footing. Blacks generally were obliged to sit at the rear of the church or in upper galleries. They faced other indignities as well, including pastors who refused to take Black infants in their hands to be baptized. One white congregation, the Ebenezer Methodist Church on Capitol Hill, became the "mother" of several early African American congregations as Black worshipers sought a more welcoming space of their own. Among these spinoff groups was the Israel Bethel AME congregation, formed around 1820 on Capitol Hill.[95] Union Bethel AME, in turn, was founded in 1838 as a branch of the Israel Bethel church to serve the Northwest neighborhood near the President's House.

Union Bethel originally met in a small house off of L Street to the east of Sixteenth, but by the 1840s it had moved a block north to M Street.[96] Union Bethel's modest church building soon became inadequate. Congregants considered building a larger church as early as 1850,[97] but several more decades passed before the new church was completed. Israel Bethel, the "mother" congregation on Capitol Hill, was set to change its name to the Metropolitan AME Church and build a large new house of worship in the early 1870s, but after disagreements among church leaders, that congregation decided instead to leave the AME fold. In its place, Union Bethel took on the Metropolitan name and proceeded to build the larger church it had long wanted. That building, started in 1881 and completed five years later, stands today as the Metropolitan AME Church on the south side of M Street, just east of Sixteenth.[98]

Metropolitan AME Church, at 1518 M Street NW, from the Historic American Buildings Survey, 1974. *Library of Congress.*

According to legend, members of the Union Bethel congregation salvaged and cleaned bricks by hand from their old building for reuse in the new church. Samuel T. G. Morsell (1823–1909), a white, Maryland-born architect and builder who had served as the city's superintendent of public works, designed the impressive new structure, which was one of the largest African American churches in the country when it was completed.[99] The red brick Gothic Revival structure, trimmed in granite, features a particularly spacious auditorium capable of seating three thousand. The large auditorium would become a focal point not only as a place for worship but perhaps more importantly as a gathering place in the struggle for civil rights. Frederick Douglass was a member of the congregation and lectured here, as did many other prominent African American leaders. Now considered the "National Cathedral" of African Methodism, the Metropolitan AME Church is said to be the oldest continuously Black-owned property in the District.

Congregations such as Metropolitan AME took great pride in their faith and their independence, especially in the Reconstruction years, when advances in civil rights seemed to come easily. Whites, when they took notice of the local African American community, routinely seemed surprised that prominent Black congregations could be as cultured as white congregations. Writing as Mrs. John A. Logan, Mary Simmerson Cunningham Logan, widow of the Civil War general, noted the sophistication of the nearby Fifteenth Street Presbyterian Church and its congregants: "Well-dressed men with fashionably-trimmed beards, and stylish women with lorgnettes occupy the pews. . . . At the church doors elegantly-dressed young colored men wait on the sidewalks for sweethearts, or drive up in carriages and traps. There is an air of refinement in this church, which is often tastefully decked with flowers, furnished with the softest of carpets, attended by polite ushers, and presided over by a clergyman who is generally a graduate of one of the great universities."[100]

In the eyes of the Black elite—those families who had lived in Washington since before the war and had acquired wealth and social standing—the wartime newcomers from the South were sometimes seen as uncouth and a hindrance to efforts to claim equality with white society.[101] Education became central to their struggle for "racial uplift," the effort to demonstrate that African Americans could achieve the same social and cultural status as whites. John Cook's Union Seminary, supported by the Fifteenth Street Presbyterian Church, was one example. Before becoming Metropolitan AME, the Union Bethel Church had opened a free school for Blacks in its basement in the 1860s. The church also founded the Union Relief Association during the war to collect clothing and other supplies for newly arrived freedmen.[102]

In 1859 Union Bethel founded the Bethel Literary and Historical Association as another vehicle for racial uplift. Under AME Bishop Daniel Payne, the Bethel Literary, as everyone knew it, was reorganized in 1881 and emerged as a key cultural center for the elite African American community in Washington. Meeting weekly on Tuesday nights, the society drew overflow crowds on a regular basis to lively discussions on a broad range of topics, from civil rights to education, science, and religion. The thirst among African Americans for intellectual discourse became a point of pride for the Bethel Literary. Originally meeting in Bethel Hall, the group later moved to the more spacious Metropolitan AME Church. Speakers included such luminaries as Frederick Douglass, Judge Robert H. Terrell and his wife, civil rights activist Mary Church Terrell (who served as president), women's rights activist Belva Lockwood, and poet Paul Laurence Dunbar, among many others.[103]

While the Bethel Literary flourished, life in the surrounding neighborhood grew more and more difficult for less affluent African Americans in the latter part of the nineteenth century. Many were gradually forced out by rising rents as Sixteenth Street became increasingly attractive to whites.[104] As Slash Run was contained in a sewer and its marshes abated, the vast area to the north and west of the White House became increasingly desirable for new, spacious mansions. Even before the statue of General Winfield Scott was erected in 1874 at the broad open space where Massachusetts and Rhode Island Avenues cross Sixteenth Street, real estate values around the square skyrocketed, from forty cents per square foot in 1871 to as much as two dollars per square foot in 1873.[105] Gentrification—a term no one used at the time—would bring an entirely new social milieu to much of lower Sixteenth Street in the final decades of the nineteenth century, disrupting its semibucolic way of life, displacing many of its longtime Black residents, and ultimately creating a much more urban environment.

TWO

Sixteenth Street from the Gilded Age to the City Beautiful

WASHINGTON SPRAWLED robustly outward during the late nineteenth century, an era that Mark Twain and Charles Dudley Warner enduringly nicknamed "the Gilded Age" for its celebration of the material prosperity that overlaid a core of corruption, exploitation, and inequality. Some cities of the era grew exponentially with new industries or transportation networks; Washington reached a critical mass as political power and financial influence coalesced in the capital of a nation reaching for world power. As the fin-de-siècle city evolved from village to metropolis, Sixteenth Street transitioned from back channel to boulevard. A Sixteenth Street address came to carry a fashionable cachet that mirrored the ambitions of an elite group of national political and local business leaders as well as a new leisure class of successful businessmen attracted by Washington's blossoming social and cultural life.

The Long Depression precipitated by the Panic of 1873 flattened growth nationally for nearly six years and provided the backdrop of insolvency that led to the abolition of Washington's territorial government and its ambitious program of public works.[1] Not surprisingly, Sixteenth Street's sparse patterns of settlement remained largely unchanged. However, by the dawn of the 1880s, even before the nation's economy fully revived, traces of a more formal and modern metropolitan life were infiltrating the land north of Lafayette Square.

"A Home for Confederate Widows"

One early landmark on the urban fringe was the Louise Home, which opened on Massachusetts Avenue between Fifteenth and Sixteenth Streets in 1871. The home was William Wilson Corcoran's memorial to his wife and daughter, both of whom had died in their twenties and both of whom were named Louise. The *Baltimore Sun* said the Southern-sympathizing Corcoran had endowed the home as a refuge

The Louise Home, opened in 1871 and known as a home for Confederate widows, was an early landmark on Massachusetts Avenue just east of what would become Scott Circle. It was torn down in 1949. *General Photograph Collection, DC History Center.*

for "destitute but refined and educated gentlewomen, many [of whom were] belles of note at the capital," but who now live "under very different circumstances."[2] Less circumspectly, the *Chicago Tribune* described it as "a home for Confederate widows," whose residents were obligated to pay only for their wardrobes and to follow paternalistic rules that included showing up punctually and tidily dressed for meals, socializing in the public parlors, and being home by 9 p.m.[3]

The home's campus resembled a rustic estate or plantation with a large manor house surrounded by two acres of gardens. Although a charitable endeavor, it was as elegant as a first-class hotel. Its appointments included fine furniture, a piano for musicales, bedroom-and-parlor suites, and an elevator to serve its upper floors. Sharing the fashionable Second Empire style of Corcoran's yet-unfinished art gallery on Pennsylvania Avenue, the four-story red brick building had a center tower whose pyramidal roof seemed lofty as a steeple. By wrapping circulatory corridors around a glass-roofed central atrium, well-established Baltimore architect Edmund George Lind (1829–1909), provided every room a window and filled a ground-floor court-yard with light.[4] In 1880 the home's thirty-six residents were attended by three white and six Black servants as well as a matron with two assistants.

Although the Louise Home garnered much favorable press, not everyone was sympathetic to faded Southern gentility.[5] The *Chicago Tribune* dismissively called its residents "dames of high degree and low purses . . . [from] the first families of the Old Dominion" and smirked that "it is better than a play to hear them boasting of their ancestors and of their families."[6] Although its Massachusetts Avenue building was replaced by a large apartment house in 1951, the Louise Home continues today as a component of the Lisner-Louise-Dickson-Hurt Home on Western Avenue NW.

"The Tin Soldier"

The first true link between the formal city represented by Lafayette Square and Sixteenth Street's undeveloped northern reaches was a statue.[7] At the Civil War's end, Washington's only public spaces with monumental equestrian statuary were Lafayette Square, with Clark Mills's Andrew Jackson, and Washington Circle, with Mills's George Washington. A statue of General Winfield Scott and a barren cross-roads seemed unlikely choices for the third such memorial.

Nicknamed "Old Fuss and Feathers" for his pomposity, General Scott (1786–1866) saw his prestige's peak between his capture of Mexico City in 1847 and rout as the Whig presidential candidate in the 1852 election. Aged, and so infirm that he could no longer mount his horse, Scott had resigned his post as commander-in-chief of the United States Army months after the attack on Fort Sumter. Yet his contributions to the Union victory in the Civil War were undeniable. He had safe-guarded Lincoln's inauguration under threat of assassination, effectively fortified Washington, and devised the "Anaconda" strategy of invasion and blockade that had crushed the Confederacy. The Virginia-born Scott's thunderous pledge to "defend . . . [the Stars and Stripes] with my sword, even if my own native state assails it" had made him an inspirational symbol of national loyalty.[8] Just months after his death in 1866, Congress resolved to erect a monument in his honor. In early 1872, space was allocated in Reservation 63, the barren rectangle where Sixteenth Street met Massachusetts and Rhode Island Avenues.[9] This location would place Scott's statue on a line of sight with the White House, as well as ironically make it neighbor to the Louise Home, with its Lost Cause associations.

Commissioned by Congress, Henry Kirke Brown, creator of noted equestrian statues in New York, spent nearly five years sculpting a mounted Scott.[10] Cast from two hundred captured Mexican cannons, the bronze statue was displayed in downtown Philadelphia while the stones for its base were quarried and its Washington site prepared.[11] Finally, in December 1873, the schooner *James H. French* unloaded the Cape Ann granite pedestal blocks at the G Street wharf in Southwest, and the gigantic stones were rolled across town on special casters to protect the paving.[12] In early February 1874, five teams of horses dragged the massive wagon bearing the statue from the B&O freight station to Reservation 63, where the figure was mounted facing south along the axis of Sixteenth Street.[13] Despite the long run-up, the monument's dedication proved a debacle. Lured by newspaper announcements, the hundreds of spectators who gathered on the cold afternoon of February 23 were waiting for speeches when the cavalry troop that had assembled at the site suddenly rode away, bringing a mystifying end to the proceedings.[14] No official explanation was ever provided, and the statue was never formally dedicated.

While a general's memorial is not supposed to be his last battlefield, nineteenth-century public statuary often proved controversial. Besides political disputes over whose memorial deserved what site, aesthetic quarrels became so passionate that the *Evening Star*'s critic, known as Arcturus Gadabout, once lamented that "Clark Mills' two equestrian subjects are denounced as if they were crimes."[15] Brown's depiction of Scott's mount was highly praised after he navigated some initial shoals. The general had usually ridden mares, and Brown's model had been his own steed, a sister of General Ulysses S. Grant's famous stallion Cincinnati. However, after being criticized for not depicting Scott on a stallion, the sculptor had simply grafted male genitals to the female equine figure.[16] The *National Republican* nonetheless waxed fulsomely about "the bronze steed . . . [which] bears all the delicate traces of a full-blooded animal."[17] The *Star* had ventured even further, stating that "criticism agrees that Brown has given us the most perfect horse yet achieved by American art. The animal is walking, as if waiting the signal to bound forward."[18]

Although no one commented on the irony of a three-times-failed presidential candidate trudging endlessly toward the White House, Brown's figure of General

Scott won much fainter praise. The sculptor had portrayed Scott on the eve of the Civil War, when, as the *National Republican* discreetly suggested, his ponderous "form and proportions . . . could not be made to accommodate the purpose of a graceful cavalry man except at an expense of truth."[19] To many, the statue seemed more antiheroic than realistic. Clark Mills and others assailed Brown for portraying Scott as "a good deal like a big pillow."[20] The perception took hold that Brown, rather than representing fact, had misproportioned "the man as too fat for the horse or the horse as too thin for the man," and by the 1910s the statue was listed as one of Washington's most ridiculous monuments.[21] An enduring legend has General Philip Sheridan, dying in his bedroom a block west, asking his brother to see that "I have a better mount than old Scott has."[22]

Whatever its aesthetic merits, the Scott statue annexed the more northerly blocks of Sixteenth Street to the formal L'Enfant city of monuments, squares, and circles. The memorial became a placemaking landmark; real estate advertisements in the 1880s often described properties as "close to the Scott Statue." The rectangular footprint of Reservation 63 became known as Scott Square and was later rounded to become Scott Circle.

Gilding Sixteenth Street

The coming of the 1880s promised a return to prosperity. The aftershocks of the Panic of 1873 were finally subsiding, along with the political tumult that had stretched from Lincoln's assassination through the impeachment crisis of 1868, the Grant administration's scandals, the disputed presidential election of 1876, the struggles surrounding the end of Reconstruction, and the convulsive Great Railroad Strike of 1877, in which some one hundred strikers were killed during harsh suppression by federal troops. As the 1880 presidential campaign opened, Republican-leaning newspapers called for the election of James Garfield to restore calm and normality; his assassination by a deranged office-seeker the following year would prove a brutal shock.

Washington had suffered during the Panic, both directly and as the nation's economic distress and unrest rippled through the political system. Yet the capital rebounded more quickly than most cities. Construction had been relatively flat in 1878, when Congress stabilized the city's governance by making permanent the new three-member appointed commissioner system, which replaced the previous territorial government.[23] But it was rising in 1880, when, shortly after Garfield's election, the *Baltimore Sun* reported that development was rapidly gentrifying the city, as "comparatively few small houses are being built, and the shabby tenements that . . . sprang up like mushrooms over all the old field have all given way to good dwelling houses."[24] With the territorial government's improvements, the *Post* noted that the carriage-owning class could now enjoy "miles of concrete pavement, intersected everywhere by ornamental parks . . . and as clean as a house floor, afford[ing] unsurpassed drives."[25]

The Washington social season had long tracked congressional sessions, which typically began in December and adjourned before summer. But the *Post* noted in 1880 that, rather than just political transients, the city was now luring "capitalists and retired merchants . . . to sell their property . . . and make their homes here" because the "winter season presents a continued round of gayety, while the elegance of its receptions and fashionable entertainments is proverbial." The elite presence was self-perpetuating, as "the wealth and refinement of its population attracts every year large numbers of strangers," and it was remaking the city as a "winter Saratoga."[26] By 1881, when new construction began a sixteen-year streak of annual increases, the local press was hailing a "Garfield boom," regularly running articles that effusively described the opulent houses under construction.[27]

Although many fine houses were rising along neighboring streets, Sixteenth Street was at first a poorer relation. In 1880 real estate maps showed its average value per square foot was often lower than on nearby streets. However, Sixteenth Street was poised for economic takeoff. Even blocks as far north as Boundary Street had such modern amenities as water mains, sewers, streetlights, and fire hydrants. Residents of even the more northerly blocks easily reached downtown by the Fourteenth Street horse-drawn streetcar line.[28]

Among the middle-class dwellings that rose on Sixteenth Street in late 1870s are the six Italianate-style brick houses at numbers 1816–1826, present-day survivors from a row of thirteen dwellings erected in 1878 by Robert A. Balloch (1831–1909). Balloch was one of many government clerks who dabbled in development—in his case with disastrous results, as he lost title to the uncompleted houses and unsuccessfully pursued the case to the US Supreme Court. These uniform houses featured embellishments that were affordable for government clerks, including protruding bays whose windows illuminated front parlors and bedrooms, decorative brick window hoods, and low mansard roofs with wrought iron cresting.

Much of the Gilded Age city was developing in rows that, like Balloch's, were built speculatively as variations on a common design and strung houses wall-to-wall across narrow lots. However, on Sixteenth Street such rows tended to be shorter and the houses more expensive than in more middle- and working-class areas. Many Sixteenth Street residents were affluent enough to commission more embellished and opulently appointed homes. An early example was 1601 Sixteenth, built in 1878 by swashbuckling westerner Captain Charles C. Huntley.

As a teenager, Huntley (1844–83) helped raise a volunteer Union regiment in his native Illinois and became its second lieutenant. In July 1864 he was captured at the Battle of Strawberry Plains and confined first in Richmond's notorious Libby Prison and later in the infamous Andersonville Prison in Georgia. After the war, he drifted around the western territories and became the contractor for a

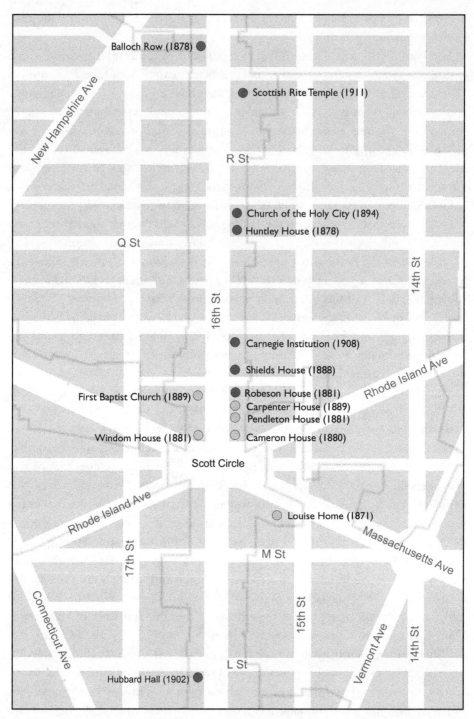

Balloch Row (1878)

Scottish Rite Temple (1911)

New Hampshire Ave

R St

Church of the Holy City (1894)
Huntley House (1878)

Q St

14th St

16th St

Carnegie Institution (1908)

Shields House (1888)

First Baptist Church (1889)   Robeson House (1881)
                               Carpenter House (1889)
                               Pendleton House (1881)
Windom House (1881)   Cameron House (1880)

Rhode Island Ave

Scott Circle

Rhode Island Ave

Louise Home (1871)

17th St

Massachusetts Ave

M St

15th St

Vermont Ave

14th St

L St

Hubbard Hall (1902)

Connecticut Ave

Key structures on Sixteenth Street in the vicinity of Scott Circle that were constructed in the late nineteenth and early twentieth centuries. Light gray circles indicate buildings no longer extant. © *Matthew Gilmore. Used by permission.*

pony express mail route between Minnesota and Montana.[29] Other mail contracts followed, and Huntley began a stagecoach line. After the Wells Fargo Company paid ten thousand dollars for these interests, Huntley established routes that transported mail and passengers across so-called Indian Country between Minnesota, California, Oregon, and Washington and linked hardscrabble gold and silver mining towns like Virginia City and the aptly named Hellsgate.[30] Huntley and a hard-riding party of scouts often escorted his coaches. Frontier newspapers considered him a genial fellow and called him a "gay boy" when in town, but he was also a ruthless competitor. A Saint Paul newspaper claimed that he had connived with postal officials to cut signatures off other contractors' endorsement petitions and append them to his own to win at least one lucrative contract.[31]

Huntley had become wealthy enough to winter at Washington's elegant Arlington Hotel (one block from Sixteenth Street on Vermont Avenue) when in 1874 he was stricken with paralysis reputedly brought on by exposure and starvation while a prisoner of war.[32] He then placed his stage operations under the management of his cousin Silas Huntley and settled permanently in Washington. He soon sued his cousin for withholding proceeds, in the process revealing that, behind the heroic figures of Captain Huntley and his plains riders, was a business built on bribery and favors rendered in the parlors of fine hotels.[33] In 1880 Silas Huntley told a court that the stage lines' profits had been offset by expenses for "getting certain things done," which included paying for territorial governors' posh rooms at the Arlington and "being friendly" to Congressmen, postal officials, and even clerks and messengers, whom "we always treated . . . very kindly in presenting them with some trifle . . . a cigar, opera ticket or dinner." Silas Huntley had also kept the press corps "very friendly" during annual postal contract reviews by hosting dinners whose fifty-dollars-per-plate cost was close to the average monthly industrial wage.[34]

Silas Huntley's courtroom revelations were reported nationally. A congressional investigation into the "star route ring" revealed widespread straw bidding and routes created to service phantom customers invented by corrupt postmasters.[35] However, neither Huntley cousin was fined or imprisoned, and Charles remained a wealthy property owner. Amid legal travails, he commissioned a fine townhouse at 1601 Sixteenth Street in 1878 and added a row of three smaller brick houses to its north two years later.

The Huntley House, which still wraps the northeast corner of Sixteenth and Q Streets, is perhaps Sixteenth Street's finest example of the Italianate style, with toothed cornices, ornamental columns, and hooded window arches. Its unknown architect apparently abhorred the idea of leaving any surface unembellished and its stable roof is topped by a spire that resembles a miniature church steeple. Unfortunately, Huntley was able to enjoy his house for only a short time before he died at age thirty-nine in 1883.[36]

While the Huntley House set an elegant standard, it was soon rivaled by a wave of newer houses. Most were substantial residences for bankers, physicians, lawyers, and other members of the city's professional classes. Like the Huntley House, such dwellings might stand wall-to-wall with neighbors, but they were larger and more embellished than typical row houses and of individualized design. While a working-class row house might have 16 to 20 feet of frontage and 700 to 1,200 square feet of living space, Sixteenth Street's greatest houses contained nearly 20,000 square feet and occupied corner lots with 100-foot frontages on each cross street. In contrast to Lafayette Square's austere Federal-style mansions, these houses were often fashion plates for the latest architectural styles. Their owners represented a new elite that mingled old money, those who had prospered in Washington, those who had gravitated to the nascent "Saratoga of the South" after becoming rich elsewhere, and a cadre that increasingly bestrode the worlds of wealth and political power. Besides being trophies for past accomplishments, these houses often staked ambitious claims to ever greater heights of power and influence.

These houses' functions were gendered and complex. Washington social life was widely seen as an extension of politics, in which receptions, dinner parties, and other gatherings created opportunities for making deals, cementing alliances, and transmitting political signals. Because formal socializing fell within what was considered the feminine domestic sphere, it was a rare avenue for women to directly participate in political life. Washington's great houses facilitated this highly ritualized behavior by following a common plan that imposed a gendered and hierarchical order on their interiors. Typically, a formal front entrance opened into an elaborately finished great hall with a grand staircase and wide fireplace whose mantel of stone or rare wood was carved into a conspicuous architectural ornament. This hall could stage informal gatherings, while its anteroom allowed household business to be transacted without letting visitors into more private domestic spaces. The grand stair, wide enough for at least two couples in evening wear to pass comfortably, led to the house's formal core on the second story. At its top was the great hall, the central area for formal entertaining. Through sliding doors, which could be thrown open during large gatherings, the hall connected the parlor, where women gathered for after-dinner conversation, the library, for masculine camaraderie, and a large formal dining room. Mary Hale, a senator's wife and famous hostess of the 1890s, noted that, although the ideal number of guests for a dinner party was twenty to twenty-four, the dining room of her Sixteenth Street home comfortably seated forty.[37] Beyond the library, a study functioned as a combination office and inner sanctum for private masculine discussions.

From the main level, the grand stair ascended to floors of bedrooms. Those on the lower sleeping floor were paired with a parlor and sometimes a private bath;

those on an upper floor might be smaller and have more limited appointments. In the most opulent houses, upper floors were served by an elevator. Servants slept on the top floor; the dormer windows in a mansard roof frequently illuminated and ventilated their rooms. A separate staircase connected this story to the kitchen, service areas, and the servant entrance on the lowest level of the house.

Newspaper articles frequently praised the appointments of such mansions and the fêtes staged within them as reflections of their owners' elevated tastes. Yet to acute observers such as novelist Henry James, the formal Washington House represented a paradox, a "self-conscious consciousness" as well as a loss of identity. James, no stranger to the salons of Lafayette Square, called Washington the "City of Conversation," where endlessly self-referential speech was a performance of a constructed public and political "self" that was atomizing and self-alienating for the actor. He portrayed the great houses that staged such conversations as disorienting spaces in which a visitor "sees only doorless apertures, vainly festooned, which decline to tell him where he is, which make him still a homeless wanderer, which show him other apertures, corridors, staircases, yawning, expanding, ascending, descending, and all as for the purpose of giving his presence 'away,' of reminding him that what he says must be said for the house." Even as these houses advanced their residents' and guests' self-inventions, social stratagems, and political ambitions, to James they were engines of depersonalization, an architectural "conspiracy for nipping the interior in the bud, for denying its right to exist, for ignoring and defeating it in every possible way, for wiping out successively each sign by which it may be known from an exterior," with a parallel effect on the individual psyche and authentic personal relations.[38]

"Calamity Circle"

In 1880 Scott Circle still marked the edge of downtown. To its south, Sixteenth Street's wood-block pavement was swept every two weeks; to its north, cleaning was monthly. Thomas Circle to the southeast was an element of the L'Enfant Plan that had been the center of a fashionable neighborhood since antebellum days. However, Scott Circle, until recently a square, was more like nearby Dupont Circle, a confluence of cross streets recently transformed into a circle and still largely surrounded by vacant land. Scott Circle's mansions would soon form continuous rows leading to these neighboring circles along Massachusetts Avenue, stretching along Rhode Island Avenue to Logan Circle, and pushing north on Sixteenth Street. As a group, these residences reflect the rapid-fire pace of development and adoption of fashionable architectural styles. Viewed individually, they vividly express the social, cultural, and political functions of mansion-building.

Northern Sixteenth Street gained its first political trophy house in 1880 when the Cameron mansion was constructed at Scott Circle. James "Don" Cameron

(1833–1918) was the son of Simon Cameron, a Pennsylvania political boss who served as Lincoln's secretary of war before being replaced for inefficiency and suspected corruption. Don Cameron, who had briefly served as Grant's last secretary of war, became a senator after his father resigned his seat in his favor. Shortly after being elected to a full term in 1879, Cameron commissioned a massive, ostentatious, and expensive house from John Fraser (1825–1906), a fashionable architect from Philadelphia and designer of the nearby Brodhead House at 1500 Rhode Island Avenue (1879) and the James G. Blaine residence at 2000 Massachusetts Avenue (1881).[39] Priced at nine thousand dollars, Charles Huntley's residence had cost about three times the price of a Balloch row house; Cameron spent more than one hundred thousand dollars on his red brick and brownstone-trimmed house, which rose five levels from basement kitchen to attic servants' quarters and was equipped with an elevator. Cameron and his much younger wife, Lizzie, were noted for entertaining; their house's grand hall had nearly the area of an average working-class row house.[40] Offering dramatic testimony to its owner's political clout, the house looked down Sixteenth Street toward the White House and in turn provided an imposing backdrop for the statue of General Scott. The presence of such elite residents called for upgrades to the street itself; bids were soon let to replace the wooden paving with asphalt between Lafayette Square and Scott Circle.[41] However, opulent surroundings and outward gaiety could not mask the Camerons' deeply unhappy marriage; Lizzie Cameron spent her time in Europe and Don Cameron soon moved to Lafayette Square.[42]

In 1885 Washington columnist Frank Carpenter, who wrote as "Carp," informed his readers that "Ohio owns Washington."[43] The capital indeed seemed a Buckeye political colony between 1868 and 1901, when Ohioans Grant, Hayes, Garfield, and McKinley held the presidency, but Carp's remark was literal. He contended that "Ohio men own more property here at Washington than the citizens of any other state."[44] Cameron's neighbor, Cincinnati lawyer-turned-Democratic-politician George Pendleton (1825–89), personified such prosperity; Carp called him "the aristocrat's aristocrat, the man whose body is nourished by terrapin and champagne."[45] Pendleton had been George McClellan's running mate in the 1864 presidential election and had spent decades in the House before being elected to the Senate in 1879. Two years later, he built a grand house to the rear of Cameron's mansion at 1313 Sixteenth. Although affluent Washington still favored Second Empire, Italianate, and Renaissance Revival styles, Baltimore architects James Bosley Noel Wyatt (1847–1926) and Joseph Evans Sperry (1854–1930) designed Pendleton's house in the exuberant Queen Anne style popular in England and just becoming fashionable in the United States. The Pendleton House helped establish a citywide trend that in 1883 led Carp to observe that "in the new buildings, the Queen Anne style predominates, and the most common material is

Scott Circle, seen here looking north against a backdrop that includes the Cameron Mansion (1880), immediately to the right of the statue, and the tower of the First Baptist Church (1889), to the left. The Cameron House was demolished in 1941, and the First Baptist Church was replaced by a Gothic Revival building in 1956. *Washington, DC, Buildings and Monuments Photograph Album, 1901, DC History Center.*

Philadelphia pressed brick. This gives this part of the city a glaring appearance of Pompeiian red, but it is on the whole pleasing and beautiful."[46]

Accentuating its red brick with deep red mortar, the Pendleton House might have struck the typical Washingtonian as wild. Unlike the rectilinear houses of the day, it was asymmetric, sprouting three dissimilar gables, a central cross-wing, and twin massive box-like oriel windows that hung from the second story of its front façade. The *Post* called it "an abode of simple elegance" with a tasteful crimson morning room, dining room in "soft shades of old gold and olive," and second-floor library flooded with light from the oriel (bay) windows.[47] The trendsetting house gained much attention. Members of Washington's social elite typically received walk-in callers on a particular day of the week; the Pendletons

The Pendleton House (1881), at 1313 Sixteenth Street NW just north of Scott Circle, helped popularize the Queen Anne style in Washington. It was demolished in 1941. *Hutchins and Moore,* The National Capital, Past and Present.

had four hundred visitors on their first such receiving day in their new home. It was called "the most beautiful [house] in Washington" by the *National Republican*, documented by pioneer architectural photographer Albert Levy, and engraved for a *Harper's New Monthly Magazine* article.[48] However, Pendleton enjoyed its splendor only briefly, as his energetic efforts to reform the Civil Service alienated home state party bosses, who ensured that he was not renominated in 1884. When Grover Cleveland named him minister to Germany in 1885, he sold the house and departed Washington for good.

Later in 1881, Wyatt and Sperry designed another Queen Anne–style house a few lots north of the Pendleton House. While Pendleton had been nicknamed "Gentleman George" for his collegial manner, his new neighbor, George Robeson (1829–97), lived in a swirl of contention. In 1869 President Grant had named the pugnacious New Jersey attorney general as his secretary of the navy. Rumored to have amassed a fortune of three hundred thousand dollars on an annual salary of about eight thousand dollars, Robeson became the target of two congressional investigations. Admiral David Dixon Porter, whom the secretary defeated in a bruising bureaucratic struggle, nicknamed him "the Cuttlefish" for his ability to confuse investigators with a cloud of ink.[49] Although the *Post* opined that "by far the boldest and most gigantic robbery that has ever been perpetrated upon this government was the system of public plunder carried on by Robeson and his accomplices," the secretary avoided indictment.[50] In 1878 he was elected to Congress from his native state. Robeson and his wife, Mary, entertained lavishly, and they likely planned their "artistic" twenty-five-room mansion at the corner of O Street to advance his political ambitions.[51] However, his aggressive pursuit of a Senate seat soon started a feud with a powerful Republican rival, who threw his support to Robeson's Democratic opponent in the 1882 congressional election. Robeson poured his own money into the campaign, and defeat found him more than sixty thousand dollars in debt. Then, as Washington diarist Mary Logan wrote, "the auctioneer's voice was heard in the drawing-room, library, dining-room, and chambers of that pretentious house, crying 'Who bids?'"[52] Mary Robeson took their children to Europe, where she obtained a divorce; "Poor Georgie" soon sold the house and retreated to Trenton.

Like the Cameron house, the Pendleton and Robeson mansions made manifest their owners' claims to newly achieved positions of power and provided social stages to advance their aspirations. While these houses were under construction, a fourth such house was rising nearby. William Windom (1827–91), a "dark horse" presidential candidate at the 1880 Republican convention, had resigned his Minnesota Senate seat to become Garfield's secretary of the treasury. In June 1881 he began building an ornate four-story mansion with an elevator and a private bath for each second-story bedchamber on Scott Circle just west of Sixteenth Street.[53]

Political rivals and Sixteenth Street neighbors: Bernhard Gillam's 1882 cartoon "The Great Congressional Tramp Bullying the Old Women of the National Household" lampooned a congressional appropriations kerfuffle. Bellicose representative George Robeson in tramp's garb stands at a door concealing his Scott Circle neighbor, frightened Senator William Windom. Fellow neighbor Senator Don Cameron hides beneath the table. Cameron, Windom, and Robeson all built mansions with frontage on the 1300 block of Sixteenth Street in 1880–81. *Library of Congress.*

Assassin Charles Guiteau's bullet, which fatally wounded the president just a week after Windom received his building permit, changed the destiny of both house and owner. Windom resigned his cabinet post and was reappointed to his former Senate seat. In 1882 he was unexpectedly defeated for reelection after his opponent circulated a photograph of his mansion, billing it a symbol of elite snobbery and corruption.[54] Windom then leased the house to Secretary of State James Blaine, who had once planned to build on Pendleton and Robeson's lots, and moved to New York.

These mansion-builders' downfalls showed the volatility and Darwinian spirit of Gilded Age politics and indelibly linked Scott Circle's mansions with hubris in the popular imagination. In the 1890s Carp noted that "the day seems to have come when the building of a big house is almost the foreshadow of political ruin."[55] The 1904 *Rand McNally Guide to Washington, DC* suggested that this curse was geographic, reporting that "Scott Circle is called 'Calamity Circle,' because every person who built a house there died shortly afterward, or met with misfortune."[56]

As the 1880s progressed, more grand houses in styles ranging from Second Empire to Queen Anne filled the 1300 block of Sixteenth Street, just north of the circle. An example of the "capitalist and retired merchant" class relocating to Washington for its social life was J. Fairfield Carpenter, who had made his money licensing German rights to the Westinghouse air brake patents. After years abroad, Carpenter decided to divide his time between Washington and his New York estate, and in 1886 commissioned his wife's cousin, architect Harry Ten Eyck Wendell (1861–1917), to design his townhouse at 1327 Sixteenth Street. The Carpenter House's façade was an extraordinary combination of white, rough-surfaced Indiana limestone blocks and bands of stone carved in swirling patterns that suggested vines and fantastic animals. Its parlor and dining room served as a personal museum for the art and artifacts collected by the Carpenters, and the *Evening Star*'s account of a reception on March 10, 1891, conveys how such spaces and their decor served as stage-sets for elaborate social ritual. Gathered in her dining room, Elizabeth Carpenter's dozen-odd women guests admired the "broad frieze . . . of delft platters and gorgeously-colored glazed pottery" from Europe displayed between the eight-foot-tall oak wainscoting and sixteen-foot-high paneled ceiling. An enormous copper tub that had once contained "the winter's bread supply for the inmates of a feudal castle" held logs for the broad open fireplace. A "monstrous clock towering halfway to the high ceiling" chimed the hours to a tune played by a mechanical harp, which varied by the day of the week. Guests sipped punch from hollowed oranges through straws, "which, tied with narrow pink ribbons, lay to the side of the cut glass dish holding the orange," ate sliced terrapin from small pewter saucepans, drank Roman punch in pink glasses, and rewarded themselves with ices molded in the form of the roses loosely scattered over the table.[57] Later that spring, Fairfield Carpenter purchased a lot on Scott Circle from the Louise Home and enclosed it with a low iron fence, creating a private park whose "well-kept lawn with its winding walks shaded from the sun by the tall trees and shrubbery is a favorite resort for his children and their friends."[58]

In 1889 a new landmark joined the 1300 block's elite residences. The First Baptist congregation, which traced its roots to a prayer meeting at the Treasury Office in 1801, had long been considered the mother church for white Washington Baptists.[59] Its move from the downtown commercial district to the corner of Sixteenth and O Streets followed the appointment of Charles Stakely, an accomplished orator from Charleston, South Carolina, as pastor. After Stakely successfully argued that moving to a developing residential neighborhood would be reinvigorating, the congregation selected a site opposite the Robeson house in what the *Star* called "the fashionable residence portion of the city [with] so many beautiful examples of modern architecture" and chose W. Bruce Gray (1849–1906), designer of nine Sixteenth Street houses, as its architect.[60]

Dedicated in 1889, the massive brick-over-stone Romanesque Revival church was among the city's grandest, with an amphitheater-like sanctuary that seated 1,300 worshipers. The *Post* called it "handsome and imposing," while the *Star* reported

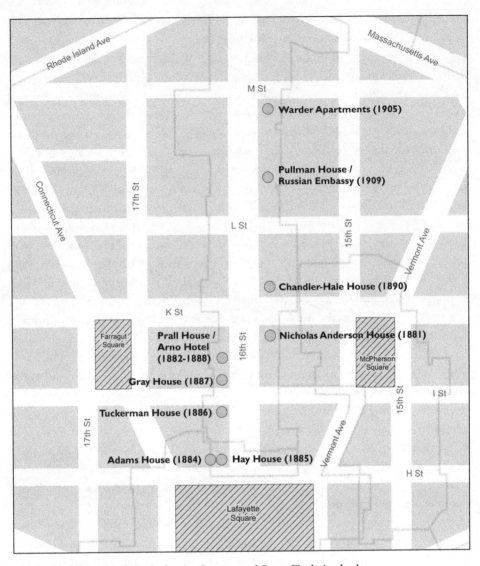

Notable buildings between Lafayette Square and Scott Circle in the late nineteenth and early twentieth centuries. Between K and M Streets, their construction contributed to the displacement of the long-established African American community. © *Matthew Gilmore. Used by permission.*

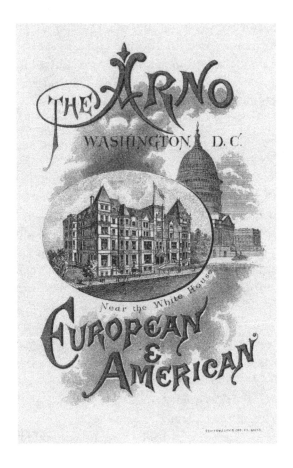

The Arno Hotel, built up from large adjoining townhouses in 1886, was located at 916 Sixteenth Street NW and remained in service until the building was demolished in 1959. *Authors' collection.*

that it represented the "the best school of modern architecture." The *Star* considered its square, 140-foot-high campanile a "very interesting experiment" because "the architect will depend entirely upon brick to give adequate expression to this characteristic of the Roman style of architecture" without relying on stone.[61] The experiment was a success; the campanile was for decades the tallest structure on Sixteenth Street and punctuated the Washington skyline for nearly seventy years.

As this elite white neighborhood coalesced around Scott Circle, a mix of substantial townhouses and mansions was springing up just north of Lafayette Square. In 1882 newspapers marveled at the house being built at 916 Sixteenth by William E. Prall, an inventor and ardent spiritualist. Prall's mansion in "the renaissance style . . . with a strong Norman feeling" was a riot in red brick, dripping with ornamental carving and dominated by a dramatic four-story square tower with a round turret. Inside its front door were entrances to separate fourteen-room residences, one for the adult children from Prall's first marriage and the other for his current spouse and their children.[62] However, by 1886 Prall and some partners had converted the house into the Arno Hotel, soon adding adjoining six-story buildings, one as rooms for tourists and transients and the other as apartments for longer-term residents. The Arno's massive presence became a selling point; its advertisements juxtaposed the Capitol with its agglomeration of turrets and gables beneath a waving "Hotel Arno" banner. The hotel and its annexes on I Street grew to include two hundred rooms, and it survived into the 1950s (see chapter 6).

Counternarratives

While the theatricality of the Prall House captured attention, three of Washington's most iconic and iconoclastic houses took shape nearby. Their story had begun thirty years earlier on the Harvard campus, where future celebrated architect Henry Hobson Richardson (1838–86) moved in the same circle of artistically inclined bons vivants as Nicholas Longworth Anderson (1838–92), the son of a millionaire Cincinnati businessman dubbed "the father of American wine," and Henry Adams (1838–1918), grandson and great-grandson of presidents. The Civil War had scattered the new graduates across the world. Richardson, a Louisianan who had entered the École des Beaux-Arts in 1860, rode out the war in Paris. After the election of 1860 Adams, who had come to Washington as his congressman father's secretary, was befriended by John Hay (1838–1905), Abraham Lincoln's junior private secretary. When war began, Adams accompanied his father to a diplomatic post in London. Anderson entered the Union Army as a private and, after being wounded three times, came out a brevet general.[63]

The four men's postwar lives followed circuitous paths. In 1877 Adams and his wife Clover settled on Lafayette Square, just a block from the house at 1601 I Street where his grandfather John Quincy Adams had lived. In Washington, Adams, supported by family wealth, wrote magazine articles and histories, as well as the novel *Democracy*, a best-seller published anonymously in 1880.

After Lincoln's murder, John Hay had stumbled through life before regaining his stride as a popular journalist and poet. In 1875 his father-in-law, a millionaire industrialist, persuaded him to move to Cleveland to manage his business affairs.[64] However, like Adams, Hay suffered recurrent bouts of depression and feelings of purposelessness. In 1879 he returned to Washington as an interim assistant secretary of state and reconnected with Adams.[65] The bond among Henry and Clover Adams, John and Clara Hay, and Clarence King, a charismatic, deeply troubled adventurer serving as the first head of the US Geological Survey, grew so intense that Clover nicknamed the group "The Five of Hearts." Most afternoons the Hearts assembled in the Adams' rented house at 1607 H Street, until Garfield's inauguration in March 1881 turned both Hay and King out of office. Eventually the ever-impecunious King set off to investigate Mexican silver mines, and Hay succumbed to a plea that he fill in for the honeymooning editor of the *New York Herald Tribune*.[66] Henry Adams's friendship with Henry Richardson had continued through the Civil War and Richardson's comet-like rise to the first rank of American architecture in the 1870s. Yet it was Nicholas Anderson who brought Richardsonian architecture to Washington. In 1880 Anderson, discontent with life in Cincinnati despite long sojourns in Europe, had settled on Lafayette Square. In March 1881, he purchased a former coal and wood yard at Sixteenth and K Streets and commissioned Richardson to design his family's home there.[67]

Building a Richardson house placed great demands upon its owner, whom the architect constantly lobbied to add layers of expensive decoration. Nicholas Anderson complained to his son about the irresistible seductions Richardson cast before him while construction lagged, and the ailing, three-hundred-pound architect's combination of neediness and boorishness as a house guest on his visits from his studio in Brookline, Massachusetts: "He bullies and nags everybody; makes great demands upon our time and service; must ride, even if he has to go but a square; gets up at noon; and has to have his meals sent to his room. He is a mournful object for size, but he never ought to stay in a private house because he requires so much attention."[68] Anderson had expected to spend thirty thousand dollars for his house but overran his budget more than threefold. Gaslights were still being fitted and doors hung when the Andersons finally moved in during October 1883, about two and a half years after the commission.[69]

Unlike the fussily detailed Prall House, the Anderson House was noted for its absence of visual clutter as well as its boldness, power, and monumental scale.[70] Indeed, critics have described it as "severely chaste" and of "massive, almost marital simplicity."[71] Its Sixteenth Street façade was framed by tower-like bays, the northernmost a rounded turret that turned the corner to K Street, where its formal entrance faced toward Cook Corner (see chapter 1). Marianna Van Rensselaer, Richardson's first biographer, suggested in 1888 that its massive steeply gabled roof was too dramatic, being "so vast [that] it strikes one more . . . as an expedient to avoid the commonplace than as an obviously sensible covering." Yet she expressed what became a critical consensus: "the building is a fine one—grand in mass, harmonious in proportions, coherent in design, and dignified in utter simplicity . . . a true conception."[72] The Anderson House pleased an aesthetically sophisticated audience; it was photographed by G. W. Sheldon for his 1884 volume *Artistic Houses* and featured in national magazines in 1885–86. The English poet and critic Matthew Arnold supposedly requested a tour while lecturing in Washington.[73] However, Washington had no ready frame of reference for what Richardson had wrought. Nicholas Anderson admitted that "public opinion seems divided," as "some are extravagant in their compliments, while others find it devoid of all beauty."[74] He concluded that "it requires severe and well-educated taste to see its grand lines and simple beauty. . . . I am delighted with it."[75]

At about the time the Andersons were moving in, Adams saw an opportunity for the Hearts to reunite. When a scheme to construct an apartment building at the

RESIDENCE OF GENERAL ANDERSON.

The Nicholas Anderson House (completed 1883) on the southeast corner of Sixteenth and K Streets NW, brought the architecture of H. H. Richardson to Washington. It was replaced by the Carlton Hotel in 1926. *Hutchins and Moore,* The National Capital, Past and Present.

corner of Sixteenth and H Streets failed, Henry suggested that he and Hay acquire the land for adjoining houses to be designed by Richardson. The wealthier Hay purchased the plot and sold the western third to Adams.[76]

Literary historian Sarah Luria has noted that Henry Adams's writing contrasted the founders' idealism and faith in democracy with his times' materialism, ostentation, and commodified social relations. As the Adamses' friend Henry James suggested, these symptoms of psychic corruption were embodied in the very structure of the Washington "great house." The Adams' home would present a counternarrative. Rather than an "anti-house" focused on social externalities, Clover Adams wrote that it would be a "spartan . . . brick box" whose center, rather than a great hall or a parlor, would have a "library—a study next to it, a dining room behind," intimate spaces for authentic personal interchange.[77] While the Adamses worried about cost, they believed that their aesthetic sophistication and emotional bond with Richardson would curb his excesses without compromising his vision and enable him to channel their values, and indeed their personalities, into a psychically satisfactory house.

Once construction began in the summer of 1884, Richardson proposed embellishments. Henry Adams bemoaned their cost but usually assented. Meanwhile, Clover Adams fell into deepening melancholy after her father's death in early 1885. An accomplished photographer, she made notable portraits of the architect and the house's stonework. Nevertheless, on December 6, 1885, her despondency led her to kill herself by drinking photographic chemicals. Three weeks later, Henry Adams moved into the parlor-less house whose form so reflected his and Clover's visions. He pronounced himself cut off from the pleasures of the world and suggested that his emotional self had died with his wife.[78]

The Adamses' tragic tale led to eternally conflicted readings of their house. To some, its twin front arches, whose carved symbols included an "Assyrian beast," suggested a mad citadel of loneliness. *The Book of Washington*, a gossipy guidebook from 1920, baselessly claimed that Henry Adams had refused a request from Clover to cut a door for the passage of spirits and dismissively described him as "as a strange man, a brooding man," who "waited for years and years for public recognition which never came," and concluded that "he so markedly shows how a man may fail even though carefully prepared to succeed."[79] Luria and others have interpreted the house less grimly, calling it a fortress-sanctuary whose arches shielded entrances that suggested the mouths of sheltering caves and whose stout brick walls and large second-story windows both confronted and surveilled the White House, denied the Adamses by despised populists like Andrew Jackson, whose statue gallops endlessly across Lafayette Square.[80]

Recent biographers have viewed Adams's self-depiction as exaggerated. While he indeed called his house a "symbolic tomb," it remained the center of a circle that included Hay, Henry James, and a host of other artistic and diplomatic figures. There was also his long-standing affair with Lizzie Cameron, wife of Senator Don Cameron.[81] The darker assessments of the house were dispelled by Adams's biographer Harold Cater, who interviewed numerous visitors and suggested that most were impressed by its cheerfulness:

> It had little about it that was pretentious and much that was practical. . . . The main living-rooms were on the floor above, and a flood of light came into them from six large south windows across the front. . . . The front stairs, designed to make climbing almost effortless led from the street level to a hall, which in turn opened into the large library. The latter served also as a drawing-room. In this room there was a fireplace of sea-green Mexican onyx shot with red. Off the library and to the rear, was the dining-room, which had an unusual fireplace in light stone carved with wild roses. . . . In all these rooms there was a sense of color and light.[82]

H. H. Richardson's Adams House (1884), located on H Street across from Lafayette Square, circa 1921. The Romanesque Revival house was a radical and controversial revision of the traditional Washington great house. It was demolished in 1926 to make way for the Hay-Adams Hotel. *Library of Congress.*

John Hay had a spectacular career as ambassador to England and secretary of state in the McKinley and Teddy Roosevelt administrations. His house followed the conventional Washington scheme, with a great hall and marble-trimmed parlor for entertaining. Its broad and busy façade featured an ungainly tower that loomed across Sixteenth Street toward Saint John's. At twelve thousand square feet, the house was twice as large as the Adams House. Its grander scale attracted greater attention. *The Book of Washington* dismissively referred to the Adams House as "tucked in" behind it.[83] Newspaper correspondent Carp frequently cast a jaundiced eye on extravagant Washington homes. When, in a November 1885 column, he turned his attention to "John Hay's palace," his readers were expecting another deflating depiction of vanity and excess.[84] However, they were surprised to learn that "it is the finest house in Washington and is one of the most wonderful combinations of brick and mortar in the world." Carp's cellar-to-roof tour vividly conveyed its expansiveness and sumptuous decoration. The great hall's white mahogany wainscoting had "a finish like that of a piano" and its staircase was "so wide that ten persons could walk up it abreast." The meshed rafters of the library's thirteen-foot ceiling held oak discs two feet in diameter, dusted with gold highlights that "show only in the grain . . . gleaming brilliantly by night, under the . . . gaslight." More functional luxuries included bathrooms with "marble wash basins with silver spigots having hot and cold water and the cutest little bathtub . . . in which to wash your feet," as well as electric servant bells.

The Cameron and Windom Houses helped establish Sixteenth Street north of Lafayette Square as a district for conventionally fashionable architecture. The Queen Anne–styled Pendleton and Robeson Houses made Sixteenth Street a stage for Washington's increasing sophistication and openness to artistic trends. Richardson's "unique conception(s)" were bold statements of their owners' personalities, the work of a nationally acclaimed architect which challenged, broadened, and deepened Washington's architectural sensibilities and reverberated throughout the city. On Sixteenth Street, the Richardsonian Romanesque became a style of choice for the most opulent and fashionable houses. The Lucius Tuckerman House, erected immediately north of the Hay House just months after Richardson's death in 1886, was long misattributed to Richardson rather than Washington's Hornblower & Marshall. The Dedman House at 1623 Sixteenth (1886) and Susan Shields House at 1401 Sixteenth (1888) soon followed as examples of citywide significance. Indeed, Richardsonianism became so established as a style that other architects' examples could find even greater favor than its originator's work. The *Star* implied that Richardson's final Washington dwelling, the Benjamin Warder House at 1515 K Street, suggested whimsy and romantic medievalism, noting, "Mr. Warder's exquisite new grotto house postulates white cross knights, aesthetic maidens wearing white rosebuds, and medieval gowns." In contrast, Hornblower & Marshall's robust Tuckerman House "presume[s] hearty

Richardson's John Hay House, which adjoined the Adams House, featured this great hall with polished white mahogany wainscoting and a grand staircase that "ten persons could walk up . . . abreast." Along with the Adams House, it was replaced by the Hay-Adams Hotel. *DC Public Library.*

nineteenth century living and plenty of it."[85] Although Richardson's quartet of Washington houses seemed built for eternity, none remained in place fifty years later. Yet as images they have become enduring architectural monuments whose imprint raised Sixteenth Street's stature as a residential boulevard.

Gentrification

As the 1880s progressed, the clusters of mansions and grand townhouses forming around Scott Circle and spreading north from Lafayette Square increasingly squeezed the African American neighborhood between them. In December 1883, a *New York Sun* correspondent assayed the social structure of Washington's African American community. In addition to elite Blacks, he wrote, the community included many middle-class "government clerks and people in comfortable circumstances who own comfortable little homes, and one of the finest streets in the city is occupied by them. This is Sixteenth Street, between the Scott statue and the White House. It is a splendid avenue, broad, well paved, and in the heart of the most fashionable part of the city." He noted that "nearly all of these colored residents own their houses and refuse to sell," but, reflecting the assumptions of the time, considered it inevitable that this "very valuable property . . . must ultimately pass out of their possession."[86]

By the decade's end, the correspondent's prediction was becoming true, as affluent whites displaced African Americans, many of whom moved to less-developed neighborhoods, like Southwest. Cook Corner, across K Street from the Anderson House, endured until 1889, when John F. Cook Jr. sold it for a price so high that the *Star* announced it would have been considered "ridiculous" a few years earlier.[87] The Cook properties were quickly replaced by a mansion of legendary grandeur built by Letitia Chandler, widow of Michigan senator Zachariah Chandler. Zachariah Chandler had been an outspoken Radical Republican who advocated for African American rights after the Civil War. A highly combative and partisan figure who became wealthy in office, he was frequently assailed in the press as a drunkard, "a howler among howling statesmen," and one of "a gang of patriots to whom the war of the rebellion was a grand harvest time, bringing them riches and honors but no sacrifices."[88] "Old Zach" was being touted as a presidential candidate when he died suddenly in 1879.

Undeterred by her late husband's controversial reputation, Letitia Chandler purchased the Cook tract to build a Washington palazzo for her daughter Mary and son-in-law, Maine senator Eugene Hale (1836–1917). Her architects, the Boston firm of Rotch & Tilden, had an impeccable pedigree as designers of Bar Harbor summer mansions and elegant Back Bay townhouses. Completed in 1891, the Chandler-Hale House was striking for its sheer size and elaborate detailing. Its greenish-yellow tile roof, resting forty-two feet above the sidewalk, and "modern" cream-colored brick and limestone façade contrasted with the red brick Nicholas Anderson House across K Street. Transparent rondels ornament whose wafer-thin diamond-shaped marble panes cast a subtle glow within and ornate plasterwork set off the Hales' collection of tapestries and Persian carpets. The house's decor captured the sensibilities of its creators' age and social class and was described exhaustively in contemporary magazines.[89] Fifteen years after the house's construction, the *Post* pronounced it still "artistic and up-to-date," and lauded the Hales' refinement in selecting a rosewood piano rather than one of the gilded instruments then in vogue.[90]

The spectacular house expressed dynastic ambitions, and it indeed launched a brilliant social career: Mary Hale became a leading hostess, entertaining royally in her dining room that could have seated a military troop. But although Senator Hale became a powerful committee chair, any higher aspirations were dashed a few years later when he opposed the war with Spain backed by Republican leaders.

The Chandler-Hale House on the northeast corner of Sixteenth and K Streets NW, seen circa 1939, was among the magnificent Sixteenth Street mansions commissioned by women. It replaced the John F. Cook residence (see chapter 1) in 1890 and was in turn replaced by the Statler Hotel in 1942. *General Photograph Collection, DC History Center.*

Nonetheless, the Chandler-Hale senatorial dynasty entered a third generation when Frederick Hale was elected to his father's seat in 1916.

In 1890 the Duke of Sunderland quipped that "I don't call [Washington] a city. It seems to me a mere park, with beautiful residences and public buildings scattered about it."[91] Over the following decades, his remark increasingly described Sixteenth Street, whose transition to a largely upper- and upper-middle-class neighborhood came at the expense of the long-established African American community. The Chandler-Hale mansion was the most opulent of numerous upscale houses built for white owners in the street's historically African American 1000 and 1100 blocks during the 1890s. A few prosperous African American residents remained in the mix. John Cook Jr. returned from Howard University's environs in 1898 to build a fine townhouse at 1118 Sixteenth, designed by white architect

Frederick B. Pyle. Cook's next-door neighbors were Anna and William Wormley, the widow and son of the famed African American hotelier and restaurateur James Wormley, who had built adjoining brick houses in 1885. However, by 1910 very few African American households remained on Sixteenth Street.

Sixteenth Street's white elite of political figures, financiers, bankers, lawyers, and physicians, more than a dozen of whom had built houses by the early 1900s, heavily represented professions that excluded women. However, the street still had women householders representing a wide economic spectrum, including dressmakers, seamstresses, boardinghouse keepers, wealthy widows, heiresses, and the matriarchs of extended families, like Letitia Chandler. In the late nineteenth and early twentieth century, they included nearly twenty women who built houses on Sixteenth Street. Besides the Chandler-Hale House, nineteenth-century mansions commissioned by women included the stately Richardsonian Romanesque house at 1401 Sixteenth, constructed in 1888 for Susan Shields, a lawyer's widow active in charities, and now the Embassy of Kazakhstan.[92] In the mid-1880s Antoinette Manney, wife of a future rear admiral, traded and subdivided plots to assemble a site for their home at 1629 Sixteenth. More modest accommodations included the brick dwelling at 1600 Sixteenth, where seventy-seven-year-old Mary Reynolds lived in a boardinghouse kept with her daughter and son-in-law, a War Department clerk.[93]

Among Sixteenth Street's women householders was a notable medical pioneer, Dr. Mary Dora Spackman (1839–1904). Spackman, a widow who supported two young children as a counter at the Department of the Treasury, became the first woman graduate of the newly formed Howard University School of Medicine in 1872. When Spackman, who, like all Howard's first half-dozen woman medical graduates, was white, applied for her medical license, it was "diplomatically explained" to her that the local law restricted them to "gentlemen." Spackman and another woman Howard graduate successfully petitioned Congress to de-gender the statute in 1875, but she was never admitted to the District of Columbia Medical Society.[94] For thirty years she practiced from her home, a modest Civil War–era brick house at 1634 Sixteenth, and at a pioneering women's clinic that treated patients without regard to color or creed.[95] When she died in 1904, no newspaper carried an obituary, but the District's women physicians held a special meeting to commemorate her path-breaking career.[96]

A National Church on an Avenue of the Elite

Despite another financial downturn, the Panic of 1893, Sixteenth Street's social stature continued to grow in the 1890s, as evidenced by the building of its first "national church," the Swedenborgian Church of the Holy City. Holy City's construction at the corner of Sixteenth and Corcoran Streets combined necessity and aspiration. The Swedenborgian faith, a Christian denomination based on the teachings of eighteenth-century Swedish scientist and theologian Emanuel Swedenborg, had been established in Washington before the Civil War. After the city's original Swedenborgian church burned in 1889, a national convention resolved that its replacement should represent the entire national denomination. Holy City might well have added to Sixteenth Street's portfolio of "modern" Richardsonian Romanesque architecture, had Pastor Frank Sewall's plans been followed. However, the building effort soon attracted Langford Warren, an influential Boston architect and Swedenborgian.

Although Warren had been H. H. Richardson's chief assistant during the building of the Nicholas Anderson House, fellow studio alumnus Charles Coolidge described him as "a Goth at heart."[97] Holy City, built in limestone to the plans of Warren with local collaborators Paul J. Pelz and Frederic W. Carlyle and dedicated in 1894, is English Gothic, a traditional style perhaps chosen to allay congregants' concerns that its design might be too flamboyant for a time of economic distress. However, there is nothing subdued about the building. Its ramparts' bestiary includes jaguars and lions, with rearing griffins at its gables. The belfry, guarded by snarling canine gargoyles, was to be surmounted by a copper spire even taller than First Baptist's campanile.[98] Although the spire was never erected, a stair-tower and two-story addition built to Warren's plans in 1911 wrapped a Gothic skin around remarkable Arts and Crafts interiors. Sewall contributed a thematic plan for the stained-glass windows of the nave and west wall, some of which were designed by his daughter, painter Alice James (1870–1955). These original windows, fabricated by Ford & Brooks of Boston, with additions by J. & L. Lamb of New York, remain vivid more than a century later.[99]

The City Beautiful

With the turn of the twentieth century, a revolutionary reconceptualization of the city's monumental core became the dominant architectural vision for the District of Columbia. Named for the Parisian architectural school that trained many of its adherents, the Beaux-Arts movement sought order and beauty by applying Classical and Neoclassical precedents to contemporary buildings. Beaux-Arts buildings did not merely copy Greek or Roman originals. They were organized by a fully rationalized plan that analyzed the building's function and symmetrically arranged its spaces around central axes, while harmonizing interior and exterior through the application of classical orders and ornament.[100] Given their expense, such highly detailed buildings were generally grand residences and major civic edifices such as Washington's Carnegie Library (1903), Union Station (1908), and John A. Wilson Municipal Building (1908).

Beaux-Arts principles were applied to Washington's cityscape by adherents of the City Beautiful movement, which achieved initial critical mass with the success of the 1893 Chicago World's Columbian Exposition and its widely admired "White City." In Washington these principles became the basis of the 1902 McMillan Plan, which re-envisioned the city core as a procession of monumental public buildings and grand boulevards arranged about the National Mall. In such a symmetrical order, every building, regardless of function or type, exerted a multiplier effect on the beauty and harmony of the city as a whole. This interlacing of Beaux-Arts architecture and urban planning has been interpreted as a reaction against urban disorder as well as a type of social control. The shared style of great houses and major civic buildings expressed upper-class hegemony, while, as historian Richard Fogelsong notes, the harmonized landscape was "a way of glorifying [economic] capital's control of the city . . . because in accepting the City Beautiful ideal and celebrating its icons, local citizens were being asked . . . to accept the leadership of the group that made these works possible."[101]

The Duke of Sutherland's 1890 quip about Washington becoming a "beautiful park" was a harbinger of the City Beautiful vision. Franklin W. Smith (1826–1911), a wealthy Boston utopian and architectural visionary, had become attracted to Washington, for which he designed the Hall of the Ancients, a cultural museum based on the Great Hypostyle Hall at Karnak, Egypt, and prepared Beaux-Arts-accented plans for the city's monumental core. In 1900 Smith presented an ambitious set of "designs, plans, and suggestions for the aggrandizement of Washington" that reflected a corollary of City Beautiful principles. Creating such aestheticized landscapes, in Smith's view, required that utilitarian functions and working-class housing be restricted to districts remote from the city center. Smith's plan included "clearance of Sixteenth street from shanties, tumble-down stables, etc." He complained that "the spacious streets of Washington, lovely in verdure at seasons, are wretchedly marred by rookeries [concentrations of slum housing], etc., intermingled with splendid dwellings. . . . On Sixteenth street, one of the most important and elegant avenues, they have been undisturbed for thirty or forty years."

Smith pushed for "legislative compulsion" to rid the avenue of inferior structures. Aware that his proposal could be considered racist, he inserted a footnote insisting that he was not objecting to the occupants of these humble dwellings and noting, "There are many colored people to be preferred as neighbors in cities to many white folks of their population."[102] Nevertheless, the practical effect of such calls for eradication of dwellings that were less than "splendid" was to force African American residents to disperse.

Smith's call for legislative action was never heeded, but pressure for displacement continued. In 1907 a *Post* real estate writer commented that "the disturbing element on the street . . . is the number of small, crude shanties which are in unpleasant contrast to the magnificent residences nearby. Efforts have been made to get rid of these, which are occupied mostly by negroes, but the attempts have been only partially successful, because of the high values set by the occupants."[103]

In 1900 "For Sale" signs reflected the displacement of the African American neighborhood on Sixteenth Street between K and M Streets NW. Both the Louise Home (*bottom left*) and the Metropolitan AME Church (*bottom center*) can be seen in the background. *Franklin Webster Smith,* The Aggrandizement of Washington.

Gentrification's march through lower Sixteenth Street was represented by several dwellings designed by French-born and École-educated Jules de Sibour (1872–1938), architect for eleven buildings that stood within two blocks of Scott Circle. De Sibour's now-altered English Gothic–accented house at 1128 Sixteenth (1909) was a forty-five-thousand-dollar speculative dwelling that replaced two small brick houses, one of which had been constructed by an African American laborer for his ten-member household in 1877.[104] The limestone-trimmed apartment house across the street at 1155 Sixteenth, designed by de Sibour and Bruce Price, emulated the finest Parisian flats.[105] In 1905 the *Evening Star* marveled that the new building was "quite unlike anything of the sort that has thus far been attempted in this city," and only a single fourteen-room apartment occupied each of its four upper floors. Each suite included a grand salon, dining room, and library facing Sixteenth Street, as well as spacious family bedrooms along M Street, and servant bedrooms, laundries, and kitchens on the east and south sides.[106] In keeping with the notion that it was a stack of discreet residences, the building was never formally named, though it became known as the Warder Apartments.

Seen here in 1923, the Warder apartment building, on the southeast corner of Sixteenth and M Streets, was one of Sixteenth Street's finest examples of the Beaux-Arts architectural style. Completed in 1906, the building was torn down in 1958 to make way for a new headquarters building for the American Chemical Society. *Library of Congress.*

Harriet Pullman, widow of the sleeping-car magnate, commissioned the mansion
at 1125 Sixteenth Street NW to advance the political career of her son-in-law,
Representative Frank Lowden. The Beaux-Arts structure, constructed in 1909, became
the Russian Embassy in 1913. Since 1994 it has served as the Russian ambassador's
residence. Historic American Buildings Survey, 1977. *Library of Congress.*

Lower Sixteenth Street's most imposing Beaux-Arts mansion, also built between L and M Streets, was commissioned in 1909 by Harriet Pullman, a society figure and widow of the Chicago railroad car magnate. Pullman intended that the house would give her son-in-law Frank Lowden, who recently had been reelected to Congress, a social springboard "so that [he] might easily reach the highest office in the land."[107] In an era in which members of Congress earned $7,500 per year, Pullman poured more than $400,000 into the house, including more than $100,000 for "finishes" that included massive plaster ornament, gold leaf, and paneling.[108] The result might have been an ornate hodgepodge had her architect not been the gifted Nathan C. Wyeth (1870–1963). Wyeth, who had spent ten years studying at the École des Beaux-Arts, cut a suave, cosmopolitan figure, teaching fencing, exhibiting prize-winning watercolors, and designing high society houses on Embassy Row, around Dupont Circle, and on Sixteenth Street, where the finest of his four early dwellings would be the MacVeagh House on Meridian Hill (described in chapter 3). Although he had practiced in Washington for less than a decade, his important public commissions already included the graceful Tidal Reservoir Inlet Bridge and the original Oval Office in the White House.[109]

The Pullman House, at 1125 Sixteenth Street, is a confection whose light-colored brick walls enclose more than fifteen thousand square feet of living space. Wyeth's design often has been described as French, although he drew upon Renaissance palazzos and eighteenth- and nineteenth-century England as well as France. The house's great stone-trimmed entrance hall had a white marble floor and grand winding stairway whose wrought iron rail trimmed in beaten gold leaf had been fabricated in France. The formal rooms on its second floor harmonized rich paneling, gilded doors, plaster carved with masks and swags, and mantles of light-veined purple marble beneath mirrors that reflected the ceiling's procession of crystal chandeliers. Its fifth floor provided accommodations for eighteen servants.[110]

However, Harriet Pullman's plans for this splendid house would carry a double irony. Its grandeur went largely unobserved because Lowden fell ill, and his family returned to Illinois before it was completed.[111] The mansion remained unoccupied until it became Czarist Russia's embassy in 1913.[112] The second irony was that, after Lowden recovered his health and became an extremely popular Illinois governor, he lost the 1920 Republican presidential nomination to Warren G. Harding after his opponents assailed his association with the Pullman fortune.[113] Could there have been a clearer symbol of such ties than having a palatial home on Sixteenth Street built by his mother-in-law?

No matter how many magnificent mansions were built, Sixteenth Street could not achieve City Beautiful grandeur through housing alone. The landscape needed a defining feature—the monumentally scaled institutional edifice. Its first such building was Hubbard Memorial Hall, the original National Geographic Society building, erected at the corner of Sixteenth and M Street and dedicated in 1904. Architects Hornblower & Marshall had originally proposed a grandiose Beaux-Arts building, but their highly embellished design was vetoed by patrons from the Hubbard and Alexander Graham Bell families. The society's headquarters, which combined office space with a library and a large auditorium, instead was built as a relatively restrained example of Florentine Revival architecture.[114]

In 1908 the *Star* noted that, "while private capital and enterprise have figured materially in increasing the comfort and beauty of the National capital from a residential standpoint, the Government of the United States and public and semi-public institutions . . . are doing their full share . . . toward building up Washington along the lines best indicated to make it in truth 'the City Beautiful.'" The news-paper was writing about the headquarters building of the Carnegie Institution, a building it considered the most important recent addition to the city, as well as a "fitting neighbor for the fine residences of the neighborhood, all of them furnish-ing valued units in the superb vista of 16th Street southward, with the White House at its base."[115]

Andrew Carnegie had endowed the Carnegie Institution in 1901 to sponsor out-standing scientists. Though the institution funded projects at laboratories across the country, its board purchased a plot at Sixteenth and P Streets in 1906 to meet its president's mandate that its headquarters be within fifteen minutes of both the White House and the Willard Hotel. Seeking an august character that would com-plement the institution's mission, the board selected the New York firm of Carrère and Hastings as its architects. Carnegie suggested that the institution should be known for the grandeur of its research rather than that of its building, but he did not impose his will on the trustees.[116] The architects, whose masterpieces include the New York Public Library, produced a grandiose Beaux-Arts building whose central portico with two-and-one-half-story Ionic columns and rotunda dome sup-ported by Corinthian columns suggest a Roman temple.

Constructed a few years after the Carnegie headquarters, the Scottish Rite Temple is one of Washington's most striking nongovernmental buildings. In 1909 the Southern Jurisdiction Supreme Council of the Scottish Rite of Freemasonry purchased four lots beside Hubbard Hall for its headquarters.[117] Yet the coun-cil's expanding visions soon outgrew this site, and in 1914 it sold its lots to the National Geographic Society for an addition to Hubbard Hall.[118] The council then purchased a larger tract at the corner of Sixteenth and S Streets and hired John

Scottish Rite Temple at 1733 Sixteenth Street NW, 1921. Completed in 1915,
it is one of the city's finest monumentally scaled private buildings. Its designer,
John Russell Pope, would go on to design the National Gallery of Art and the
Jefferson Memorial. *Authors' collection.*

Russell Pope (1874–1937) as its architect, with architect of the capitol and freemason Elliott Woods as his advisor.

The Scottish Rite Temple was the first Washington public building designed by Pope, a graduate of the École des Beaux-Arts whose later works include the National Archives, the original National Gallery of Art building, and the Jefferson Memorial. He based the temple on the Tomb of Mausolus at Halicarnassus, the burial place in modern Turkey of a Persian king, designed by Greek architects in approximately 350 BCE. This model was an ironic choice; Scottish Rite Freemasonry celebrated the exploits of Scottish crusaders, who during the crusades had largely expunged the remnants of Mausolus's tomb, mining its marble slabs for fortifications and burning its exquisite statuary for lime.[119]

Like the Carnegie Institution and National Geographic Society Headquarters, the temple was intended as a place for research, teaching, and administration. While it is Neoclassical in form, Pope interwove masonic symbolism throughout. Its colonnade of thirty-three Ionic columns, each thirty-three feet high, commemorates the thirty-three degrees of Scottish Rite ritual. Double-headed eagles, a primary masonic symbol, appear everywhere from the bronze medallions on the great staircase to the four corners of the temple's pyramidal roof.[120] The entrance is flanked by gigantic figures of Boaz, the sphinx of power, and Jachin, the sphinx of wisdom, carved in place from immense blocks of limestone by A. Alexander Weinman, designer of the Mercury dime and the Liberty half-dollar.[121]

The temple contains some of the most beautiful monumental spaces in Washington. In the atrium, Pope's palette of polished stone includes French white Botticino marble with a border of green-infused marble from the Isle of Timos for the floor, green Windsor granite from Vermont for the eight massive Doric columns of the inner portico, and white limestone for the walls. A double-spiral white Italian Botticino marble stair lined with Egyptian figures sculpted by Weinman in Vermont black marble rises from the atrium to the temple room, the building's ceremonial heart and meeting place for the Supreme Council. Its dome, which soars almost one hundred feet above its marble floor, is a Guastavino vault formed of interlocking terracotta tiles.[122]

Since it is "by studying and passing through the various . . . degrees, the Mason [moves] out of the darkness of ignorance into the light of knowledge," Pope studded the temple with symbols of light and illuminated the temple room with banks of windows whose amber-tinted panes become progressively lighter from bottom to top to suggest a celestial glow. At the dome's apex is a massive eight-sided skylight, which besides casting natural light throughout the council chamber, functioned in a natural system of air conditioning when the atrium doors were open.[123] Although built for a regional jurisdiction, the temple has become a national symbol of Freemasonry and is one of the most famous masonic buildings in the world.

The construction of these grand organizational headquarters buildings marked Sixteenth Street's ascendance from byway to Beaux-Arts boulevard. Designed by architects of the first rank, these buildings' architectural sophistication conveyed that they served organizations of more than local scope. That their officials chose Sixteenth Street is a testimony to the street's growing association with power and influence. However, as impressive as these they were, the apex of Sixteenth Street's redevelopment as a seat of the City Beautiful movement would be to the north, on Meridian Hill.

THREE

Mary Foote Henderson and the Rise of Meridian Hill

THE PERSON WHO HAD THE greatest ambitions for Sixteenth Street's development is undoubtedly Mary Foote Henderson (1842–1931). Wealthy and influential, she once lived in a castle across the street from what would become Meridian Hill Park. While other streets also benefited from the influence of the rich and powerful—Massachusetts Avenue, for example, owes a good part of its Gilded Age prestige to the efforts of banker and philanthropist Charles Glover—none of the city's other major arteries had such a determined and impassioned advocate. Henderson and her husband, former senator John Brooks Henderson (1826–1913), worked tirelessly to bring notable residents, buildings, and parkland to Meridian Hill and to the entire length of Sixteenth Street, lifting it to the ranks of the city's most stately and impressive avenues.

Henderson's push to elevate Sixteenth Street was based on a vision that excluded the interests and aspirations of many of the street's other property owners and residents. It was a racist and elitist vision that made no room for those of limited means—primarily African Americans—even if they had been living on Sixteenth Street much longer than she had. It was an uncompromising vision of white wealth, prestige, and exclusivity.

The African American Community on Meridian Hill before the Hendersons

By 1867, as cities across the country began pushing outward to create residential enclaves away from their central business districts, hopes were high for developing Meridian Hill and other previously rural spots around Washington as suburban residential neighborhoods. In that year, Richard M. Hall and John R. Elvans, businessmen who worked with the Freedmen's Bureau to subdivide lots in the Barry Farm tract in Southeast Washington to give to recently freed people as homesteads, laid out the Hall and Elvans subdivision of more than four hundred home lots on

Hall and Elvans Subdivision of Meridian Hill, 1867. North is at the top of the map.
Library of Congress.

Meridian Hill.[1] Densely platted, these small lots were intended to accommodate concentrated groups of modest rowhouses, such as were built in many other parts of the city. The subdivision's boundaries encompassed Champlain Avenue (Champlain Street) on the west, Columbia Road on the north, Fourteenth Street on the east, and Boundary Street (Florida Avenue) on the south. The future extension of Sixteenth Street, then called Meridian Avenue, ran through the middle of the tract, jogging slightly to the west to avoid running directly through the site of the old Commodore Porter mansion. The new subdivision had limited success, however. While investors bought and sold lots here for many years, little housing stock was actually built, especially on the steep hillside at the southern end of the tract. Most development was along the ridge to the north, where modest, two-story frame dwellings were constructed, either in rows or occasionally as freestanding houses.

One concentration of such houses stood in the block at the northeast corner of the subdivision. White landowners owned many of these houses, renting them to working-class African Americans, a few of whom were able to purchase their homes. During and after the Civil War, African Americans had begun settling on Meridian Hill in some numbers. The first were likely the formerly enslaved, who gravitated toward military installations and hospitals where they could find work and support from the army-run Freedmen's Bureau. From these humble beginnings a community gradually developed. Census records from 1900 show that the residents of this block had working-class occupations such as chauffeur, plumber, porter, stable worker, coalyard laborer, and laundress.[2] "There was a regular settlement up there, and many very fine families lived up there," recalled Gladys Scott Roberts, who was born on Meridian Hill, during an oral history interview in 1984.[3]

Roberts's father was Edmond W. Scott, who purchased his home on Meridian Hill in 1884, initially moving in with his mother, Lucy (a Virginia native), and three siblings. Scott's brothers and sister moved out in the 1890s, and Lucy died in 1902, but by then Scott had married Imogene Magruder. By 1910 the couple was living in the house with their three children, including Gladys, the youngest. Scott was working then as a "helper" at the Bureau of Engraving and Printing. Federal jobs such as his were a lifeline for many Black Washingtonians from Reconstruction days until the Woodrow Wilson administration.

The Scotts' next-door neighbor was Daniel Briles, who had been born around 1850 and possibly was enslaved before the Civil War.[4] Briles purchased the two-story frame house at 1510 Erie Street (Euclid Street) sometime before 1892. He and his wife, Georgiana, shared their home with another younger couple and their son; all five were originally from Virginia. For his living, Briles operated a neighborhood market out of a small one-story building a few doors down from his house. He undoubtedly knew all his neighbors well.

Around the corner from the Scotts and Brileses lived Daniel and Maggie Dixon, at 2426 Columbia Avenue (Fifteenth Street). Typical for renters, their tiny

Frame houses on Meridian Hill at 2400, 2402, and 2404 Columbia Avenue (Fifteenth Street NW), which were demolished around 1913 to make way for Meridian Hill Park. *US Commission of Fine Arts.*

two-story house had five occupants, according to the 1910 census: beside Daniel (occupation unknown) and Maggie (a laundress) were eleven-year-old daughter Ophelia; seventeen-year-old daughter Elsie; Elsie's husband, James Banks (a lumber driver); and Banks's brother Jared (a porter at a grocery store)—all sharing a living space of perhaps seven hundred square feet. Like many of their neighbors, the elder Dixons had been born in Virginia.

In its earlier days, this multifarious community was anchored by the Wayland Seminary, an institution of higher learning to train African American preachers and educators that was founded in 1867 by the American Home Baptist Mission Society. Originally located at Nineteenth and I Streets NW, it moved to a handsome new building on the west side of Columbia Avenue, a block south of where the Dixons would live, in 1876. The four-story brick building with fashionable mansard roof and central tower, called Parker Hall, was a notable landmark in the neighborhood and was constructed entirely by African Americans. Inside its walls a generation of Black churchmen were trained and sent to congregations around the country. In 1897 Baptist leaders decided to consolidate Wayland Seminary with other similar institutions to form the Virginia Union University in Richmond, Virginia. Local African American Baptists were divided on the wisdom of this action, with many arguing that the successful and prestigious seminary should remain in the nation's capital. However, move it did, and around 1900 its former building on Meridian Hill was razed.[5]

Another Meridian Hill institution was the Home for Friendless Colored Girls, located in a frame building on Erie (now Euclid) Street just west of Sixteenth Street. Carolyn Taylor, an African American house servant, founded the shelter in 1886, after she discovered two young girls eating out of a slop barrel in an alley while she was on her way to work one morning. Starting in a single rented room, the home was supported by the Women's Union Christian Association, which depended almost exclusively on contributions from within the African American community, as white donors were few. While First Lady Frances Folsom Cleveland became a supporter, attending a benefit concert in 1896 at the Metropolitan AME Church that raised funds for the home, her appeals to Congress for financial assistance went unanswered.[6] Sadly, Carolyn Taylor died the following year when she fell down the steep embankment in front of the home on Erie Street and broke her neck.[7] The home remained on Erie Street until sometime in the early 1900s.

The Hendersons' Lives before Settling on Meridian Hill

It is unknown whether John or Mary Henderson took any note of Carolyn Taylor's passing, the accident occurring just a couple of blocks north of their grand home. Though firmly established on Meridian Hill in the 1890s, the Hendersons had spent much of their lives in other places. Mary Henderson, born on July 21, 1842, in the Finger Lakes town of Seneca Falls, New York, was from a highly accomplished family of lawyers and politicians. Her mother, Eunice Newton Foote (1819–88), was arguably the first to describe what is today known as the greenhouse effect in a scientific paper, which was read by Smithsonian Institution Secretary Joseph Henry at the 1856 American Association for the Advancement of Science Conference.[8] Both of Mary's parents attended the 1848 Seneca Falls Convention on the rights of women, chaired by their friend and neighbor Elizabeth Cady Stanton, and signed its Declaration of Sentiments.

Studying at what became Skidmore College and a finishing school in New York City, Mary dutifully met the expectations of her social milieu by acquiring the social graces, becoming fluent in French, and developing an abiding taste for the arts. In 1865 her father took a position as an examiner at the US Patent Office (he would later be appointed commissioner) and moved the family to Washington.

In the spring of 1868, as the capital plunged into the bruising impeachment battle between President Andrew Johnson and Senate Republicans, newspaper squibs told of a romance between Missouri Senator John B. Henderson and "a young lady" who was eventually revealed to be Mary Foote. The politically mercurial Henderson, who was more than fifteen years Mary's senior, was noted for coauthoring and cosponsoring the Senate resolution that became the Thirteenth Amendment to the Constitution, abolishing slavery.

In May 1868 Johnson's impeachment trial ended with an acquittal by one vote, with John Henderson among the seven Republicans who joined a unanimous Democratic caucus in voting not guilty on all counts. Then, on June 25, Mary Foote married John Henderson in an elaborate ceremony attended by President Johnson, General Ulysses Grant, and Supreme Court Justice Salmon Chase.[9]

Outrage over the impeachment verdict cost John Henderson his seat in the November 1868 elections, but he determined to rebuild his fortunes by moving his family back to Missouri. After his 1872 campaign for governor ended in a stinging defeat, the family settled in Saint Louis, where John practiced law and became wealthy through speculation in real estate, railroads, and highly discounted Civil War bonds. When Congress voted to redeem the bonds in gold rather than greenbacks, he became instantly rich.

While running the family's elegant Pine Street home with the aid of three servants, Mary Henderson became a hostess and society doyenne, publishing a guide to entertaining, *Practical Cooking and Dinner Giving.*[10] As was expected of a woman of her stature, she became a patron of the arts and involved herself in charitable work, cofounding the Saint Louis Women's Exchange, which aided impoverished women and their children. She also helped found the Missouri State Suffrage Association, which successfully lobbied the legislature to include a women's suffrage provision in the new state constitution in 1875.[11]

In the 1880s tragedy struck the Henderson family. Their infant second child, Maud, had died of measles a decade earlier, and in an undated letter Mary Henderson described how their third child passed from rambunctious spirits to an agonizing death in a matter of days. She wondered whether her son's illness may have resulted from eating cheese, but she settled on bungling by the family physician as the main cause. Shortly after this loss, Henderson wrote *Diet for the Sick: A Treatise on the Values of Foods* (1885). Her book, which was respectfully reviewed by newspapers in Chicago and New York, presented a holistic view of the relationship between diet and disease, and prescribed regimens of bland foods for various illnesses. Henderson would remain a champion of strict diet control for the rest of her life.

Meanwhile, John Henderson, nearing age sixty, remained a fiery political maverick. He twice violently brawled with opposing attorneys in the courtroom, breaking one lawyer's hand by throwing him against a radiator and pummeling another who had struck him with his walking stick. His political skirmishes with President Grant and James G. Blaine pleased some Republicans, and he began to make his way back onto the national stage. In 1884 he was mentioned as a candidate for vice president and adroitly presided over the Republican National Convention. Although the Democrats' victory squelched any immediate hopes of high office, John Henderson remained hooked on Washington politics, and soon the Hendersons decided to move back to Washington permanently, this time without an elected office.

By 1887 the couple was staying at the elegant Arno Hotel on lower Sixteenth Street while searching for a site to build a permanent residence.[12] Upper Sixteenth Street—beyond Boundary Street (Florida Avenue)—was still sparsely developed, but real estate promoters touted it as "fast becoming one of the most desirable residence streets" in Washington.[13] John Henderson purchased several lots along the narrow road that would later become the extension of Sixteenth Street north of Boundary Street. Even before construction of the Hendersons' massive Seneca-sandstone mansion began, John Henderson joined other well-to-do local landowners in forming a Meridian Hill Improvement Association to lobby Congress for public funding to aid in the development of the neighborhood's infrastructure.[14]

Henderson—well connected on Capitol Hill—was adopting a common technique increasingly used by wealthy whites to influence real estate development in the nation's capital. While granting African American men in the District the right to vote in 1867, Congress soon took it away for all District males by abolishing home rule just seven years later. A three-member board of commissioners, appointed by the president and confirmed by the Senate, was established to run the city. White landowners were generally quite pleased with this arrangement. Taking away the popular vote had effectively eliminated the ability of the city's Blacks, as well as immigrants and others with limited resources or political connections, to

Mary Foote Henderson, circa 1895.
In the 1890s, Henderson was a well-
established Washington society doyenne
famous for her formal vegetarian
dinners. *Hinman,* The Washington
Sketchbook.

participate in city government. The wealthy whites couldn't vote either, of course, but they retained the unique ability to exert influence through their business and political connections with the DC commissioners and in Congress.[15] At stake was the 50 percent of the cost of running the city that the federal government had pledged to contribute on an annual basis. Landowners like John Henderson would try their best to control how that money was spent.

By April 1888 construction of the Henderson home on Meridian Hill was underway, with Mary Henderson taking a dominant role in overseeing the work. The Hendersons chose Springfield, Massachusetts, architect Eugene C. Gardner (1836–1915), noted for his designs for country villas and one of the earliest American architects to have a national practice. Gardner's best-selling 1882 home design book, *The House That Jill Built, after Jack's Had Proved a Failure,* told how a wife's clearheaded analysis of a house's functions overcame her husband's dysfunctional design preferences. Perhaps Mary Henderson had read the book and thought this architect was just the one she would like to work with.

Boundary Castle, as they called it, was a sprawling brownstone pile on a six-acre estate that was much in keeping with the wistful, Romantic aesthetics of the late Victorian age. Supposedly modeled after a castle Mary Henderson had seen in Germany, the original three-story Romanesque Revival house had a square footprint and a four-story central tower, but embellishments were many.

Boundary Castle as it appeared in the 1890s. While the castle was demolished in 1949, the turreted retaining wall still stands along Sixteenth Street. Fifty Glimpses of Washington.

The house's overall shape was hard to decipher amid all the swells, bays, towers, and bows.[16]

In 1892 the mansion's sprawl was extended west with a huge service wing featuring crenelated battlements that made it look even more castle-like. Matching battlements were added to the main house in 1902, completing the structure's medieval-fantasy appearance. Press accounts routinely admired the "stately" castle on the hill overlooking the city.[17]

The Hendersons quickly settled into their grand mansion as they continued to pursue myriad social and political causes. They sometimes shared each other's crusades. In 1896 John supported Mary by signing an anti-vivisection petition, while Mary returned the favor by writing a popular pamphlet endorsing the gold standard, a key Republican plank. John Henderson was alternately mentioned as a possible presidential candidate, attorney general, or secretary of the interior. None of these came to pass. Nevertheless, he continued to be seen as a Republican elder statesman and kept his name before the public by sponsoring the John B. Henderson Drum and Bugle Corps, a troop of boys in Zouave uniforms that paraded and entertained at fraternal and political gatherings across the city. In 1897

The drawing room at Boundary Castle. *General Photograph Collection, DC History Center.*

rumors circulated that newly elected president William McKinley was considering appointing him a district commissioner. If there was ever a chance of Henderson playing such a direct role in city politics, it presumably vanished when he began assailing McKinley's imperialist policies.

Meanwhile, Mary Henderson was an active hostess at Boundary Castle. The Hendersons' first formal dinner, held in February 1890, was in honor of the many international delegates who were in town for the first Pan-American Conference, where a wide range of inter-American affairs were discussed. The dinner drew a rave review from the *Post*'s society reporter, who marveled at Henderson's elegant attire—her Felix gown of old rose velvet trimmed in gold—as well as the lavish furnishings of her castle: the "mellow" Moorish entrance hall, plush-lined picture gallery used as a ballroom, and grand oak-paneled dining room hung with oak-leaf embroidered tapestries.[18] An invitation to dine with the Hendersons became a highly sought-after status symbol.

Mary Henderson remained an impassioned evangelist of clean living, growing increasingly fanatical about it over time. In her 1904 book, *The Aristocracy of Health*, she rhapsodized—somewhat incoherently—about her vision of the human body reaching an ideal state "when blood-corpuscles are no longer disintegrated, spiculated, and pale, but round, red, and rich laden; when the body-machine is no longer oppressed with the clinkers of surplus material; when reserve forces are no longer wasted or dissipated by avoidable devitalizing expenditures." Such a state would result when an individual ceased to ingest any and all poisons, which according to Mary included not just alcohol, coffee, and tobacco but also spices and other condiments, such as pepper. Her heavily prejudiced view was that such poisons had led to the decline of humanity. She seemed to suggest that Germans, for example, were degenerate for drinking beer. "The violation of hygienic laws has been so general and long-prevailing that human degeneracy has come to be accepted as the appointed lot of humanity. Human life is but an apology, a makeshift, a compromise," she insisted.[19]

By the time her screed on poisons was published, Henderson was famous for her unusual dinners featuring strictly vegetarian cuisine and no alcohol. A 1905 fête included a fruit soup, mock salmon in hollandaise sauce, broiled slices of pine-nut Protose (a meat substitute made of peanut butter, wheat gluten, and corn starch, among other things), unfermented "wine" from Catawba grapes, iced fruit, and Kellogg gelatin for dessert. As reported in the *Washington Post*, the printed menu cards for this dinner included "figures corresponding to each item on the bill of fare, showing the number, kind, and proportion of the food units, or 'calories,' contained in each dish."[20] Like all meals prepared by Henderson's accomplished English chef, it was claimed that the uninitiated couldn't tell that they weren't eating meat or fish. In any event, none of her elite guests would have dreamed of complaining about the unusual cuisine.

In May 1906, after joining the Independent Order of Rechabites, a Christian temperance society, Mary decided to dispose of the plentiful and expensive stocks of fine wine that John had accumulated over the years in Boundary Castle's cellar. Mary's butler was also a Rechabite, and he had asked for the use of the castle grounds for a group assembly. With her acquiescence, members of the Rechabite tent brought armfuls of wine bottles up from the castle's cellars and smashed them on a large rock on the front lawn. There was so much wine that it ran down into the gutter on Sixteenth Street. The newspapers loved the story. With racial insensitivity typical of the day, the *New York Times* reported, "Along the gutter down the hill Negroes gathered, and with tomato cans and other utensils scooped up what they could of the liquor and drank it. As they enjoyed themselves they sang old-time plantation melodies, while the Rechabites within the courtyard sang stirring temperance hymns."[21]

John acquiesced to Mary's newfound zeal for temperance. Frail at age eighty, he allowed the Rechabites to name their local tent in his honor. He fell seriously ill with a kidney ailment sometime in 1906 and disappeared from the public eye until his death in 1913.[22]

It was shortly before John Henderson fell ill that Mary Henderson's Meridian Hill building campaign began to take wing. Henderson's ambition to transform her neighborhood was not atypical for wealthy landowners of her era. Many embraced the City Beautiful movement, an ideology of radical physical change that aimed to remake the congested and unhealthy cityscapes of America into pristine, orderly expanses of parks, boulevards, and monumental architecture (see chapter 2).

The Senate Park Commission, known informally as the McMillan Commission, was chartered in 1900 to create a plan for developing Washington as a worthy capital of the powerful nation that the United States had become. In its highly influential 1902 report, the commission focused on enhancing the National Mall with white Neoclassical monuments and broad open spaces but also recommended that increased parkland be set aside around the city, including a proposed park on Meridian Hill.[23]

As a staunch supporter of the City Beautiful movement, Mary Henderson enthusiastically applied the McMillan Plan's concepts to her vision of an aggrandized Sixteenth Street. She declared that "each section of the thoroughfare will be a dream of beauty; long, impressive vistas; beautiful villas, artistic homes, not only for American citizens, but diplomats of foreign countries. Whatever there is of present civic incongruities will be wiped out. It will be called Presidents Avenue."[24] The result, she believed, would be magnificent: "Stretching in an absolutely straight line from the White House to the District line, leading to and bordering Rock Creek Park, this street, seven miles long and reaching an elevation of 202 feet from the Potomac, could—with perfect surface grades and drains, no railway [i.e., street-car] lines, be developed into a national boulevard, such as the Champs-Élysées at Paris or the Unter den Linden at Berlin."[25]

On a practical level, what could Henderson do to turn her vision into a reality? She decided to attack the problem one grand residence at a time. By buying up house lots and speculatively building mansions on them, she hoped to spur others to follow her lead, especially the officials of diplomatic missions, which she hoped would cluster on Meridian Hill. Nearly as soon as they had moved into Boundary Castle, the Hendersons had begun acquiring additional building lots along Sixteenth Street. In 1905 Henderson began her first speculative house project, a large residence on the northwest corner of Sixteenth and Euclid Streets, financed from the Hendersons' own funds.

Later nicknamed the "Pink Palace" for its distinctive color, the mansion at 2600 Sixteenth Street was designed by George Oakley Totten Jr. (1866–1939), one of Washington's preeminent architects of the Beaux-Arts era. Born in New York City, Totten grew up in Newark, New Jersey, and earned degrees in architecture from Columbia University in 1891 and 1892. He won a scholarship from Columbia

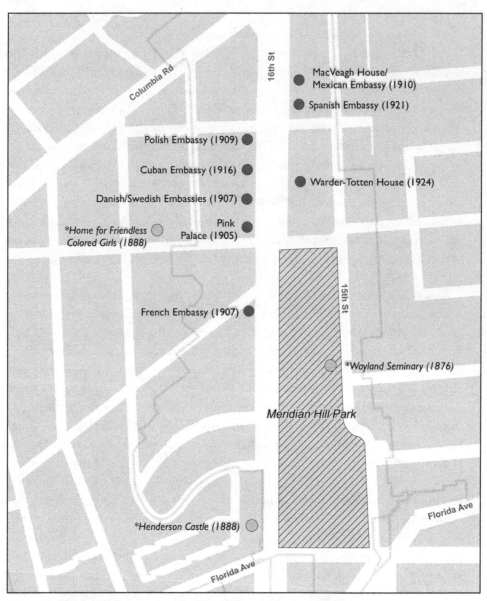

Sixteenth Street buildings in the Meridian Hill neighborhood, between
Florida Avenue and Columbia Road NW. Construction of Meridian Hill Park
in the early twentieth century displaced previous residents, many of them
African Americans. Light gray circles indicate buildings no longer extant. ©
Matthew Gilmore. Used by permission.

The 1906 Pink Palace, on the northwest corner of Sixteenth and Euclid Streets NW, as it appeared in 1921. *Authors' collection.*

Caricature of architect George
Oakley Totten by Clifford
Berryman. *Authors' collection.*

to travel to Paris to study at the École des Beaux-Arts, where he became imbued
with the design principles of the Beaux-Arts style. Totten settled in Washington
in 1895 to serve as chief designer within the Treasury Department's Office
of the Supervising Architect, a job that involved him in many federally funded
construction projects. Then in 1898 he moved into private practice and began
focusing on residences for wealthy clients.[26]

Mary Henderson came to know Totten when she hired him to supervise the remodeling of Boundary Castle in 1902. Totten designed the castle-like crenelated
battlements that completed the original structure's design "along the lines of the
old Norman architecture."[27] Pleased with his work, Henderson made Totten her
"official" architect, beginning with the Pink Palace project in 1905. He would go
on to create more than a dozen expensive, elaborately ornamented residences on
or around Meridian Hill as well as on Massachusetts Avenue and elsewhere in the
city, many of which became embassies.

The Pink Palace's exterior is in a distinctive Venetian Gothic style, replicating
the decorative elements of the great palazzos of fifteenth-century Venice. Faced
in white marble with terracotta trim, the façade originally featured ornate Gothic
windows, spiraled corner pilasters, decorative stringcourses, and elaborate balconies balanced on the heads of roaring lions with long, flowing manes.[28] Inside, the

house was equally lavishly decorated, although the style was Beaux-Arts. When it was completed in 1906, its presence at the crest of Meridian Hill was quite striking, with the only other comparable large structure being the newly completed Kenesaw Apartments several blocks further north (chapter 4).

Just as Boundary Castle's interior featured a variety of styles, so Mary Henderson took an eclectic approach to the houses she built on Meridian Hill. Observers have speculated that she chose the Venetian style for the Pink Palace to entice the Italian Embassy. The Italians, however, were comfortably ensconced in a mansion near Dupont Circle and would not move to Sixteenth Street until 1925, when they built their own Renaissance Revival mansion a block to the north.[29] Instead, the Pink Palace's first tenant was Oscar Straus, President Theodore Roosevelt's secretary of commerce and labor. Straus acknowledged that his new house was somewhat removed from what was then the city's leading fashionable residential area around Dupont Circle, but he wrote in his diary that "what we lose in convenience as to location, we gain in cheerfulness and healthfulness of the situation, which will be of special importance when the spring and summer months come."[30] After Straus's term ended, the house was occupied briefly by Treasury Secretary Franklin MacVeagh, followed by Delia Spencer Field, widow of famed Chicago merchant Marshall Field, who gave lavish parties at the house in the 1920s.[31] In 1949 the house was acquired by the Inter-American Defense Board, which has kept its headquarters there ever since.

Mary Henderson believed that "as [Sixteenth Street] was on a line with the White House and centrally in touch with the state and other governmental departments, it seemed especially desirable as a location for our foreign representatives."[32] To entice foreign delegations, she built several more houses along the street's west side, the next being an exuberant Beaux-Arts mansion at the corner of Sixteenth Street and Kalorama Road, which the Hendersons leased to France upon its completion in 1907. The French were the first foreign legation to move into what would become a Henderson-sponsored enclave of embassies around and just north of Meridian Hill. This was the second of Totten's thirteen commissions for Mary Henderson.

Sited near the crest of Meridian Hill, the mansion had a commanding view of the city below. Architectural historians Sue Kohler and Jeffrey Carson have called the structure "almost appallingly elegant." Its two main façades, facing Sixteenth Street (the east side of the building) and to the south, are ornately decorated, with heavy Neoclassical cornices supporting a mansarded top floor and attic. The shape of the flamboyant tower at the southeast corner has reminded some observers of a thermos bottle.[33] Most of the building's extensively carved exterior decoration is of terracotta.

Like many of its rivals, the new French Embassy was designed first and foremost for entertaining. As one passed through great, wrought iron gates into the

French Embassy building at Sixteenth Street and Kalorama Road NW, completed in 1907, pictured circa 1925. The Pink Palace can be seen in the distance. Meridian Hill Park is across the street. *Library of Congress.*

entrance hall, the marble staircase at the far end of the hall beckoned with its elaborate wrought iron balustrade. Immediately at the top of the staircase on the second floor was the grand salon, the embassy's largest room, a great rectangular reception hall with a balcony overlooking Sixteenth Street that was originally finished "in the modern French style with woodwork in white and gold."[34] Luxurious Oriental carpets graced the quarter-sawn oak parquet floor, the walls were hung with silk, and a shimmering crystal chandelier hung from the ceiling.

Ambassador Jean Jules Jusserand (1855–1932) and his wife, Elisa, moved into the new embassy in December 1907 and held their first formal dinner in January, hosting senators, diplomats, and other high officials. The dining room table was "decorated with great quantities of brilliant and vari-colored tulips," according to the *Post.*[35] It would be the first of many such events.

After the French Embassy building was completed, Henderson had Totten design an unusual duplex of mansions just north of the Pink Palace. The two houses, at 2620 and 2622 Sixteenth Street, were in a Spanish Renaissance Revival style, taking inspiration from the Palacio de Monterrey in Salamanca, Spain. The smaller of the two, 2622, featured an ornate tower that served as a sunroom, with windows on all sides.[36] These two mansions were first occupied by the Danish and Swedish embassies, although other legations (including, fittingly, the Spanish) leased them at later times. Only the towered building, which is now the Embassy of Lithuania, still stands.

Just up the street, the next addition to Henderson's eclectic petting zoo of residential palaces was a Totten-designed Beaux-Arts residence on the southwest corner of Sixteenth and Fuller Streets, completed in 1910. The *Post* reported in 1909 that the mansion would be "occupied by the ambassador of one of the large European empires as soon as completed," but in fact it's unclear who, if anyone, lived in the building for the first decade of its existence.[37] Henderson finally sold the building to the Polish government in 1919, just as Poland gained its independence in the aftermath of World War I. Carefully restored in 1978, the building remained the Polish Embassy at the time of this writing. In 1909 Totten also designed an Elizabethan Revival style building for the lot to its immediate south.[38] It has been suggested that perhaps Henderson had the British Embassy in mind for this spot.[39] However, the house was never built, perhaps because of the trouble Mary Henderson faced in finding an occupant for the future Polish Embassy building. Henderson eventually sold this lot to the government of Cuba, which built its embassy here in 1916 and has occupied the site ever since.

The Cuban Embassy was designed by the short-lived architectural firm of Macneil & Macneil, headed by Robert Lister Macneil (1889–1970). Macneil created a Neoclassical structure with a columned portico and engaged Neoclassical pilasters adorning its limestone façade, described as "in the style of Louis XV" by the *Post*.[40]

Through the 1940s, the Cuban Embassy was one of Washington's brightest social spots, especially during the term of Ambassador Pedro Fraga in the late 1930s. "It ranked with the best embassies in town in terms of glamour and prestige," Hope Ridings Miller, the *Washington Post*'s society editor, explained many years later. "The Cubans frequently held moonlit garden parties in the back, with rumba music and the finest food imaginable. The elite constantly went to parties there because it was quite a social center."[41] Gloria Vanderbilt was among the notables said to have danced in the ballroom to the accompaniment of the twenty-one-piece Cuban orchestra.

Meanwhile, in 1915, George Oakley Totten Jr. built his own house and studio on a large lot stretching from Fifteenth to Sixteenth Street in the block above Euclid Street. It was a fairly modest, Arts and Crafts–style structure, far less imposing than the houses he designed for Mary Henderson. Part of the house stills stand, but it is not visible from the street. The house was originally approached via a horseshoe drive off Fifteenth Street. Its large garden on the Sixteenth Street side featured a magnificent panoramic view of the city that would be blocked in 1941 with construction of the Meridian Hill Hotel between the Totten House and Euclid Street.

The Cuban Embassy, completed in 1916 at 2630 Sixteenth Street NW, as photographed in 1923. *Authors' collection.*

In 1924 Totten dramatically expanded his house when he acquired major elements of the 1886 Benjamin Warder mansion, then standing at Fifteenth and K Streets, and reconstructed it in the space on Sixteenth Street behind his house.[42] The Warder mansion, an eclectic structure finished in Ohio sandstone, was designed by Henry Hobson Richardson and is the only one of the four Washington mansions he designed that survives, the other three being the Anderson, Hay, and Adams houses (discussed in chapter 2). The Warder mansion, the largest of the four, was the home of Benjamin H. Warder (1824–94), an industrialist from Springfield, Ohio, who had made his fortune in manufacturing farm implements. Warder moved to Washington in 1884, built his mansion on K Street in 1886, and spent the last ten years of his life investing in DC real estate and contributing to charitable causes. His house has many of the signature Romanesque Revival elements for which Richardson is noted, including heavy, rounded arches, decorative columns, and a prominent, castle-like tower.

Totten's acquisition of the landmark house was an impulse purchase. As he explained to the *Evening Star,*

> I had an ardent admiration for the house, and was greatly dismayed while passing one day to see workmen taking it down. Upon inquiry I learned that it was being wrecked

Warder-Totten House at 2633 Sixteenth Street NW, pictured in 2020. George Oakley Totten moved the H. H. Richardson–designed 1886 mansion here from its original location at Fifteenth and K Streets NW in 1924. *Authors' collection.*

to make room for an office building, and that the material was for sale. . . . I felt an instant desire to save this building, and immediately bought everything that was available. This included much of the beautiful oak and mahogany interior and the entire exterior except the doorway and gate.[43]

As reconstructed by Totten on Sixteenth Street, the Warder house is faithful to the original on the exterior, although the interior was substantially altered to create four independent apartments. Totten never intended to live in the building himself but instead aimed to rent it out as apartments, which he did for many years.[44]

More mansions were being built along Sixteenth Street as well. Totten designed the house that would become the Spanish embassy, on the northeast corner of Sixteenth and Fuller Streets, as a speculative project for Mary Henderson in 1921. Henderson intended it to be a memorial for her late husband and her son, John B. Henderson Jr., who had just died at age fifty-two. Sprawling and castle-like, the limestone mansion features a large, arched Neoclassical portico and two upper stories that appear to step back dramatically from the street, giving the house the look of an ornate country villa. Though the building features Beaux-Arts detailing, the overall design is eclectic, and it seems mostly intended to contrast dramatically with its many grand neighbors. Kohler and Carson, in their authoritative study of Sixteenth Street architecture, state flatly that "the excellence of [its] design is very much in doubt."[45]

When it was built, however, it was "one of the showplaces of upper 16th street," envisioned as an embassy but drawing no immediate takers.[46] In January 1923 Henderson offered it to the US government for use as the home of the vice president. First Lady Florence Harding was said to have been enraged by this idea, exclaiming, "Do you think I am going to have those Coolidges living in a house like that? A hotel apartment is plenty good enough for them."[47] A Senate committee politely declined Henderson's offer, citing the expense of maintaining the house.[48]

The house stood empty for several years until Spain purchased it for its embassy in 1927. Henderson claimed that she had "countless offers" for the mansion but "bided my time until some government should select it as its embassy."[49] Inside, the Spanish decorated a glass-vaulted interior fountain room with hand-painted tiles from Valencia and Seville as well as wrought iron grilles from Toledo, giving it a distinctively Spanish appearance. The house remained the Spanish Embassy for many decades and now serves as the embassy's cultural office.

Like the Cuban Embassy, the MacVeagh House just north of the Spanish Embassy was conceived and built independently of Mary Henderson. It stands, however, as a testament to the traction that Henderson's vison for Meridian Hill had gained in the early twentieth century, spurring others to build elegant houses there as she had. While Treasury Secretary Franklin MacVeagh and his wife were living temporarily in the Pink Palace, Emily MacVeagh hatched the idea of building a new house and presenting it to her husband as a surprise Christmas present in 1910. MacVeagh was a wealthy Chicago industrialist, having made his fortune in the wholesale grocery business, and thus his wife was able to spare no expense in building a dream house for him. She hired Nathan C. Wyeth (1870–1963), a highly successful and well-connected architect, to design the house. Wyeth, a Chicago native, was also designing the Pullman House near Sixteenth and M Streets (see chapter 2).[50]

The MacVeagh House's Italian Renaissance Revival design is restrained on the exterior but lavishly decorated on the interior. The music room—supposedly modeled on one in the French royal palace at Fontainebleau—featured a built-in pipe organ. Rare tapestries adorned the walls of the library, and the walls and ceiling of the drawing room were "papered" in fourteen-karat gold leaf. Although it appears that Emily MacVeagh was unable to keep the new house a complete surprise, the couple happily settled in in early 1911.[51] Tragically, Emily died just five years later, and the heartbroken Franklin soon moved out. In 1921 he sold the house to the Mexican government for use as its embassy. Mexican ambassador Manuel Tellez then embarked on extensive renovations to the interior, including

The former Spanish Embassy on the northeast corner of Sixteenth and Fuller Streets NW, pictured in 2020. Constructed in 1921, it now serves as the embassy's cultural office. *Authors' collection.*

commissioning the painting of a number of colorful murals of Mexican life and history.[52] At the time of this writing, the mansion served as the Mexican Cultural Institute of Washington, DC.

A New Mansion for the President?

For City Beautiful proponents, the unique vantage point of Meridian Hill—its dominating location and spectacular views of the city—cried for something truly monumental. As early as 1868, Senator Oliver P. Morton had proposed purchasing land on Meridian Hill for construction of a new executive mansion to replace the White House.[53] In March 1900 Mary Henderson brought renewed energy and enthusiasm to the idea when she wrote a long article for the *Evening Star* promoting it. The old White House should be preserved as a relic, she argued: "We have outgrown it as a man outgrows the shoes he wore as a child." In its place, a new, much

· PROPOSED ·
· EXECVTIVE MANSION ·

Sketch of a proposed Executive Mansion on Meridian Hill, by architect Paul J. Pelz, 1898. *Library of Congress.*

grander mansion should be built on Meridian Hill, a site "finer than the hill on which the Capitol is built, and double its height; finer than any of the seven hills of Rome."[54] Henderson took inspiration from the exuberantly ornate Library of Congress building, designed in part by Paul J. Pelz (1841–1918) and completed in 1898. That same year, Henderson had commissioned Pelz to produce drawings for her proposed new President's House. Adopting a Beaux-Arts style similar to what he used for the Library of Congress, Pelz designed a massive, sprawling temple-like complex, which the *New York Times* called a "pretentious structure."[55] Later in 1900 wealthy Boston idealist Franklin W. Smith included the proposal in his report on the "aggrandizement" of Washington, published by the US Senate. Smith included a drawing of an even more elaborate building that straddled Sixteenth Street. In fact, the street itself would be relegated to a narrow tunnel passing underneath the massive complex.[56]

Henderson lost the fight for the new executive mansion. Just as she was promoting the idea, the McMillan Commission was at work on its own proposals. While supportive of creating new parkland all around the District, the commission envisioned concentrating the city's monuments on the National Mall. Major public buildings and monuments would be positioned along or near this axis, not scattered throughout the city as they had been during the nineteenth century. In 1910 the US Commission of Fine Arts was established to review and advise on the design of new structures for the city in conformity with the McMillan Plan. Staffed with former members of the McMillan team, the Commission of Fine Arts was resolute in promoting the plan's goals, and Henderson stood little chance of changing its views. The White House would stay where it was, and Sixteenth Street, despite being one of L'Enfant's grand avenues, would not become a monumental axis on par with the National Mall.[57]

Eviction

Opulent mansions were a vital element in the plan to transform the neighborhood, but Mary Henderson still needed something more, a central focal point of beauty and elegance to punctuate her enclave. When they moved into Boundary Castle around 1890, the Hendersons had perceived themselves surrounded by a neglected wasteland. Mary later boasted of her accomplishments in clearing the old frame houses that stood in the blocks on the opposite side of Sixteenth Street. "At the time of our settling here Washington was building in another direction, and this neighborhood was neglected. . . . Temporary shanties had been allowed to spring up. The first thing we knew we were surrounded by a slum district stretching from Scott Circle to Meridian Hill. Upper Sixteenth Street, it seemed, had become a dumping ground for the entire city, and authorities did not appear able to prevent it."[58]

Contemporary white commentators invariably referred to the frame dwellings inhabited by African Americans as "shanties," which they denigrated as "ramshackle," "dilapidated," or "filthy." Mary Henderson liked to call them "temporary." These characterizations reflected more the writers' wish that such dwellings would disappear than any actual assessment of their physical condition and certainly took no account of the intentions of the houses' inhabitants. While some of the houses were indeed poorly maintained, others were kept in excellent condition.[59] Of course, this mattered little to people like the Hendersons.

John B. Henderson became president of the Meridian Hill and Lanier Heights Citizens Association, an all-white group of property owners living west of Sixteenth Street. At a June 1899 meeting of the group at Boundary Castle, a resolution was adopted that complained of the neighborhood's "dilapidated, dangerous, and unhealthy shanties," concluding, "this territory in its present condition, and as it has been allowed to remain, is a disgrace to the city, and it is becoming, by way of comparison with the surrounding sections, a public nuisance, which should be abated by the authorities."[60]

With the desires of these powerful landowners clearly articulated, it was only a matter of when and how the less well-to-do, predominantly African American residents of Meridian Hill would be pushed out. The end came when the federal government finally agreed to build a formal park on Meridian Hill. The McMillan Commission, perhaps in deference to Mary Henderson's lobbying efforts, had endorsed the idea of a small Meridian Hill park. On its map of areas recommended for new parkland across the District, the commission marked a circular area around the extension of Sixteenth Street at Meridian Hill as an ideal spot for public parkland, a circle that included the Hendersons' property.

If the government had followed the commission's recommendation precisely, Henderson's imposing Boundary Castle would have been condemned, seized, and torn down. Nevertheless, Henderson was pleased that the commission had endorsed the idea of a park on Meridian Hill, having concluded that the steep hillside that used to mark the southern half of the site could not be developed anyway. She became the primary proponent for the establishment of Meridian Hill Park as one of America's first public parks laid out in the formal European tradition.

In 1906 the first hearing was held on acquiring land for Meridian Hill Park and funding its construction. Mary Henderson was a principal witness. "There are three reasons why the special parking space on Meridian Hill should be taken at once," she testified. "First, because there is no park near; second, because it commands one of the finest city views in the world, comparable with that of Athens from the Acropolis, and of Paris from the Arch of Triumph; third, in the interest of the proper development of Sixteenth street."[61]

Ever parsimonious about investing in the District, Congress was slow to respond but in 1910 finally passed legislation authorizing the acquisition of the land needed for the park.[62] Two years later, the federal government condemned and purchased all sixty-four of the private lots that filled three city blocks on the east side of Sixteenth Street, from W Street north to Erie (Euclid) Street. These lots had been owned by thirty-eight individuals or other entities, but only nine of the owners were residents.

Most of the 150 or so individuals who had been living on this land were renters, like the Dixons on Columbia Avenue, and had little say in how disputes were settled. The Dixons ended up moving to 608 Fairmont Street NW, just east of Georgia Avenue. Others, such as the Brileses and the Scotts, tried unsuccessfully to fight the condemnation.[63] In May 1912, just as the government was moving to seize the properties on Meridian Hill, Georgiana Briles died. Her widower, Daniel Briles apparently refused to move out of their longtime home. In November 1912, the DC court ordered him to leave, threatening to send in marshals to evict him from the premises. Briles himself died a few months later, in March 1913.[64]

Edmond and Imogene Scott, the Brileses' next-door neighbors, hired an attorney to fight the government in court. "My father was a bit of a fighter, so he fought the government up on Meridian Hill," recalled Gladys Scott Roberts. "He had just had his home remodeled, so he fought to keep his home. I think he fought harder than anybody." Eventually, he gave in, however, and accepted the government's offer, moving his young family to a rowhouse at 1447 S Street NW. Daughter Gladys knew that Mary Henderson was to blame for the debacle: "She saw to it that the whole settlement moved, and it was quite tragic."[65]

Building Meridian Hill Park

With the previous inhabitants gone, design work on the new park was soon underway, inspired by the elegant, formal gardens of Renaissance Italy. George E. Burnap (1885–1938), a landscape architect working for the Office of Public Buildings and Grounds, developed the initial design in 1914. Burnap planned the park's two-part layout, composed of a formal upper terrace overlooking cascading falls that spilled through a series of basins into a lower park. The lower park was divided into a reflecting pool and plaza at its base, with wooded coves and intimate gardens flanking the cascading series of water basins. However, Burnap moved on to private practice in 1917, leaving the lion's share of the detailed planning and design of the park to his protégé and former student, Horace Peaslee (1884–1959). Peaslee was trained as an architect and designed several private homes in the Washington area. He would also work on the preservation and restoration of the circa 1800 Dumbarton House, now a museum in Georgetown, as well as Saint John's Episcopal Church (discussed in chapter 1), and other landmarks. But Peaslee's greatest achievement was undoubtedly Meridian Hill Park.

The models for the park were the formal gardens of several noted Baroque Italian villas, including the Villa Borghese in Rome and the Villa d'Este in Tivoli, which Burnap and Peaslee visited on various trips to Europe between 1914 and 1929.[66] Burnap and Peaslee designed the upper terrace as a great, open lawn space, bordered on its two long sides with shrubbery and meandering paths. Originally, Burnap planned a concert pavilion and a fountain surrounded by an octagonal garden for the upper terrace, but they were dropped early in the park's development. Instead, visitors would be drawn inexorably to the balustrade at the southern end of the upper terrace, where they would be rewarded with extraordinary views of the city below. "That undoubtedly will make it a great visiting point for all tourists and out-of-town visitors, as well as a favorite gathering point for Washingtonians on hot summer evenings," the *Evening Star* anticipated in 1914.[67]

Construction progressed in fits and starts over more than two decades, chronically hampered by a lack of funds. One of the earliest features to be completed was the massive retaining wall along Sixteenth Street, which allows the upper terrace to be flat. When first built, the two-section wall seemed alarmingly out of place to some observers. "If there is a useless expenditure of money going on anywhere in Washington it is the construction of that wall, uglier than a mud fence," groused Representative James Robert Mann of Illinois in 1915. "You might as well put a pig in a parlor as to put this retaining wall on 16th street."[68]

Work crept slowly along for the next ten years. By 1926 the park was nearly in a state of crisis. Although the upper terrace had been laid out, little progress had been made on the cascade of water basins that was supposed to bring grace to the sloping lower section. The red clay of the hillside had been formed into bare terraces, but there was nothing in place to keep them from slowly washing away after each rainfall. Instead of one of the city's most elegant public places, the barren field of mud and cliffs of clay were frequently a site for burning trash.[69]

Lieutenant Colonel Clarence Sherrill, director of the Office of Public Buildings and Grounds, appealed to Congress and the president to reinvigorate the project.[70] While some elements of the original design were dropped, such as the planned concert pavilion on the upper terrace, the effort was back on track by 1928, when the park's annual appropriation jumped from twenty-three thousand dollars to ninety-two thousand dollars. The increased funding lasted for three more years, allowing most of the planned work to be completed. The cascade finally was installed, as were the reflecting pool and formal gardens at its base.

Beginning in 1933, the Depression-era Public Works Administration contributed to the renewed effort, ensuring that all the landscaping and other details were finished, and the park officially opened to the public in 1936.[71] Mary Henderson, who died in 1931, was never able to see the final result.

One of the unique features of the park is its innovative use of concrete. Architect Peaslee was fascinated by the stone pebble mosaics in the formal Italian gardens that had inspired the park's design. Peaslee worked with John Joseph Earley (1881–1945), an architectural sculptor who ran a plaster and stucco studio, to come up with a form of concrete that would convey the elegance of the original but avoid its prohibitive cost. Through patient experimentation, Earley developed a method of forming concrete with a surface of exposed pebble aggregate that created an elegant, finely crafted appearance in what otherwise would have been ugly concrete. Vast quantities of Potomac River pebbles were sieved to produce evenly sized pebble aggregate. After a section of concrete contacting the aggregate had sufficiently dried, the forms were removed and the concrete was scrubbed with steel brushes dipped in acid to remove traces of mortar and reveal a colorful, mosaic-like pebbled surface. The technique was used to create several different textures for a variety of surfaces, including walls, balustrades, pilasters, urns, and obelisks.[72]

The park is home to a rather motley assortment of statues and monuments. One that is not there is the Lincoln Memorial, though not for want of effort. When Congress finally approved funds to build a memorial to Abraham Lincoln in February 1911, Mary Henderson made sure that Meridian Hill was one of three sites (along with the Mall and the plaza in front of Union Station) considered. The Commission of Fine Arts remained staunchly in favor of the site on the National Mall, which had been specified in the McMillan Plan and was part of its vision

Aerial view of the lower portion of Meridian Hill Park, 1976. The cascade and fountains have been drained for winter. *Library of Congress.*

for the city's monumental core. Nevertheless, the independent Lincoln Memorial Commission, which was in charge of the memorial's development, wanted to consider alternatives. The commission solicited architect John Russell Pope to prepare drawings for each of the proposed sites.[73]

Pope prepared an evocative design for Meridian Hill, featuring a Parthenon-like memorial on a tall pedestal. It would have made for a stunning landmark on top of the hill. Henderson wrote a passionate letter, published in all the city's major newspapers, arguing that Meridian Hill would be a much more prominent and dignified location than flood-prone Potomac Park, where the memorial would have to be constructed on land reclaimed from the Potomac by the Army Corps of Engineers.[74] But her pleas were in vain. The Lincoln Memorial would be built on the National Mall.

Instead of a memorial to Abraham Lincoln—one of the country's greatest and most beloved presidents—Meridian Hill Park would host a monument to his immediate predecessor, James Buchanan. Buchanan, in contrast, was one of the least respected of the nation's chief executives, often blamed for failing to prevent the Civil War. One could conclude that the decision to substitute Buchanan for Lincoln added insult to injury, but it does not appear that Henderson took it that way; she was happy to get a presidential memorial in the park.

More than just a statue, the Buchanan Memorial includes a large surrounding cove, known as an exedra, with the seated Buchanan on a pedestal in the center and carved allegorical figures of Law and Diplomacy at either end. No such memorial would ever have been built if not for the bequest of Buchanan's adoring niece, Harriet Lane Johnston. Even at that, Congress was slow to accept the gift and almost ran out the fifteen-year limit set in Johnston's bequest. In temporarily blocking the bill at one point, Representative Clarence B. Miller of Minnesota said, "I would like to have someone tell me, if he can, what distinguished services Buchanan rendered anybody that will justify erecting a monument costing the enormous sun of $100,000 to be paid for by anybody, in Meridian Hill Park, one of the showplaces-to-be of the land."[75] Representative Irvine Lenroot of Wisconsin later echoed his sentiments: "The best thing we can do for Mr. Buchanan is to forget him."[76] Nevertheless, the measure was approved in 1918. The memorial was not completed until 1930, however, due to delays in constructing the rest of the lower part of the park.

The Commission of Fine Arts also sanctioned an assortment of less prominent memorials to be placed in the park. With foreign embassies taking root all around it, the park was a logical place to celebrate international relations. In 1921 a group of French women in New York City donated a statue of Joan of Arc as a commemoration of French-American amity. The statue, a copy of one located at Reims, France, was installed in the park in late 1921 but had not yet been dedicated when Italy's Dante Alighieri slipped in ahead. Carlo Barsotti, editor of an Italian American newspaper in New York, donated a copy of a statue of Dante that had been unveiled in New York that same year. The Fine Arts Commission rushed to set up a dedication ceremony for the Dante statue while Italian officials, who had been attending an international conference on disarmament, were still in town. The dedication was held December 1, 1921, a short distance away from the Joan of Arc statue, which wasn't dedicated until January 1922. French and Italian diplomats graciously attended each other's ceremony. At the Dante unveiling, a veritable "international love feast" took place, with the French and Italians brushing aside differences they had aired during the arms conference and pledging friendship with the United States and each other.[77]

After twenty-six years of effort and a final infusion of cash from emergency appropriations, the park was completed in the fall of 1936.[78] Park service officials

Ceremony at the unveiling of the Joan of Arc statue, January 1922. Meridian Hill Park was still under construction. *Library of Congress.*

Youngsters admire the armillary sphere in this view facing north from the foot of Meridian Hill Park in 1936. The cascade, drained of water, is directly behind the sculpture. *Library of Congress.*

were proud to be able to finish the beautiful landscape, which served as a civic achievement for the people of Washington at a time when most of the government's investment in the city was going into the massive office buildings of the Federal Triangle. Aristocratic as the park's design origins may have been, it was an immediate hit with neighbors from all walks of life. And as we shall see, both the neighborhood and the park were in for dramatic changes in the coming years.

The park had just been completed when a large sculpture of an armillary sphere was unveiled at its southern end in November 1936.[79] The six-foot sphere, mounted in an exedra, was a replica of an ancient astronomical instrument. The delicately entwined metal rings of the sphere offered a striking contrast to park's heavy masonry walls and fountains. Meticulously designed by sculptor Carl Paul Jennewein, it also served as an accurate sundial. It was donated to the park by Washington artist Bertha Noyes in honor of her sister, Edith.

The establishment of Meridian Hill Park may be one of Mary Henderson's most enduring accomplishments, but it certainly did not mark the beginning or end of her ambitions for Sixteenth Street. Henderson was intensely concerned with the street's physical layout, its name, and how it was to be decorated with sculpture. For example, in 1888 the DC commissioners had decided to create a new traffic circle at the intersection of Sixteenth Street, U Street, and New Hampshire Avenue, located just two blocks south of Boundary Castle. Called Hancock Circle, the new circle was laid out, and admirers of Civil War General Winfield S. Hancock began raising funds to erect a statue of him at its center.[80] Alas, no statue would stand in Hancock Circle.[81] Preventing the Sixteenth Street installation were the streetcars of the Rock Creek Railway, which by 1893 were riding along rails that ran down the center of U Street, slicing Hancock Circle into two crescent-shaped fragments. In 1896, as plans were drawn to remove the circle's remains, Mary Henderson gathered more than one hundred signatures on a petition to save them, arguing that the two crescents could be beautified with floral plantings.[82] Henderson lost the battle, and the circle was removed, leaving the wide and complex intersection that remains there today. She later wryly commented that "the rejoicing surrounding property holders had hardly finished paying for the actual building of this circle when they were called upon again to pay special taxes for its removal."[83]

She would have greater—if only temporary—success in her efforts to have the name of Sixteenth Street changed to something she felt was worthier of such a magnificent boulevard. It was a topic that had been frequently debated but never resolved. As early as 1894, the Senate had entertained a proposal to change the name to Executive Avenue, perhaps at the urging of Mary Henderson, but no action was taken. The movement gained momentum in 1903 with the formation of the Sixteenth Street Improvement Association, a group of influential residents that included Cabinet officers, Supreme Court justices, senators, and representatives, as well as the Hendersons and Secretary of State John Hay. The group considered the Executive Avenue moniker as well as several other options. Supreme Court Justice Henry Billings Brown preferred White House Avenue. Another leading candidate was John Hay's favorite, Avenue of the President.[84]

For several more years a wide assortment of new names was bandied about, with little consensus. Meeting in 1907, Mary Henderson's complementary Women's Sixteenth Street Improvement Association endorsed the idea of changing the street's name but, like their men counterparts, couldn't agree on what it should be.[85] Meanwhile, the DC commissioners favored Washington Avenue. Supreme Court Justice Alexander Hagner liked Lafayette Avenue. And an article in the *Washington Post* claimed that many people preferred Fourth of July Avenue.[86]

Mary Foote Henderson, circa 1923. Henderson was nearing the end of her building career. Meridian Hill Park, across Sixteenth Street from her castle, was still under construction. *Authors' collection.*

Amid the proliferation of ideas, Mary Henderson began lobbying for the name Avenue of the Presidents, pointing out that the recently deceased John Hay had also chosen that name. She dismissed complaints that the name was too long, arguing that it had no more syllables than Pennsylvania Avenue (true only if you pronounce the state's name as "Penn-syl-van-i-a").[87] She pushed Senator Jacob Gallinger, head of the District committee, to take up the matter in Congress, and he introduced a bill, which never passed.

With no action on the Hill or by the DC commissioners, the Sixteenth Street Improvement Association decided in March 1909 to start calling the street Avenue of the Presidents, regardless of the official designation.[88] Shortly thereafter, they convinced two of the three commissioners to change the name of the street north of Florida Avenue (the boundary of Washington City). However, the following year, with a new commissioner installed, the board reversed its decision, arguing that only Congress could change the street's name. While the association claimed that the majority of homeowners on the street supported the name change, some plainly disagreed. Dr. A.A. Snyder of 1126 Sixteenth Street, wrote to the *Evening Star*, "I saw notice of a meeting of residents of that street in the home of some one, and the meeting seemed to be occupied by the speech of one lady and to have accepted without dissent her wishes in regard to the changing of the name of 16th street."[89]

Mary Henderson renewed her pressure on Congress.[90] Finally, in early 1913, Senator William Alden Smith of Michigan slipped an amendment to change the name into the annual DC appropriations bill. With little official debate, the change took effect in early March.

Soon distinctive glass street signs with elegant blue lettering were installed along the newly rechristened avenue. Maps and addresses changed. Newspaper advertisements beckoned with fancy new homes on the Avenue of the Presidents. And then it all changed back again, as if it had been a dream. In December, Representative Thomas Sisson of Mississippi inserted a provision in the 1914 DC appropriations bill changing the name of the avenue back to Sixteenth Street. Mary Henderson tried frantically to cajole congressmen into voting against the reversal, reportedly inviting many of them to an elegant dinner at Boundary Castle, but her efforts failed.[91] Just as the original name change had been enacted with little debate, so the reversal likewise happened just as efficiently, taking effect in July 1914. The *Washington Post* interpreted the move as congressional chastisement of the District for its overweening desire to be more cosmopolitan than it really was. "The sonorous words calculated to create a mental vista of embowered grandeur and illimitable spaciousness have been discarded," the newspaper observed with dripping sarcasm.[92]

It probably hadn't helped that Mary Henderson's vision for Sixteenth Street didn't stop at just its name. Part and parcel with the renaming effort was her plan to erect forty-six monumental bronze busts of all of the presidents and vice presidents along the avenue, one in each block.[93] Passersby would be able to reflect reverently on the myriad achievements of each of the country's presidents as they made their way north. Fortunately, the pretentious idea languished throughout the short-lived Avenue of the Presidents era. The Commission of Fine Arts formally nixed the proposal in 1916.[94]

Henderson never gave up on changing the name, however. By the mid-1920s, she was at it again, pushing the name Presidents' Avenue as a slightly less ponderous alternative. Bills were introduced in Congress, but, as had happened so often in the past, no action was taken. To this day, Sixteenth Street carries the same simple name it began with.

While the name was never changed again, some people still envisioned the street as a monumental avenue, a boulevard suited to commemoration. In February 1920 Charles Lathrop Pack, president of the American Forestry Association, proposed that Sixteenth Street be lined with trees to commemorate the men of the District who had died during the Great War.[95] On Memorial Day of that year, the American Legion dedicated the first of 507 Norway maple trees that were planted along Sixteenth Street between Varnum Street and Alaska Avenue. Next to each stood a small concrete block sporting a copper shield engraved with the name of a DC soldier who died during the war.[96]

The neat rows of trees spaced forty feet apart were said to be impressive when they were first planted, but they did not last. The memorials were being vandalized or crushed by careless truck drivers as early as 1929. By the 1960s some of the trees had died, and thieves had stolen most of the copper plates from the concrete blocks when the value of copper had risen markedly. In the 1980s *Washington Post* columnist Bob Levey tried to work with the American Legion to restore the memorials but encountered resistance from the DC government. Today, the original trees are all gone, and only a few of the concrete markers remain, sunken out of sight into the ground.[97]

FOUR

Sixteenth Street in the Automobile Age

WHILE MARY HENDERSON was building Sixteenth Street mansions in pursuit of her aspirations, the early twentieth century was bringing profound changes that would open up the street to a variety of new houses, new apartment buildings, and new places of worship. Physically, the road more than doubled in length in the early 1900s as it was extended from Piney Branch to the Maryland border. The range of people and organizations that influenced the street's function and appearance broadened as well, as real estate developers sought to build houses and apartment buildings appealing to a much wider range of buyers than those for whom the Victorian townhouses and mansions below Florida Avenue had been designed. The proliferation of automobile and bus traffic brought new opportunities for dispersed working and living arrangements as well as new traffic and congestion challenges.

Before it was extended past Piney Branch, Sixteenth Street's undeveloped path through the countryside had been a haven for nature lovers and eccentrics. The best known of these was Allen B. Hayward (1839–1922), who chose to build and live in a treehouse along the future route of Sixteenth Street in the early 1880s. Hayward was a Civil War veteran who had lost his right arm in the Battle of Cold Harbor, near Richmond, and after the war gained employment as a clerk in the US Pension Office. In 1907 he explained his decision to move to the banks of Piney Branch: "One summer I got tired of the awful heat and the disagreeable smells and the sickening sights of the city; so I decided to go out and build me a little house among the trees near Mt. Pleasant. I see enough of people during the day time, and I thought I would get away from them at night."[1]

Hayward constructed his tree house in a hillside cluster of sturdy oak trees near Piney Branch, just north of where the Woodner Hotel stands today. Standing partly on stilts and partly attached to several trees, Hayward's boxy, two-level wooden house hung thirty-five feet above the ground, the dining room and kitchen

Airy Castle was on the west side of Sixteenth Street just before Piney Branch, near the present-day site of the Woodner apartment house. *Authors' collection.*

suspended beneath the main living quarters. A heavy canvas tarp served as a roof. Inside were all the comforts of home, including a carpet sewn from remnants, dozens of pictures on the walls, assorted tables and chairs—everything a recluse could want. Hayward dubbed his home Airy Castle, and, after it was written up in the newspapers, it became a minor tourist attraction, with hundreds of visitors in the summer months. Hayward even began charging an admission fee. A guest register on a small table inside the house included the names of the many congressmen, government officials, and prominent Washingtonians who had come to see the "Man in the Tree" for themselves.[2]

Hayward lived in this tree house for only a few years, moving to a larger one at Forest Glen, Maryland, around 1890. Though he remained at Forest Glen until his death in 1922, Hayward was always associated with the treehouse on Piney Branch, which served after his departure as the centerpiece of Airy Castle Park, a retreat where dances, concerts, and picnics were held in the 1890s. Then the park was gone. By 1900 a new era of development was gathering steam.

The March of Progress

Washington had been rapidly expanding beyond the old boundaries of the L'Enfant-designed city throughout the 1880s and 1890s. Key arterial roads in the northwest quadrant of the District—including Eleventh Street, Fourteenth Street,

Connecticut Avenue, New Hampshire Avenue, and Massachusetts Avenue—all were being extended into the rural countryside as developers saw opportunities to build suburban homesteads in bucolic settings away from crowded downtown streets.[3] Existing country roads, such as the dusty Seventh Street Road and the Georgetown-Rockville Road (Wisconsin Avenue) saw rapid development as well. The extension of electric streetcar routes in the 1890s was a key factor in providing convenient, economical transit to enable the new developments. Builders advertised that their homes had all the restful advantages of country living while still being within easy reach of downtown via the streetcar lines. Early suburbs within the District of Columbia that blossomed in this era included Mount Pleasant (including what is now Columbia Heights), Eckington, Bloomingdale, Congress Heights, and Cleveland Park.[4]

Though it never hosted a streetcar line, Sixteenth Street would be among the straightest of the major roads that were extended to the District's borders. Full grading and paving of the entire stretch would happen fitfully, however. The first major segment, up Meridian Hill from Boundary Street (Florida Avenue) to Mount Pleasant, began in the 1870s when steps were taken to grade the steep Meridian Hill escarpment. This segment of the road was originally called Meridian Avenue and jogged to the west for several blocks to avoid the remains of the old Porter mansion. By the mid-1880s, a straighter route up the hill to Columbia Road had been staked out, although it was narrower than the original part of Sixteenth Street to the south.

In the late 1880s, an additional segment was laid out from Columbia Road to Park Road in Mount Pleasant. This new segment did not continue due north. Instead, it angled to the west to avoid plowing through the houses that had already been built in Mount Pleasant.[5] For a while, Sixteenth Street ended in the heart of this quiet enclave of frame houses, but the angled detour would be only temporary.

The desire to extend Sixteenth Street further to the north came in the 1880s and 1890s as the streetcar line on nearby Fourteenth Street was repeatedly extended, bringing more and more potential homeowners to lots carved from the once-rural areas beyond Mount Pleasant and Columbia Heights. When it was first constructed during the Civil War, the Fourteenth Street streetcar line ended at Boundary Street; it was extended up the hill to Park Road in 1892. Once connected to downtown, the Fourteenth and Park Road terminus became the commercial center of Mount Pleasant, accelerating residential development on adjacent blocks, including Sixteenth Street. Then, in 1906, the line was extended again, this time to Decatur Street, where a large carbarn was built that still stands.[6] This extension brought streetcar riders to areas north of the Piney Branch valley.

As Fourteenth Street grew, powerful landowners, including Thomas Blagden, the wealthy owner of the Argyle estate north of Piney Branch, pushed for Sixteenth Street to likewise be extended. In 1896 Blagden corralled some twenty other landowners to agree with him to donate the land for a full, 160-foot-wide, straight-line extension of Sixteenth from Piney Branch all the way to the Maryland border, a distance of about three and a half miles. "It is to be doubted if ever before have property owners given so liberally of their lands with so little prospect of immediate return," the *Evening Star* marveled—though in truth the owners anticipated a hefty financial gain.[7] The *Washington Post* noted in 1898 that the DC commissioners considered the extension of Sixteenth Street to be "one of the most important of the several measures recently introduced for the extensions of streets in the suburbs."[8] Finally, in 1899, Congress gave its approval.[9]

Fully $1 million was set aside for the project, which the *Washington Post* claimed was the most expensive of its type that the federal government had funded in DC.[10] The *Post* noted that the Feds had a special interest in the project:

> It is proposed to have a broad boulevard, not especially for the accommodation of the residents along the street, but as the magnificent entrance to Rock Creek Park. Leading as it does, from the White House to the park, it is bound to be the principal driveway to the big government reservation north of the city. It is planned not for the present alone, but for the future, and is to be more of a national than a local improvement.[11]

Though not specifically recommended in the McMillan Commission's report, the extension of Sixteenth Street was seen as playing an important role in the beautification of the city and the enhancement and interconnection of its parks.

Congress established Rock Creek Park as the country's third nationally chartered park in 1890, after several decades of consideration. With real estate development rapidly expanding in the District, the window of opportunity to preserve a large tract of unspoiled parkland had been closing just as rapidly, as the case for such a park grew more compelling. Banker Charles Glover, *Evening Star* editor Crosby Noyes, and other prominent Washingtonians began lobbying hard for the park.[12] In 1888 Noyes complained in the *Star* that "when we come to the matter of that indispensable feature of a first-class city, a great public park supplying a health and pleasure resort for all classes, the comparison of Washington to the European capitals of London, Paris, Berlin, and Vienna, with their thousands of acres of parking [i.e., parkland], is most humiliating."[13] Then, in one fell swoop, the creation of Rock Creek Park remedied that problem, vaulting Washington into the ranks of world capitals with large central parks.[14] Within the United States, the park gained parity for Washington with New York City's Central Park, mapped out in 1857, and Boston's Emerald Necklace of parks, conceived in the 1870s.

The extension of Sixteenth Street was to play a key role in connecting Rock Creek Park with the center of the city, adding to the prestige of both the park and the street. Sixteenth Street forms the eastern border for much of the park above Military Road and serves as the most direct connection between downtown and the park.

Work on the Sixteenth Street extension was carried out in discontinuous segments, all eventually linked together. South of Piney Branch, the straightening of Sixteenth Street in 1903 resulted in dozens of Mount Pleasant homes being either razed or moved to new locations.[15] When workers were grading the street just north of Columbia Road, they found the remains of an old coffin and human body, adding to the disruption.[16] After the new road was finished, the old, angled segment of Sixteenth Street was renamed Mount Pleasant Street. Meanwhile, work on clearing and grading segments of the street north of Piney Branch began simultaneously in the early 1900s.

Spanning Piney Branch

The deep Piney Branch valley posed a natural barrier to completing Sixteenth Street as a seamless north-south artery. By 1904 the path of the street beyond Piney Branch had been cleared but not paved. To get to it, traffic was still obliged to follow the narrow, steep track of old Piney Branch Road down one side of the valley, cross a ford through the creek (pedestrians could use a rough wooden bridge), and then climb an equally steep incline on the other side. At the edge of Thomas Blagden's property, a small signboard was tacked to a tree stating, "Center of 16th street." Looking south across the valley from this vantage point, a traveler could see the Washington Monument looming up in the distance. All that was needed was a bridge to span the valley. In March 1904 Theodore Noyes, editor of the *Star*, joined Blagden, Mary Henderson, Charles Glover, and some two dozen other distinguished Washingtonians in petitioning Congress to fund such a bridge.[17]

"The Commissioners want the longest, widest, and best-looking bridge that can be had for the money," the *Washington Post* reported in 1905.[18] Never enthusiastic about spending on the District, Congress appropriated just fifty thousand dollars, which was not enough to cover a bridge big enough to span the full width of Sixteenth Street. In response, DC engineer W. J. Douglas decided to construct the bridge in two phases. The first would be a narrow two-lane bridge that he hoped would support some traffic on a temporary basis until additional funds were available to widen it. The concrete, single-span bridge that was completed over Piney Branch in 1907 was the first parabolic arch bridge constructed in the United States, projecting "strength and beauty," according to Douglas.[19] To save money, it featured a hollow interior of concrete pillars supporting concrete crossbeams over which the roadbed was laid.[20]

However, the bridge was never opened to the public in its original narrow configuration, the approaches on either end unfinished. Instead, the twenty-five-foot-wide segment stood "like a big white monument in the surrounding woods" for two years until additional funds were appropriated for finishing the bridge with a twin arch to be built alongside the original.[21] When it finally opened in 1910, the

Piney Branch Bridge as seen from the Piney Branch Parkway that runs beneath it, 1993. Note that the bridge was built in two parallel sections. *Historic American Engineering Record, Library of Congress.*

complete bridge had cost approximately $135,000 and featured a sixty-foot-wide deck spanning the two separate arches.

DC bridge officials still wanted the bridge to look stately and ceremonial, despite the meager funding. The completed structure featured a handsome Neoclassical balustrade at street level and a pebble-dash finish that foreshadowed the look of the walls and ornamentation in Meridian Hill Park (see chapter 3). Alexander Phimister Proctor (1860–1950), a New York sculptor who specialized in animals, created the two pairs of bronze Bengal tigers that grace the ends of the bridge. Proctor modeled the sculptures from live animals at the Bronx Zoo. Army Captain Edward M. Markham, the District's assistant engineer commissioner, said he believed that the animals would "add much to the beauty and artistic adornment of the bridge," helping to build up Sixteenth Street as one of the city's grand avenues.[22]

Combined with the extension of the streetcar line on nearby Fourteenth Street, the opening of the bridge and subsequent grading and paving of Sixteenth Street

Advertisement from the *Evening Star*, May 21, 1910, promoting development on Sixteenth Street. Real estate agent Ephraim J. Totten was of no relation to architect George Oakley Totten Jr. *Library of Congress.*

to the north ushered in a prolonged period of rising property values and extensive residential development, including many large, beautiful houses in new subdivisions such as Mount Pleasant Heights, Argyle Park, and Sixteenth Street Heights. The *Star* reported in October 1910 that property values along the extension of Sixteenth had risen 500 percent since 1904 and were still going up. "Almost the moment after the money was appropriated for that bridge you could feel the prices jumping," real estate attorney Shelton T. Cameron remarked. Almost all of the property on Sixteenth Street came with covenants restricting development to single-family houses.[23]

Dawn of the Automobile Age

According to the *Washington Post*, the first horseless carriage rode the streets of the nation's capital on April 2, 1897, and was an immediate sensation, startling pedestrians and horses alike. "People ran to the windows and front [of the automobile] to see it pass, and the trip caused more excitement than a circus and was more amusing," the *Post*'s reporter observed.[24] The particular machine in operation that day ran on compressed air, but gasoline-powered vehicles were not far off. In May 1900, just three years later, automobiles were beginning to appear around the city.

Early motorists at the beginning of the twentieth century bought and rode automobiles chiefly for amusement—commuting would come later. Motorists enjoyed cruising the long, broad stretch of Sixteenth Street after it was extended into the sparsely populated suburbs north of Piney Branch. Here was a strip where one could have the freedom to test out the full capabilities of one's fancy new machine, perhaps traveling as fast as twenty or twenty-five miles per hour. By the 1910s, one of the city's first gas stations, owned by the Dome Oil Company, opened at Sixteenth and Taylor Streets, just a short distance north of the Piney Branch Bridge. The station doubtless fueled many a joyride on upper Sixteenth Street.

Even more fun than driving on Sixteenth Street were Washington's first automobile races, which were held at the Brightwood racetrack in October 1903. The hard, trotting track for horses proved to be ideal for the era's cars, none of which were custom-made racing machines. Proud amateur owners competed with "automobiles of nearly every style sold in Washington," including gasoline, steam, and electric models ranging in size from "light runabouts to great touring cars."[25] The *Washington Post* made much of the fact that the cars were free to race at high speed on the enclosed track because it was not subject to traffic laws. The danger of the track's tight curves was an added attraction for the roughly five hundred attendees. Fortunately, no serious accidents were reported. Big winners on race day were a Cadillac, Winton, and Saint Louis, along with a Stanley Steamer from Baltimore. The top speeds they reached were around thirty miles per hour.[26]

The Brightwood track, however, would be short-lived. It lay directly in the path of the Sixteenth Street extension. The track held its last horse race just days before workmen knocked down the track's fences in October 1909 and laid Sixteenth Street straight through the middle.

Meanwhile, adequate lighting for the Sixteenth Street extension grew in importance as more automobiles traveled along the pitch-black thoroughfare at night. Members of the Piney Branch Citizens' Association argued in 1913 that Sixteenth Street in the vicinity of the Piney Branch Bridge was "an inviting rendezvous for loving couples, but is absolutely unsafe for automobile traffic at night." With no sidewalks yet constructed north of the bridge, pedestrians simply walked in the street. Finally, in 1914, after a youth walking in the street at night was killed by an automobile, forty-one new hundred-candlepower incandescent lights were installed between the bridge and Madison Street, north of the former Brightwood track site.[27] Further improvements in lighting, paving, and sidewalks were made through the early 1920s.[28]

Meanwhile, the downtown segment of Sixteenth Street was growing much more densely populated. A 1903 *Washington Post* article noted that much progress had been made in transforming Sixteenth into a "noble highway," largely through the efforts of prominent residents such as John Hay, whom the newspaper called "an enthusiastic Sixteenth street advocate," and the numerous senators and Supreme Court justices who lived in or owned mansions on the thoroughfare.[29] These wealthy denizens had little idea that their way of life would soon vanish. They wanted only to enhance the park-like, City Beautiful–style street they had so assiduously developed, preserving it as a sedate and dignified boulevard lined with residential mansions, manicured lawns, and an atmosphere of quiet elegance. Large institutions, denser housing, and increasing traffic would soon shatter that vision.

Nevertheless, a Herculean—and successful—effort was undertaken to preserve Sixteenth Street from commercial development. Through the efforts of Mary Henderson and her supporters, the concept of limiting development on Sixteenth Street was widely accepted by the turn of the twentieth century. A litmus test came in 1904 with the case of the William King & Son Coal Company. The company, which previously had operated a coalyard and woodyard on Sixteenth Street, by this time had just a small one-story office at 1151 Sixteenth, south of L Street. King petitioned in November 1904 to build a driveway next to his office, but powerful Sixteenth Street residents raised a hue and cry, and the DC commissioners quickly rejected the proposal. The *Washington Post* editorialized that "there is enough room in Washington for business offices without marring the appearance of Sixteenth street. Let us have at least one boulevard in the city which will be free from blemish throughout its entire length."[30] William King's tiny office would remain on Sixteenth Street until 1947, but few other commercial businesses would be allowed. In 1905 the DC commissioners followed up by surveying property owners on limiting the future development of the avenue. The response was overwhelmingly in favor of banning commercial enterprises.[31]

The residential character of Sixteenth Street would soon be more fully protected when the city's first zoning regulations were adopted. Zoning as a means of city planning caught on across America in the 1910s. The first National Conference on City Planning and the Problems of Congestion had been held in Washington in May 1909. Here early planners, including Frederick Law Olmsted Jr., offered examples of tightly regulated town planning in Germany and Switzerland that they argued could be applied to American cities. Beautifully landscaped residential neighborhoods would attract the wealthy, stimulating property values and economic development.[32] From the planners' viewpoint everybody would win under a comprehensive, well-thought-out zoning scheme, even though an unspoken goal was to exclude African Americans from affluent areas.[33] Taking up

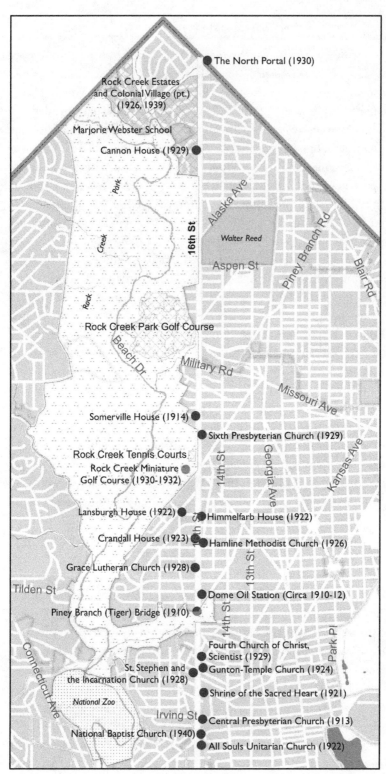

The North Portal (1930)

Rock Creek Estates
and Colonial Village (pt.)
(1926, 1939)

Marjorie Webster School

Cannon House (1929)

Alaska Ave

16th St

Walter Reed

Piney Branch Rd

Blair Rd

Aspen St

Park

Creek

Rock

Rock Creek Park Golf Course

Beach Dr

Military Rd

Missouri Ave

Somerville House (1914)

Sixth Presbyterian Church (1929)

14th St

Georgia Ave

Kansas Ave

Rock Creek Tennis Courts
Rock Creek Miniature
Golf Course (1930-1932)

Lansburgh House (1922)

Himmelfarb House (1922)

Crandall House (1923)

Hamline Methodist Church (1926)

Grace Lutheran Church (1928)

13th St

Tilden St

Dome Oil Station (Circa 1910-12)

14th St

Piney Branch (Tiger) Bridge (1910)

Connecticut Ave

Fourth Church of Christ,
Scientist (1929)

Park Pl

St. Stephen and
the Incarnation Church (1928)

Gunton-Temple Church (1924)

National Zoo

Shrine of the Sacred Heart (1921)

14th St

Irving St

Central Presbyterian Church (1913)

National Baptist Church (1940)

All Souls Unitarian Church (1922)

Early twentieth
century churches,
houses, and other
structures on
upper Sixteenth
Street between
Harvard Street
NW and the
Maryland border.
Rock Creek Park,
just west of the
Sixteenth Street,
is a major feature.
© *Matthew Gilmore.*
Used by permission.

the cause, Congress in 1919 directed the District to enact comprehensive zoning regulations.

DC already had restrictions on new construction, most notably the Height of Buildings Act of 1899, which kept buildings from being built taller than the Cairo apartment house, completed in 1894 just off Sixteenth Street on Q Street. Zoning went further, specifying how buildings could be used—residential, commercial, or industrial—and blocking off specific areas of the city for each type of use. New constraints on height and use, as well as rules on how much of a lot a building could occupy, went into effect in the District in September 1920.[34] The entire length of Sixteenth Street was zoned for residential use, an exceptional constraint for a major thoroughfare in the heart of the city. The section of Sixteenth from Lafayette Square to M Street was the only residentially zoned street in the area immediately north of the White House. Other major thoroughfares, such as Massachusetts Avenue and Connecticut Avenue, featured residential zoning as they moved away from the center of the city but were commercial in the downtown area.

Allowable under the residential zoning regulation were noncommercial facilities such as churches and other nonprofit institutions. The Scottish Rite of Freemasons and the Carnegie Institution had built imposing headquarters buildings on Sixteenth Street in the early years of the twentieth century (see chapter 2). In the same architectural vein, the somewhat more modest Jewish Community Center arose at Sixteenth and Q in the mid-1920s.

Fewer than twenty thousand Jews lived in Washington in the 1920s, and their social lives largely centered around their individual synagogues. A central facility was needed for social, cultural, and recreational activities to support the entire community. A Young Men's Hebrew Association (YMHA), modeled after the YMCA, had been formed in 1911, and a Young Women's Hebrew Association (YWHA) had followed it in 1913, but these were small groups with limited facilities. By 1921 the movement to build Jewish Community Centers in major American cities was well underway, and a special meeting of national and local Jewish leaders was convened to plan for such a center in Washington.

The center would have national significance for American Jews, but it would also be emblematic of the well-established Jewish presence in the nation's capital, and thus a prestigious and dignified location was of paramount importance. The site on Sixteenth Street fit the bill perfectly and was soon acquired. Local community leaders persuaded real estate developer Morris Cafritz (1888–1964) to lead the fund-raising campaign for the new building.[35]

Though Cafritz reportedly was "swamped with offers of aid," several years passed before construction began.[36] Prolific local architect B. Stanley Simmons (1872–1931) designed the classically columned four-story limestone and granite structure. Notably, the center's highly conventional Beaux-Arts design features no Star of David or other distinctly Jewish emblems, just the words "Jewish Community

The Jewish Community Center, located on the southeast corner of Sixteenth and
Q Streets NW, around the time of its completion in 1925. *Library of Congress.*

Center" carved in the limestone entablature over the entrance. The design avoids iconography that would emphasize the uniqueness of Jews, instead emphasizing their integration with the rest of the community.[37]

President Calvin Coolidge attended the May 1925 groundbreaking for the center, giving a rare speech in which he lauded the contributions of American Jews throughout history in building the country, counting them as "buttresses of national solidarity" and denouncing, in contrast, the "demoralizing influence of privilege enjoyed by the few."[38] Coolidge didn't mention the Ku Klux Klan by name, but its influence at the time was alarming. The Klan would march in an officially sanctioned parade on Pennsylvania Avenue just three months later.[39]

Opened in February 1926, the Jewish Community Center quickly became a focal point of activity on Sixteenth Street, hosting meetings and events for Jewish and non-Jewish organizations alike. "Sunday afternoons, hundreds of young people were there, and the guys were trying to date the girls and so forth," one patron later recalled. "The steps were full of people. That was the gathering place and the meeting place."[40] The center's role as a social unifier would in later years extend beyond just bringing together Washington's Jews. In 1942 the center became the city's first integrated music venue when a jazz concert was held there, performed by an ensemble of African American and white musicians and attended by both Black and white audience members. The concert was organized by Ahmet and Nesuhi Ertegun, sons of the Turkish ambassador, who loved jazz and found that after they had finally succeeded in staging an integrated concert at the Jewish Community Center, other sites slowly began to come available for integrated performers and audiences.[41]

Taming Traffic

By the 1920s centralized facilities like the Jewish Community Center made sense in part because it was easier for people from all over the city to take transit—buses, streetcars, and automobiles—to a central location. Unlike previous generations, twentieth-century Washingtonians would live in one area, work in another, and socialize in a third.

As mentioned in chapter 1, it was unusual that a major artery like Sixteenth Street should not have its own streetcar line. In response, Sixteenth Street became the first route for a modern bus line in the city. The first true buses in the modern sense of the word—(relatively) comfortable gasoline-powered vehicles, with pneumatic tires and seating for twenty riders—began operating on Sixteenth Street when the Washington Rapid Transit Company was founded in 1921. The Public Utilities Commission, which regulated transit in the District in those days, approved the new route because it did not directly compete with streetcar lines running on other major arteries. The new line, the forerunner of the current

S2 Metrobus line, was wildly popular, serving thousands of commuters in its first year.[42] Additional buses were added as fast as they could be procured. By the mid-1920s, Sixteenth even sported a small fleet of double-deck buses that featured a winding stair at the back leading up to an open-air top deck, much like some of the modern tour buses that circulate downtown.[43] The street's lush lines of trees had to be carefully pruned to avoid striking passengers riding in the upper compartments of the buses.[44]

Traffic tie-ups, compounded by the new buses, became commonplace on Sixteenth Street in the 1920s. The *Washington Post*'s automotive columnist, Si Grogan, complained in 1923 that there was more traffic at the intersection of Sixteenth, U, and New Hampshire Avenue during the evening rush hour than at any other intersection in the city.[45] Grogan suggested putting a policeman at the intersection to direct traffic, but three years later the city went a step further, installing the city's first network of traffic lights on Sixteenth Street between Lafayette Square and Irving Street. The system, controlled from a box at Scott Circle, was synchronized in the simplest way: all traffic on Sixteenth Street had green lights for forty-five seconds or so, depending on the time of day; then all traffic on the side streets had thirty seconds of green lights. Traffic Director M. O. Eldridge predicted that the new system would "greatly reduce accidents on Sixteenth street and be welcomed as a boon by pedestrians, who now fear to cross this heavily traveled thoroughfare."[46]

When the signals were turned on in January 1926, chaos was the immediate result. Most drivers were confused about how to proceed, especially if they wanted to make a left turn. A month later, the clumsy initial timing scheme was changed to a synchronized system, whereby an automobile traveling at the proper speed in smooth-running traffic would be able to traverse the entire length of Sixteenth Street without stopping.[47] The modern traffic era was underway.

Apartment Living Comes of Age

More and more people were living on Sixteenth Street, and they were no longer building grand mansions—at least not on the portions of the street south of Piney Branch. Instead, apartment living increasingly became the order of the day. As James M. Goode described in *Best Addresses*, Washington in the early twentieth century came to embrace luxury apartment living in a way that few other cities did. On the one hand, the lack of a large-scale industrial base meant that there was little demand for the kind of inexpensive tenement housing being built for factory workers in other large cities. On the other hand, the seasonal and transient nature of politics and the workings of the federal government enhanced demand for more upscale, hotel-like accommodations. For those who could afford it, apartment living was often the answer. Several apartment corridors developed, particularly after

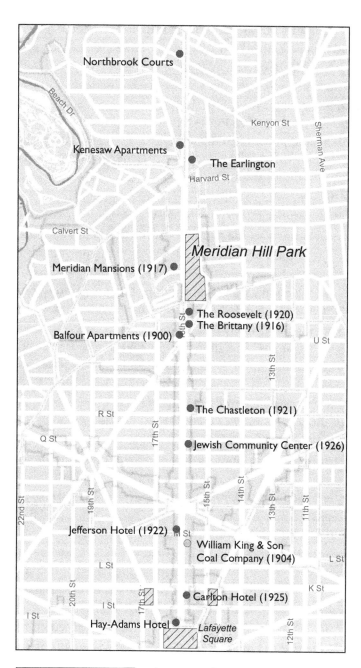

Apartment houses built along Sixteenth Street in the early twentieth century. © *Matthew Gilmore. Used by permission.*

Legend

extant

- ○ No
- ● Yes
- ⬚ Historic_Districts

zoning regulations were instituted in the 1920s, including on Fourteenth Street, Connecticut Avenue, and Columbia Road NW, all of which were streetcar routes.[48] Sixteenth Street, marketed as "the best residential street in Washington," followed. It had the advantage of accessibility via bus (and the Fourteenth Street streetcar) without the noise and commercial hurly burly of the streetcar routes. Some of the city's finest apartment houses and hotels soon rose along Sixteenth Street.[49]

The city's first apartment buildings, such as the residential Arno Hotel discussed in chapter two, appeared in the 1880s and were essentially extended versions of Victorian townhouses, large brick or brownstone structures with elaborate towers and bays. By the turn of the century, apartment living in Washington had reached a golden age.[50] Instead of intricate Victorian piles, the new apartment houses were stately Beaux-Arts structures in line with the aesthetics of the City Beautiful movement. They offered spacious suites with accommodations for both guests and servants and hotel-like amenities such as public dining rooms.

Apartment buildings were generally designed as either apartment houses or apartment hotels. The hotels were intended for individuals (men, almost exclusively) wishing to book extended stays in Washington, who might have more permanent homes elsewhere. Their suites generally did not include kitchens. Instead, they would take their meals in the building's dining room and could also take advantage of a full range of hotel-like services, including daily maid service and fresh linens. In contrast, apartment houses featured dining rooms and other communal amenities, such as barber shops, drug stores, and dry-cleaning establishments, but did not offer maid or linen services. Most had kitchens in every unit.

An early example of a DC apartment house was the Balfour (originally known as the Westover), located on the prominent northwest corner of Sixteenth and U Streets NW—the busy intersection where the short-lived Hancock Circle had come and gone just a few years earlier. Rising six stories, this "beautiful and substantial flat" cost an extravagant one hundred thousand dollars to build in 1900, making it one of the most expensive apartment houses built in DC. Clad in stately limestone up to the second floor, it originally towered over its lightly developed neighborhood.[51] Its Neoclassical portico, heavy cornice, and many decorative flourishes reflected the standard that the best of the city's new buildings were expected to meet.[52]

With building lots on lower Sixteenth Street harder and harder to come by, developers began eyeing the wide-open stretches along upper Sixteenth Street (beyond Meridian Hill) as a potential new luxury residential destination. First up was a triangular lot that had been formed where the old, angled extension of Sixteenth Street (renamed Mount Pleasant Street) veered away from the new, straightened thoroughfare. It was this triangular lot that a group of real estate investors eyed for development of a large apartment house. The attractiveness of the site was enhanced when the Capital Traction Company extended its Connecticut Avenue streetcar line (now Metrobus route 42) along Mount Pleasant Street in

1903, providing ready transportation for the planned apartment house's residents. Irving Street was called Kenesaw Avenue at the time, and the new apartment house was to be known as the Kenesaw.

John B. Henderson was an investor in the project; he may have hoped the large building would spur greater development of Sixteenth Street above Meridian Hill. But local residents in Mount Pleasant feared that the planned seven-story structure would ruin the neighborhood's appeal as an enclave of suburban, single-family homes. Senator William Morris Stewart of Nevada, a powerful silver magnate with real estate interests elsewhere in the District, introduced a bill in Congress in 1904 to condemn and seize the property so that it could be turned into parkland. Stewart and other proponents of this scheme likened the parcel of land at Irving Street to the many triangular lots downtown that were preserved as open parkland, owned and maintained by the federal government.[53] After the bill failed to gain traction in Congress, largely due to its cost, several Sixteenth Street residents filed suit to prevent construction of the new building, arguing that "the erection of apartment houses . . . will change the character of the street, and be injurious to all who have bought and held property and borne assessments on the theory that it was to become a boulevard."[54] The legal challenge failed, however, and in 1905 construction of the Kenesaw was allowed to proceed. In a gesture of goodwill, its owners donated the southern end of the property for a park.

The Kenesaw, now called the Renaissance, towered over its neighbors, offering scenic views from virtually all of its apartments. Hotel-like in design, the brick and limestone Beaux-Arts building included two public parlors, two restaurants, and a café on the first floor as well as shops on the English basement level to the rear of the building facing Mount Pleasant Street.[55] Its construction meant that upper Sixteenth Street would no longer be reserved exclusively for single-family houses.

Notable among the large developments that followed the Kenesaw was Meridian Mansions, at 2400 Sixteenth Street. Located just a block north of Henderson's Boundary Castle, the large apartment hotel, completed in 1917, was considered among Washington's most sophisticated. Built by prolific developer Edgar S. Kennedy (1864–1953) and designed by his longtime collaborator, Alexander H. Sonnemann (1872–1956), the seven-story building was massively out of scale on Mary Henderson's carefully curated Meridian Hill.

Henderson initially tried to block the project, but in the days before zoning she was no more successful than the opponents of the Kenesaw had been. She later told columnist Mayme Ober Peak that when she found she couldn't prevent the building's construction, she tried to get it to conform to her vision for Meridian Hill:

> The corporation which built it was certainly very decent. . . . I was delighted at the opportunity of helping design an apartment house that could spread out instead of up, with ample facilities for sunlight and air. There wasn't an apartment in Washington where an outdoor woman could live happily. I worked with Major Totten in designing

Kenesaw Apartments, now called the Renaissance, on the southwest corner of Sixteenth and Irving Streets NW, pictured in 2020. The building was constructed in 1906. *Authors' collection.*

A 1920s postcard view of Meridian Mansions, constructed in 1916 at
2400 Sixteenth Street NW. *Authors' collection.*

the suites in ells, each with the sunroom opening on a loggia. There is also a water garden on the roof. Ten senators live there now, and their personal interest and influence
are worth a good deal to us up here [on Meridian Hill].[56]

At a cost of nearly $1 million, the sprawling, 33,000-square-foot structure featured 190 apartments, comprising more than 500 rooms, more than 200 bathrooms, and 54 porches. The first floor featured a grand lobby, large foyers, and
wide marble stairways, as well as a dining room and two ballrooms, all trimmed in
mahogany. Amenities included a sizable refrigerating plant (so that tenants would
not need to order ice), electric power and gas for cooking, separate chauffeurs'
and servants' quarters above the spacious garage, roof gardens, and tennis courts.
A massive power plant on Kalorama Road offered free electric power for lights and
for charging electric automobiles in the garage during the winter months.[57]

The posh residential complex quickly became an emblem of social status. Senators,
congressmen, and diplomats all lived here, playing out their meticulously choreographed social lives in the 1920s with extravagant parties and receptions.[58] Most
notably, Tomáš Masaryk (1850–1937), the champion of Czechoslovakian independence from the Austro-Hungarian empire and first president of Czechoslovakia,
lived at Meridian Mansions from July to November 1918—shortly after the building opened—and ran a diplomatic mission from his apartment there. In October
1918 Czechoslovakian independence was finally declared, and the flag of the new
nation flew for the first time from Meridian Mansions. Other diplomatic missions

headquartered at Meridian Mansions included Bolivia and Jordan, in addition to the residences of dozens of diplomats from other countries.

In 1922 the Kennedys sold Meridian Mansions, but they bought it back two years later. The ownership shuffle would be the first in a long series of turnovers as the grand apartment hotel weathered economic and social upheaval. The Kennedy brothers were devastated financially by the Great Depression, and in the early 1930s they finally lost control of the building to their creditor, the Metropolitan Life Insurance Company.

Hotels and Apartments of the Harry Wardman Era

Harry Wardman (1872–1938), perhaps Washington's most prolific real estate developer, built some four hundred apartment buildings and probably 4,500 houses throughout Washington during his career, including more than a dozen apartment houses on Sixteenth Street. Born in Bradford, England, the son of textile workers, Wardman decided to seek his fortune in Australia, where opportunities were thought to abound, when he was twenty years old. When he discovered he would have to wait a month for a ship to Australia, he instead stowed away on the next ship leaving port, which was bound for New York City. He arrived in America with just seven shillings in his pocket and landed his first job as a salesman for John Wannamaker in Philadelphia, where he also bought a set of carpenter tools and learned how to build stairways.

Wardman found work as a carpenter in Washington in 1895, bicycling to job-sites with his tools strapped to the handlebars. Known to builders as a good "trimmer," he got his big break in real estate when he hooked up with a tailor named Henry Burglin to obtain financing from the local Home Savings Bank to build a row of frame houses at Ninth and Longfellow Streets NW, in the then-suburb of Brightwood.[59] Wardman and his partner each made five thousand dollars on the deal, and Wardman used his profits to launch his real estate empire. He was soon building houses throughout the northern quadrants of the city.

Wardman's first Sixteenth Street project was the Earlington, a four-story brick apartment building at 3033 Sixteenth, constructed in 1908. It was designed by Albert H. Beers (1859–1911), an architect from Bridgeport, Connecticut, who came to Washington around 1903. The building stands just north of the intersection with Columbia Road and almost across the street from the Kenesaw, which was completed just three years earlier. It features a heavy, richly decorated cornice and a U-shaped design intended to maximize light and air for individual apartments.

After architect Beers died unexpectedly from pneumonia in 1911, Wardman turned to Frank Russell White (1889–1961) as his principal designer. White, a native of Brooklyn and former apprentice in Beers's office, designed several Sixteenth Street apartment buildings for Wardman, including the stately, seven-story

Lillian and Harry Wardman. Undated photo. *Library of Congress.*

Somerset House at 1801 Sixteenth Street (1916), as well as Northbrook Courts, a pair of visually striking buildings at Sixteenth and Newton Streets, completed in 1917. Northbrook Courts' decorative flourishes, including commanding limestone balconies and elegant plasterwork in their two lobbies, set them apart from other buildings.

Another Wardman effort from this era was the Brittany, a Flatiron-like building that occupies a triangular lot bounded by Sixteenth Street, V Street, and New Hampshire Avenue. Construction of this seven-story tan pressed-brick building was reportedly begun the same day Wardman acquired the tract from its previous owner.[60] Its architect was Albert M. Schneider (1884–1924), a native Washingtonian who lived across the street at the Balfour. One individual who was decidedly unhappy about the Brittany's construction was Mary Henderson, who didn't care for all the apartment buildings proliferating on Sixteenth Street. Just the previous year she had bought property adjacent to the Meridian Hill Park site to prevent Wardman from building an apartment house at that location.[61] Though her husband had invested in the Kenesaw project, Mary believed that all of the city's triangular plots, created by diagonal thoroughfares such as New Hampshire Avenue, should be reserved as parkland.[62] "Who gave Mr. Wardman or anyone else the privilege of building on that triangle or on any of our triangles anywhere?" she demanded to know.[63]

World War I brought a massive influx of new residents to the city, many of whom remained after hostilities ended. The city had been growing steadily since the Civil War, but its population took a big jump—from 331,069 in 1910 to 437,571 in 1920—during the war years. New construction couldn't keep up with the demand. In fact, housing options across the city actually declined as government agencies leased apartment buildings and converted them to temporary offices. On Sixteenth Street, a handsome new apartment building was nearing completion on the southwest corner of Sixteenth and P Streets in November 1917, when the government took it over for the offices of A. Mitchell Palmer, custodian of alien property (and future attorney general), and his staff.[64]

By 1919 the city was in a full-blown housing crisis, with an estimated shortage of two thousand homes. "An army of homeseekers is daily traveling the length and breadth of the city in a vain effort to find a place to lay its head," the *Washington Post* reported.[65] Wardman and other developers responded to the demand with large new apartment house projects, including several on Sixteenth Street.

One of the most prominent of these was not a Wardman effort. It was the eight-story Chastleton, at Sixteenth and R Streets, the city's largest apartment house when it was completed in 1921. Begun as a 155-unit structure in 1919, its developer, the S. W. Strauss Company of New York, decided that same year to double its size, to 310 units, noting that the applications it had received for the original building were more than enough to fill the addition as well.[66]

The Chastleton offered affordable living in an elegant building at a time when any apartment was hard to find. Its English Gothic Revival design was extraordinarily decorative. The giant three-story front portico, complete with Gothic tracery, niches, gargoyles, and faux buttresses, opened into a two-story lobby ringed with second-floor balconies and crowned with an ornate, strapwork ceiling. The plasterwork in the lounge and spacious dining room were the most elaborate of any Washington apartment house to date.[67]

The Strauss Company sold the building shortly after it was completed for $3 million, setting off a protracted series of transfers as one investor after another tried, and failed, to make enough money to offset the expense of the building's massive mortgage. The Chastleton's tenants were often unhappy with their rates,

Letterhead drawing of the Roosevelt, 1931. The block-long hotel and apartment house at 2101 Sixteenth Street NW was completed in 1920. *Authors' collection.*

occasionally clashing with management at rowdy tenant association meetings in the 1920s. In 1926 Harry Wardman became one of the building's long line of owners, converting about a quarter of the building's residences into hotel space for transient guests. It's unclear whether the conversion resulted in higher profits; Wardman would give up the building six years later.

The Chastleton was not the Strauss Company's only mammoth postwar apartment project. In 1919 the company underwrote the mortgage for another, even larger apartment hotel that developer John W. Weaver had been trying to build since the previous year. The result was the Hadleigh Apartment Hotel (now the Roosevelt), on the east side of Sixteenth Street just south of W Street. The eight-story building was the first on Sixteenth Street whose façade spanned an entire full-size block, from V to W Street, just south of Meridian Hill Park. The Hadleigh's flexible layout of seven hundred rooms was divided into two top floors of large apartments (up to seven rooms each) and six lower floors of smaller one-, two-, and three-bedroom units, sizes that were much smaller than had been customary in previous buildings. The smaller units were available both to short-term (hotel) guests as well as longer-term residents, with hotel services available as desired. In announcing the project, the Strauss Company observed that "people have found that living compactly has many advantages and conveniences that can be obtained in no other way."[68]

Despite the compact size of many of the units, the building boasted the latest in luxuries and amenities and was considered one of the finest in the city when it opened.[69] The elaborately decorated lobby featured a Florentine entrance loggia and the main lobby's walls and columns were decorated with colored stonework created by the John J. Earley studio (see chapter 3). The individual apartments had elegant touches as well: the fold-up Murphy beds in the smaller units were finished in mahogany, and the kitchenettes included up-to-date electric ranges and refrigerators. Every apartment was equipped with a recently introduced invention known as a Receivador—a compartment in the corridor wall with doors on the inside and outside where residents could deposit items, such as laundry, for retrieval by service staff.[70]

Mary Henderson was outraged when she heard of the plans for the Hadleigh. While she opposed any large apartment house that would dominate Sixteenth Street and obstruct the views from Meridian Hill that she had so carefully curated, the Hadleigh was especially obnoxious. Its height, she felt, threatened to ruin the panoramic vistas of the city that were to be the highlight of Meridian Hill Park. Working with Charles Moore of the Commission of Fine Arts and Carl E. Mapes, chair of the House Committee on the District of Columbia, Henderson saw to it that a bill was ushered through Congress in November to restrict the height of the Hadleigh to seventy-five feet, its height without the rooftop pavilions.[71] As a result, the rooftop pavilions were never constructed. The following year, the city's first zoning ordinance would set an eighty-five-foot limit for buildings on residential streets like Sixteenth Street.

In 1924 the building's name was changed to the Roosevelt, after Theodore Roosevelt. Like the Chastleton, the Roosevelt changed ownership several times, and was briefly owned by Harry Wardman beginning in 1926. While fashionable in the 1920s, the Roosevelt's high rents would lead to increasing vacancies by the 1930s.

While the Chastleton, Roosevelt, and other large residential buildings played counterpoint to the middle-class row houses lining Sixteenth Street above Scott Circle, the blocks south of the circle were still the domain of the wealthy. The northwest corner of Sixteenth and M Streets—opposite the National Geographic Society's distinguished Hubbard Memorial Hall (1902) and catty-corner to the elegant Warder Apartments (1905)—had been home to African Americans who lived in frame houses and held out resolutely until the early 1900s (see chapter 1). Real estate maps show that the lots on this corner were cleared of these houses over the next decade. During the Spanish Flu pandemic of 1918, the American Red Cross built an emergency ambulance station here.[72] Then in 1922, the Jefferson, a luxury residential hotel, rose in its place.

The Jefferson was the work of Jules Henri de Sibour, who had designed the Warder Apartments earlier in his career. It reflected lower Sixteenth Street's continuing elite residential cachet in the early 1920s. Designed in a restrained Beaux-Arts style, the building could accommodate seventy-five families in spacious,

Temporary Red Cross Ambulance Station on the northwest corner of Sixteenth and M Streets NW, established during the Spanish Flu pandemic of 1918. *Library of Congress.*

well-appointed units and featured elegant Renaissance Revival decoration in its interior public spaces. It was converted to a hotel in 1954 and continues to operate as a boutique hotel today.

As Washington's most prolific developer, Wardman was always moving on to something new, investing the profits from his last effort in new projects. In the late 1920s, just before the start of the Great Depression, Wardman was going great guns. It was in this period that he produced his two crowning achievements on Sixteenth Street: the Carlton and Hay-Adams hotels, Jazz Age monuments to wealth and affluence.

The Ritz-Carlton hotel chain had been looking for a spot for a hotel in Washington since the early 1920s. Then, in 1925, Harry Wardman announced that he would be building a new Carlton Hotel on Sixteenth Street. Noting that he had originally planned to put it at Sixteenth and H Streets, the site of the historic Hay and Adams mansions, Wardman said, "he ha[d] received so many requests that this historical residence and landmark be left intact that the original plans changed and, for the present, at least, to preserve the John Hay home." Instead, Wardman would build

The Carlton Hotel, shortly after its opening in 1926. Located on the southeast corner of Sixteenth and K Streets NW, the hotel replaced the Nicholas Anderson House (see chapter 2). *Authors' collection.*

the Carlton on the southeast corner of Sixteenth and K Streets. Of course, that site was also occupied by a landmark of its own—the Nicholas Anderson mansion— also designed by Henry Hobson Richardson. Apparently, the Anderson House drew less affection than the Hay and Adams houses.[73]

With the Carlton, Wardman constructed a jewel of a hotel. Designed by Mihran Mesrobian (1889–1975), the handsome Italian Renaissance Revival structure rivaled the best hotels in Europe. Rooms featured unheard-of luxuries, including a baby grand piano in corner suites and a telephone in every bathroom. Public amenities, such as the immense lobby, were richly decorated and meant to convey the comforts of a country estate house. The new hotel "will cater to high-class national and international tourists," the *Post* explained when the project was first announced. "The most unusual feature of the Carleton is the beautiful Italian patio, which will occupy the center of the building at the rear. . . . A fountain of graceful and elaborate design will play in the center among the ferns and palms, while an orchestral concert will be given every evening."[74]

Mesrobian, an Armenian American born in Turkey, had as a young man been architect for the Ottoman sultan and had served with distinction in the Turkish army in World War I. After many of his extended family members disappeared during the Armenian genocide, Mesrobian moved to the United States, settling in Washington in 1921 and becoming Harry Wardman's principal architect. The Carlton Hotel, based on elements from the Palazzo Farnese in Rome, was one of his signature accomplishments. Wardman seems to have been uninterested in turning a profit on this expensive, relatively small hotel; it was a showpiece of what he could achieve, meant above all to impress. Legend has it that one of Wardman's friends told him, "Harry, the only reason you built the Carlton was to entertain your friends. It's too small to be a hotel, too big to be a club."[75]

Before the Carlton was even finished, Wardman lifted the stay of execution on the Hay and Adams mansions, announcing plans for a new boutique hotel on that site. "The John Hay house has lately been purchased by Harry Wardman for the purpose of erecting thereon a huge hotel," Mary Henderson wrote in January 1926 with obvious disdain. She also commented on the Carlton: "A rumbling in the air, and in a jiffy Harry Wardman purchased the Nicholas Anderson house, on the ashes of which another hotel project is now half way up in the air."[76] Others complained as well, but like developers everywhere, Wardman seems to have been unconcerned. While objections were often raised about the demolition of historic buildings like the Hay, Adams, and Anderson houses, no legal mechanisms existed at the time to protect such structures. Ultimately, owners were free to tear them down if they wished.

If any small hotel could rival the newly built Carlton in European-style luxury and elegance, it was the new Hay-Adams House, located directly across Lafayette Square from the White House—about as perfect a location for a high-class Washington hotel as anyone could ask for. Also the creation of Mihran Mesrobian, the Hay-Adams was originally envisioned as a kind of annex to the Carlton, designed to accommodate a relatively small number of long-term guests. When first announced in 1926, the planned "apartment hotel" was to be called the Carlton Chambers and would feature all the comforts of the best continental hotels.[77] However, by the time it opened two years later it was christened the Hay-Adams, in honor of the houses it replaced.

The hotel featured two hundred rooms on eight floors. Its Beaux-Arts design included a mix of Neoclassical elements from English and Italian Renaissance sources. The eclectic design extended to the interior rooms, which were "treated in six modes, having the Tudor, Elizabethan, and Italian styles as the basic motifs, and finished in green, buff, light blue, orange and mauve."[78] The elegant lobby,

The Hay-Adams Hotel, completed in 1928 on the northwest corner of Sixteenth and H Streets NW, pictured in 2020. The hotel replaced the John Hay and Henry Adams Houses (see chapter 2). *Authors' collection.*

richly dressed in walnut wainscoting, arched coves, and a coffered ceiling, had an exclusive, club-like atmosphere. The hotel's restaurant, called the Tudor Room, had an old English feel—mahogany paneling, heraldic banners, leaded glass windows. Harry Wardman himself lived on the top floor. Other residents included department store magnate Julius Garfinckel, writer Sinclair Lewis, aviator Amelia Earhart, and actor Ethel Barrymore.

Wardman was riding high. In 1928 newspapers reported he was once again raising capital—$11 million this time—by floating a bond issue, essentially mortgaging his apartment and hotel properties. It proved to be his undoing. The financial crisis that ignited the Great Depression struck the following year, and in 1930 Wardman was forced to declare bankruptcy, relinquishing all his major properties, including the Carlton and the Hay-Adams, at auction. His last major project, completed that year, was a contract with the British government to construct its new embassy on Massachusetts Avenue NW.

Wardman had always been a gregarious man, "happiest when surrounded by a crowd," as described by Carl Bernstein in a 1969 *Washington Post* article: "An avid baseball and prize fight fan, he made a practice of hiring private cars for big fights and transporting a coterie of formally attired friends and diplomats to the pugilistic wars, then back to [his great mansion at] Woodley Road for a ball."[79] All that was gone by the 1930s. Asked if he planned to rebuild his empire, Wardman said, "No sir, I'm through with that. I thought I was a rich man and then I woke up and found I didn't have a nickel." He was exaggerating just a bit. He continued building houses until his death, at sixty-five, in 1938.

Denizens of Suburban Sixteenth Street in the 1920s

Developers added hundreds of new houses to the upper reaches of Sixteenth Street in the 1920s, as more segments of the road were finished. By 1910 the street had been graded as far north as Military Road, and in the following decade it was extended to Alaska Avenue.[80] A hill just beyond Alaska Avenue slowed further development for a time, but in 1925 the street was cut through the hill and extended to Kalmia Street.[81] The last segment, from Kalmia Street to the District line, was not opened until 1930. Sixteenth Street finally became a regional artery at that point as it connected with key Maryland highways such as Colesville Road, Columbia Pike, and the newly constructed East-West Highway. A host of new Maryland commuters welcomed the invitation to use Sixteenth Street as an expressway to and from their downtown jobs.[82]

With Sixteenth Street slicing through the woods of upper Northwest, builders once again saw the opportunity to construct new houses of all types. Houses built on the new stretch in the 1920s included semidetached and freestanding buildings as well as row houses, many in the popular Colonial Revival style. They typically offered more room and more yard space than the older Victorian rowhouses south of Meridian Hill. Residents for whom postwar apartment living had been too confining soon found new options, often at reasonable prices, if they were willing to move further out. With buses to downtown running frequently, the suburban lifestyle on upper Sixteenth Street became a practical option.

Morris Cafritz, the prominent developer who had led the effort to build the Jewish Community Center on lower Sixteenth, was an enthusiastic participant in the development of suburban Sixteenth Street. In 1927 he built a showhouse at Sixteenth and Farragut Streets, just south of Colorado Avenue, in a lavish Spanish Revival style that evoked the exoticism of the Old World and conveyed a sense of escape from worldly troubles. Dubbed El Cortijo ("the farmhouse"), the house was designed by Harvey Warwick (1893–1972), an architect skilled in adapting

Star pitcher Walter Johnson shakes hands with Clark Griffith at Griffith Stadium in 1930. Both men lived on Sixteenth Street. *Library of Congress.*

romantic styles to luxury homes and apartment buildings. Its rambling, country-villa design featured a Spanish tile roof and exterior walls faced in a type of Portland cement called morene, which imitated stucco. El Cortijo was marketed in a special paid section in the *Washington Post* in January 1927 that stressed the mansion's stylistic innovation. "The public is becoming more educated and appreciative of color, design, atmosphere and the setting of houses of the better class," the ad asserted.[83]

Several of Washington's more prosperous businessmen and entrepreneurs of the Roaring Twenties sought lots on upper Sixteenth Street to build ostentatious houses celebrating their success. One was Clark Griffith (1869–1955), owner of the Washington Senators baseball team, who built a mansion at the corner of Sixteenth and Decatur Streets in 1926.

Born in rural Missouri, Griffith had grown up small and sickly in a family that relied on wild game for much of its subsistence. When he was a small child, a hunter's stray bullet had killed his father. Short of stature at five-foot-six, he nevertheless became a professional baseball pitcher while still a teenager, earning the nickname "the Old Fox" for his mastery of the slow breaking ball and the trick pitches he allegedly enhanced by gouging the baseball with his spikes.[84] In 1912 he joined his fourth team, the Washington Nationals (also known as the Senators), as their manager. Griffith improved the team's record and in 1920, with the help of a wealthy backer, gained full ownership of the club. Four seasons later, his Senators beat the New York Giants in their first appearance in the World Series.

With the fame of his team as well as soaring attendance at Griffith Stadium (on Georgia Avenue just south of Howard University), in May 1925 Griffith purchased the large lot at the southwest corner of Sixteenth and Decatur as the site for an "imposing residence."[85] Up until that point, he and his wife, Addie, and two adopted children had lived in a three-story townhouse at 3035 Sixteenth Street (since demolished), across the street from the Kenesaw Apartments, where Griffith's star pitcher, Walter "Big Train" Johnson, stayed when he was in Washington. Griffith's two adopted children had been born to Addie's widowed sister-in-law, who had five more children. In November 1925 the Griffiths brought the other five children home to live with them as well, making the need for a more spacious home urgent.[86]

Griffith's architect for the mansion, James Cooper (1877–1930), was a designer of English Revival style country estates and mansions for fashionable subdivisions like Foxhall Village.[87] The handsome Elizabethan Revival home he built for Griffith was redolent of tradition and ancestral heritage. Its castle-like main block, connected to a steep-gabled wing by a hyphen, gave the appearance of a manor house that had been expanded over multiple generations of distinguished residents. Son Calvin Griffith recalled the house as "so damn beautiful," with brick set in diamond patterns and "light posts all around . . . that were round, looking like baseballs."[88]

Griffith's grand house was soon a gathering spot for Washington's sporting, business, and political elites, but it came to symbolize the pinnacle of a career with a long downward slope. The Nationals/Senators never again did as well as they had in their 1924 world champion season, and attendance dropped off.[89]

Baseball teams in the 1920s were strictly segregated. The players of the Negro Leagues were markedly better than their white counterparts, though they received little recognition for their feats. When the largely anemic Senators weren't playing at Griffith Stadium, the outstanding African American players of the Washington Grays regularly took to the field. Even after Jackie Robinson broke baseball's color line by joining the Brooklyn Dodgers in 1947, Clark Griffith remained staunchly opposed to allowing African Americans to join his team. It was not until late in the 1954 season, in which Washington finished a distant sixth, that Cuban outfielder Carlos Paula became the first Black Senator. Shortly after the following season, Griffith was dead.

The Clark Griffith House on the southwest corner of Sixteenth and Decatur Streets NW, constructed in 1926, pictured in 2020. *Authors' collection.*

At Sixteenth and Buchanan Streets, just three blocks south of the Griffith mansion, stands the former home of theater mogul Harry Crandall (1879–1937). Crandall was one of the city's richest men, but he would lose much of his wealth in the Great Depression. A native Washingtonian, he was endowed with keen instincts and fortuitous timing. Dropping out of school after the fourth grade, Crandall took his first job, at a grocery store, at age twelve. Later he worked as a telephone company test operator and ran a livery stable business on the side. One day, while sitting in one of the city's cramped little nickelodeon theaters, Crandall realized that "moving pictures were the coming thing."[90] Starting with the small Casino theater on Capitol Hill in 1907, Crandall acquired theaters and made steady profits, slowly expanding his business from owning to building. His comfortable, well-ventilated theaters with elegant trappings drew capacity crowds.

Soon he was the largest movie theater operator in the city. One of his projects was the 1,800-seat Knickerbocker Theater at Eighteenth Street and Columbia Road NW, in what is now the heart of Adams Morgan. In 1922 the Knickerbocker's roof collapsed during a massive snowstorm, killing ninety-eight of the several hundred patrons who were watching a new comedy that evening. Though Crandall was cleared of any blame in the accident, it would haunt him for the rest of his life. Nevertheless, he continued to open neighborhood theaters throughout the city, making him one of the District's wealthiest men.

In 1923, the year after the Knickerbocker disaster, Crandall built the mansion at Sixteenth and Buchanan and moved there with his wife and three daughters from their old home, a townhouse at 3321 Sixteenth Street, not far from Clark Griffith's old townhouse. The new house was designed by famed theater architect Thomas W. Lamb (1871–1942) of New York City, who had designed several theaters for Crandall, including the Tivoli Theater in Columbia Heights. For Crandall's mansion, Lamb created a Georgian-style brick house with extensive limestone detailing around the windows, water table, quoins, and chimney. Intended for entertaining, the formal rooms on the first floor included a Victorian drawing room, grand ballroom, and a richly paneled library. Crandall's book collection was considered one of the best private libraries in the city.[91]

By 1925 Crandall was said to be worth $6 million, and he decided it was time to merge his business with a large national theater chain, the Stanley Corporation. At first, Crandall continued to run his theaters as part of the Stanley organization. But consolidation was sweeping the industry, and by the end of the decade Stanley had merged with Warner Brothers. The stock market crash in 1929 hurt Crandall's finances, forcing him to sell his remaining interest in the theaters to Warner Brothers. Ultimately, this is what did him in. While outwardly as cheerful as ever, by 1937 Crandall was a broken man. He secretly rented a room at the Parkside Hotel on Franklin Square downtown, quietly went there one evening, and turned on the gas. When police found his body the next morning, he had left a note of explanation: "You don't have to look for the cause of me taking my life. I'll tell you I have not committed any crime. Have no love affairs. Not insane. Have very good health. No. None of these are the reasons. Only it is I'm despondent and miss my theaters, oh so much."[92]

Other 1920s showhouses line upper Sixteenth Street as well. Directly across from the Griffith House on the southeast corner of Sixteenth and Decatur stands the Paul Himmelfarb House, designed by George Oakley Totten, Mary Henderson's favorite architect, and completed in 1922. Himmelfarb was an oil industry executive and real estate investor. Also on or near Sixteenth are the frame country-style house of local plumbing magnate, Thomas Somerville, at 5600 Sixteenth; the Tudor Revival home of restaurateur Thomas Cannon Jr., owner of the popular Cannon's Steakhouse in Northeast, at 7700 Sixteenth; and the three grand

The Harry Crandall House, now the Embassy of Cambodia, was constructed in 1923 on the southwest corner of Sixteenth and Buchanan Streets NW. *Authors' collection.*

Tudor Revival mansions a block west of Sixteenth at 4801 Blagden Avenue that were home to family members of department store owners James and Gustav Lansburgh. Remarkably these houses and many others reflect the affluence and business success of entrepreneurial Washingtonians rather than the transplanted wealth of outsiders.

The Street of Churches

Sixteenth Street's unique qualities played to the ambitions of local religious communities almost as much as those of the city's businessmen and entrepreneurs. The 1920s saw a boom of religious construction along Sixteenth Street. "Sixteenth street northwest, long known as the street of the embassies and legations, is winning a new name now as the street of the churches," the *Evening Star* reported in 1924.[93] Since the late nineteenth century, affluent white congregations had been following their members as they moved from older downtown neighborhoods to spacious suburban homes, and the early twentieth century saw an accelerated migration of white Washingtonians to upper Northwest. Houses of worship sprang up throughout these neighborhoods, but for many congregations Sixteenth Street had a special draw. As an exclusively residential thoroughfare, the street offered a dignified and appropriate setting, free of commercial distractions such as stores, restaurants, and taverns. It was also a wide, easily accessible avenue with a cachet of national importance and dignity that had been amplified by Mary Henderson's tireless efforts. For local congregations, Sixteenth Street offered pride of place, demonstrating that they were leading community organizations. In addition, for large national religious denominations, the symbolic link to the White House made Sixteenth Street an ideal location for building a house of worship to express a national presence.

The highest concentration of new religious structures was in the blocks above Meridian Hill. The National Baptist Memorial Church, at the intersection of Sixteenth Street and Columbia Road NW in 1907, had been one of the earliest to locate here. It was just a modest, neighborhood Sunday school when it started. In fact, organizers were surprised to find some one hundred people show up to the Immanuel Baptist Bible School's organizational meeting. Soon a complete, new parish was formed. Immanuel Baptist Church moved into a frame house on the northeast corner of Sixteenth Street and Columbia Road as a temporary house of worship and in 1909 constructed a two-story Gothic Revival school building at some distance from the corner that would serve as the first part of a larger church complex.[94] Part of that stone structure can still be seen along Sixteenth Street just north of the main church building.

A larger church would be built, but it was not the Gothic Revival structure that Immanuel Baptist had planned. Instead, church leaders in the 1910s began promoting the idea of building a national church that would serve as a memorial to Roger Williams, founder of the first Baptist congregation in America, on the unbuilt corner portion of the property. The Sixteenth Street location was seen as a perfect spot for a national memorial. Both the northern and southern Baptist conventions in the United States supported the idea, contributing more than three hundred thousand dollars to jumpstart construction of the church.

The National Baptist Memorial Church project officially began with much fanfare in 1921, when President Warren G. Harding broke ground by cutting a neat square of dirt from the site.[95] The focus on Roger Williams was eventually dropped to keep the memorial broadly representative of the whole country. The majestic, limestone-clad structure, its columned tower prominently rising at the sharp corner of Sixteenth Street and Columbia Road, was completed in 1926 and dedicated in 1933, when both northern and southern Baptist conventions were meeting in Washington.[96]

Nearby, at Fifteenth and Irving Streets, the Central Presbyterian Church was another pioneer, moving from its longtime home at Third and I Streets NW in 1914.

The National Baptist Memorial Church, completed in 1926, is seen in this late 1920s aerial view, facing northeast from Sixteenth Street and Columbia Road NW. The Shrine of the Sacred Heart is the white building in the distance.
Gordon B. Bradley Photograph Collection, DC History Center.

The old building, a distinguished Victorian Gothic Revival structure completed in 1885, was sold to the Mount Carmel Baptist Church, an African American congregation. President Woodrow Wilson was a member of Central Presbyterian, and he laid the cornerstone for the new Classical Revival structure just off Sixteenth.[97] The church, which stills stands, though in a much-altered condition, is of brown tapestry brick and includes a classical pedimented façade with six limestone columns. Wilson, the second president after William Howard Taft to have an automobile while in the White House, must have enjoyed riding his Pierce-Arrow out Sixteenth Street to Central Presbyterian. The location was much farther outside the central city than previous presidents had ventured for Sunday worship.

A block further north on Sixteenth stands the Shrine of the Sacred Heart, a Roman Catholic memorial also with national aspirations. In the late 1890s the local diocese of the Roman Catholic Church formed a new parish for the growing suburb of Mount Pleasant, which met on Fourteenth Street near Park Road beginning around 1897. But this was never intended to be just another community parish. Instead, Sacred Heart would be for Washington what the Sacré-Cœur basilica is for Paris, a "temple dedicated to the human heart of Christ and similar to the great national shrines of Europe."[98]

A permanent site for the shrine was acquired just off of Sixteenth Street at Park Road, and the cornerstone was laid in 1921. Completed the following year, the Shrine of the Sacred Heart was designed by Frederick V. Murphy (1879–1958) and reportedly cost $1 million to build, a remarkable sum for the time. Murphy, a graduate of the École des Beaux-Arts in Paris and founder of the School of Architecture at Catholic University, was a prominent local architect, sharing a practice with Walter B. Olmsted (1871–1937), whom he met when the two worked as young men for the supervising architect of the Treasury.[99] Murphy chose an Italian Romanesque Revival style, which was typical of Catholic churches in the early twentieth century. The style evoked the period before the Reformation, when all European Christians were Catholics, and also helped to visually distinguish Catholic churches from Protestant churches, many of which had adopted the Gothic Revival style. Other Catholic churches in Washington in the Italian Romanesque style include the Basilica of the National Shrine of the Immaculate Conception, Saint Matthew's Cathedral, the Franciscan Monastery, and a number of parish churches.

Massive and imposing, the Shrine of the Sacred Heart is built of white Kentucky limestone and is crowned with a Spanish tile roof and polychrome dome emblazoned with four Latin crosses, giving it an Italian ambiance.[100] Passing through the arcaded front portico of polished Milford granite columns, the visitor enters a cavernous central nave capable of seating 1,200 worshipers. Columns and rounded Romanesque arches separate the nave from the side aisles, all of them decorated

The Shrine of the Sacred Heart, at Sixteenth Street and Park Road NW, at the time of its completion in December 1922. *Authors' collection.*

with colorful, inlaid, mosaic-like patterns produced by the John J. Earley studio, which had worked on the Chastleton and Meridian Hill Park (see chapter 3).[101]

The church's dedication in December 1922 was a lavish event, full of elaborate religious ceremony. Despite the fact that the expensive building had been funded largely by contributions from wealthy, conservative donors, the speakers at the dedication emphasized tolerance and inclusiveness. The *Washington Herald* reported that, "while no attack was made on the Ku Klux Klan as an organization, each of the speakers flayed it in their appeals for a larger clarity of thought and liberality of ideas on the part of the American people."[102] The politically powerful KKK of the early 1920s was avowedly anti-Catholic, and church leaders looked to institutions like Sacred Heart, neighborhood-based and yet with a broad appeal, to serve as a counterweight in the struggle for a more tolerant society.

Very different in matters of faith and yet strikingly similar in its goal of tolerance and acceptance, the All Souls Unitarian Church was another major addition to the collection of Sixteenth Street religious institutions in the early 1920s. The Unitarians, though small in number, have had a long presence in Washington. Their name comes from their fundamental belief in a single God rather than the concept of the trinity embraced by other Christian creeds. Their first church in Washington, designed by Charles Bulfinch, was built on the northeast corner of Sixth and D Streets NW in 1820. By 1908 the congregation was in a tall-spired,

Victorian Gothic church at Fourteenth and L Streets NW and was looking to build a larger church. Its most famous congregant, President Taft, had been inaugurated that year and was a faithful attendee, sparking greater attendance from the public at large. However, the effort to locate and build a new church would take many more years.

Like many other organizations, both religious and secular, the Unitarians saw a presence on Sixteenth Street as having national significance and prestige. In 1913 the church acquired a large lot near Sixteenth and R Streets NW, adjacent to the site where the Scottish Rite Temple was being constructed. In February Taft, wearing a heavy fur-lined coat, laid the cornerstone for the projected new building there in a festive ceremony, declaring that "the site which has been selected, and the edifice which has been designed and projected, all insure an opportunity for greatly increasing the influence of Unitarianism in this Capital and in the country."[103] But the English Gothic–style church complex planned at this location was never built. Instead the site remained empty and the building project delayed until after World War I.

By 1919 the posh Chastleton apartment building was under construction next to the church site, and its developers coveted the Unitarian site for an expansion of the Chastleton. After much debate, church members agreed to sell it to them. Key to the deal was Mary Henderson's offer to supply a new site for the church on property she owned on the southeast corner of Sixteenth and Harvard Streets NW.[104] While still located on prestigious Sixteenth Street, the church would have a more spacious site here, in a growing part of the city.

Completed in 1924, the All Souls Unitarian Church was designed by Boston architect Henry R. Shepley, a grandson of Henry Hobson Richardson. Colonial Revival in style, it is modeled on James Gibbs's famous Saint Martin-in-the-Fields church, prominently located on Trafalgar Square in London. The Unitarians had wanted a structure that would "typify Unitarian ideas and ideals."[105] Shepley's design fit the bill in part because of the close association between the Colonial Revival style and New England, where Unitarianism began in America. The structure's light and airy interior, continuing the New England Neoclassical look, is devoid of religious symbols or decorations. In addition to the main auditorium, the church featured wings to the rear for a library, classrooms, and meeting rooms. Fittingly, the soaring central tower held a bell cast in 1822 by Paul Revere's son.[106]

At the very end of the decade, another major national church was added to the Sixteenth Street collection, the Universalist National Memorial Church, located at S Street, midway between Scott Circle and Meridian Hill. Scholars surmise that the church's solid-looking Romanesque Revival design was a compromise between church elders, who preferred the traditional Neoclassical Revival style, and Boston architect Charles Collens, a specialist in ecclesiastical buildings, who preferred Gothic.[107] Construction began in 1928, when workmen demolished eight row

All Souls Unitarian Church at Sixteenth Street and Harvard Street NW is modeled after London's Saint Martin-in-the-Fields. *Library of Congress.*

houses on the site to make way for the new building. In 1929 a ceremony was held to dedicate the church's tower to "world peace, international justice, and brotherhood," and the full church was dedicated the following year.[108]

Other distinguished Sixteenth Street churches from the 1920s include Gunton Temple Memorial Presbyterian Church (now the Canaan Baptist Church), a striking Romanesque Revival edifice at Sixteenth and Newton Streets; the handsome Gothic Revival Hamline Methodist Church at Allison Street (now the Simpson-Hamline United Methodist Church), completed in 1926; Grace Lutheran Church, equally handsome and Gothic in the style of English parish churches, completed in 1928 at Varnum Street; Saint Stephen and the Incarnation, a red brick early English Gothic edifice constructed in 1928 just off Sixteenth Street at Newton Street; and the Fourth Church of Christ, Scientist (now the Trinity AME Zion Church), an imposing limestone-faced Neoclassical temple completed in 1929 at Oak Street and designed by Chicago architect Howard L. Cheney (1889–1969), who also designed Washington National Airport's main buildings.[109]

As the prosperous 1920s gave way to the Great Depression, Sixteenth Street stood on the verge of more change. Modern apartment houses and hotels were crowding out the old Victorian mansions. Respected churches and other institutions were increasingly claiming their spots. The onset of hard times would mean more upheaval for the street's residents and institutions alike.

FIVE

Moderne and Modern in the
1930s and 1940s

T HE 1930S AND EARLY 1940s pitted continuing ambitions for modernity
against the bleak prospects of depression, fascism, and war. Washington felt
the Great Depression's pains, as the city's total value of building permits, a measure
of the health of the local economy, plunged to record lows in 1933–34. However,
these pains were less severe and of shorter duration in Washington than in the rest
of the nation. In 1935 Washington's total permit value rebounded to about 84
percent of its 1929 level. Surely Los Angeles, Baltimore, and Philadelphia, whose
respective permit values were 35 percent, 25 percent, and an appalling 12 percent
of their 1929 totals, would have happily traded places with the nation's capital.[1]
By the boom year of 1939, Washington's annual building permit value was more
than 25 percent higher than in 1929. Even while construction was plunging, the
city's population had swelled. Although this trend is often ascribed to increased
government employment during the New Deal, the city's population also had increased substantially during the Hoover years. In 1940 the District had 36 percent
more residents than in the previous census, making the 1930s its highest growth
decade since the Civil War.[2] As miserable as the city's situation may have seemed,
the Depression was plainly less desperate in Washington than elsewhere.

These trends rippled along Sixteenth Street, accelerating changes and disrupting patterns that had been evolving for decades. In the early thirties, the street
finally became a continuous boulevard linking Lafayette Square with suburban
Maryland. As Mary Henderson's ambitions and influence waned, a new generation of stylish high-rise apartment buildings appeared on Meridian Hill, and the
run-up to war spurred both new construction and the transformation of old neighborhoods. While war froze building, it changed how Sixteenth Street's landscape
was perceived and inhabited. Mobilization affected virtually every aspect of life,
promoting civic engagement and unifying disparate neighborhoods.

Even as Meridian Hill Park took final shape in the mid-1920s, it was becoming evident that, although Mary Foote Henderson had won the battle for the park, she would lose her war for Sixteenth Street's civic soul. Although the street had almost forty apartment houses by the early twenties, Henderson's vision of an elite residential enclave still held sway over Meridian Hill, whose long slope remained dominated by large houses and embassies. However, Henderson, who had turned eighty in 1922, was becoming increasingly isolated. Her husband, John B. Henderson, had died in 1913 after a half-dozen years completely bed-ridden; newspaper articles had referred to Mary as his widow even while he was still living. Their son, John, wrote his mother earnest letters that advocated selling family landholdings to liquidate "the debt that hangs over us like a funnel shaped cloud" and to redecorate the castle's dated and shabby great hall.[3] Mary had taken in a young immigrant from Okinawa named Jesse Shima. After her son's sudden death in 1923, she made him manager of her business affairs, majordomo of the castle, and host at her parties. Shima slept in John Henderson's bedroom, ate meals with Mary, and accompanied her on daily walks.[4]

Mary continued to write letters to newspapers on topics as varied as public architecture, women's bathing suits, and meat-eating's relationship to cancer, but her causes seemed more the expressions of an eccentric personality than bold civic visions.[5] Her death in 1931 was bracketed by protracted legal battles involving her granddaughter, whom she had disinherited. In 1937 the castle was purchased by a Texan named Bert L. Williams and converted to the Castle H Swim and Tennis Club, with a bar in its ballroom and rooms-to-let upstairs.[6] In the late 1940s, a neighbor, *Washington Post* publisher Eugene L. Meyer, became irritated by late-hour revelry, bought the dilapidated castle, and tore it down.[7]

Washington Comes to the Fair

As Mary Henderson's influence waned, market forces overrode her powerful will, and new architectural styles supplanted her decorous Beaux-Arts vision. "Art Deco" has become shorthand for the fusion of avant-garde artistic movements with industrial design that crystalized into a style at the Paris Exposition Internationale des Arts Décoratifs et Industriels Modernes of 1925. In architecture, Art Deco evolved into a family of Moderne styles that shared streamlined planes conveying a sense of motion, lively color accents, bold geometric forms, and machine-age materials like polished aluminum. "Moderne" suggested modernity and glamor, as well as the flamboyance of downtown nightclubs and the gleaming aluminum half-lozenges above apartment house entrances.

Mary Henderson's cortege leaves Boundary Castle on July 30, 1931. *DC Public Library.*

The Moderne-style Park Tower apartment building at 2440 Sixteenth Street NW, completed in 1929, contrasts with the 1907 Beaux-Arts old French Embassy building, representing two distinct epochs on Meridian Hill. *Authors' collection.*

Although Washington was stereotyped as stodgy and slow to follow trends, the new style appeared in fashionable apartment houses within two years of the Paris exhibition's close. Sixteenth Street's Moderne age began with a luxurious apartment building in the heart of Mary Henderson's embassy district in the summer of 1928, three years before her death. Developer-builders Z. Thomas Goldsmith and William Keller advertised Park Tower, at 2440 Sixteenth, by presenting sketches of its dramatic "skyscraper-moderne" façade, whose window ribbons running between limestone pilasters pulled the eyes upward to a loggia-gallery at the top of its ziggurat roofline.[8] Park Tower wrapped a side wing behind Henderson's French Embassy on the corner of Kalorama Road, and its variegated façade, dashed with color-accented brick, multihued tile, and green marble panels, contrasted sharply with the Beaux-Arts embassy's chalky limestone walls.

Park Tower was planned for a new mix of Meridian Hill residents. Its eighty-seven original units included efficiency-like bachelor apartments as well as expansive three-bedroom suites with separate living and dining rooms as well as private porches.[9] Rents were only about half those at nearby Meridian Mansions, and its residents, who included a congressman, physicians, lawyers, managers, and salesmen, represented the upper-middle class more than the affluent elite. In 1930 only one Park Tower family had a live-in servant, while at Meridian Mansions one family was attended by a staff of four.

Park Tower's fresh style marked the coming of a new generation of architects. William Harris, its twenty-seven-year-old designer, had received his first commission while still a student at the Carnegie Institute of Technology. In 1929 he reprised Park Tower's Moderne façade at the Ravenel, near the corner of Corcoran Street just north of Scott Circle. Soon afterward, the Great Depression struck, and the Ravenel proved the next-to-last apartment building erected on Sixteenth Street for a half-dozen years.

Street of Dreams

Although the stock market had collapsed in September 1929, national economic indicators improved in early 1930, leading some to regard the crash as a short-term correction that mostly punished greedy speculators. A spirit of cautious optimism perhaps infused the crowd that assembled at the District line on May 16, 1930, to watch Maryland Governor Albert C. Ritchie and a host of civic leaders dedicate the North Portal. The portal project had been designed by the newly formed National Capital Parks and Planning Commission as a major regional traffic artery. Besides completing Sixteenth Street's "missing link" between Kalmia Street and the District Line, it was to furnish a hub for radiating roads linking Lafayette Square to Rockville, Gettysburg, and Baltimore.[10] The portal had been envisioned as a grand replica of Rome's Piazza del Popolo, but what spectators saw was considerably more modest; a traffic circle that connected lower Sixteenth Street, Eastern Avenue, and Colesville Pike, which ran through downtown Silver Spring, with a block-long northern leg of Sixteenth Street that ended at East-West Highway, a new connector with Bethesda. Although Sixteenth Street would not reach further north to Georgia Avenue for years, the ceremony's speakers excitedly drew parallels between the new junction and communication innovations like radio and the airplane. The rough-hewn rock marker at the circle's center, a substitute for a once-planned pool that was to be fed by a cascade running along Sixteenth Street, won praise for symbolizing the new unity between Maryland and the District.[11]

Like many ambitious projects, establishing this long-dreamed-of direct link between downtown and the wilds of Maryland had an unintended consequence; Sixteenth Street became a favored route for rumrunners and a scene for not-infrequent police car chases. One "thrilling . . . nip-and-tuck" chase featured gunplay worthy of the gangster movies that captivated Depression audiences.[12] At about three o'clock on the morning of February 28, 1932, Montgomery County Officer Lawrence Dixon and his partner were patrolling the rural roads north of Silver Spring when they encountered two sedans speeding along without taillights. When the police car drew even with the lead sedan, Dixon pointed his pistol at the driver and ordered him to stop. He was greeted with a guffaw, and a fifteen-mile chase ensued, with the sedan blasting dense clouds of smoke from a backseat generator and swerving from shoulder to shoulder to prevent the police car from drawing alongside. After firing his pistol in the air, Dixon began shooting at the sedan's tires and gasoline tank with a rifle. The sedan was riding on two rims when the cars reached East-West Highway in Silver Spring and passed Metropolitan Police Lieutenant Frank Varney and his wife, wending their way home from a night out with friends. Varney signaled Dixon to pursue the sedan into the District and joined the chase, now a procession that included a dozen thrill-seekers lured by the sound of gunfire echoing in the dead of night. Even after Dixon shot out a third tire, the "rum car" kept rolling and swerving down Sixteenth Street, its driver ignoring shouts to stop or be shot. Finally, as the last gas seeped from its riddled tank, the sedan, which had absorbed nine bullets, blew a huge billow of smoke and ground to a halt near Military Road. Two men jumped out and vanished into the fields and brush on the edge of Rock Creek Park. While the officers searched, at least one spectator filched a half-gallon jug of moonshine. The pursuit was Patrolman Dixon's second to end on Sixteenth Street in just two days.[13]

On the Frontier

Sixteenth Street's northern reaches were developing slowly even before the Great Depression brought residential building in the city to a virtual halt. Here the street's long boundary with Rock Creek Park had created an urban frontier, as the park's expansive tracts, reserved for retention in their natural condition, made it difficult for adjoining neighborhoods to achieve critical mass and imposed a barrier to the street's west.[14] North of Peirce Mill, only the Military Road Bridge provided a direct vehicular link to the developing Connecticut Avenue corridor. What development there was capitalized on the area's character as a sylvan enclave. In 1928 the Marjorie Webster School of Expression and Physical Education fled the urban temptations of Thomas Circle to settle on an estate-like, six-acre campus on Kalmia Street just west of the Sixteenth Street right-of-way. Webster's two-year women's college and business school thrived in the new location, weathering the Depression by offering swimming lessons in its large indoor pool and inaugurating classes in radio announcing, play production, and public speaking. By 1940 its graduating class had nearly quadrupled.[15]

The private Marjorie Webster School, which left downtown in 1928 for this sylvan setting just west of Sixteenth Street at Kalmia Road NW, pictured in 2020. It is now the Lowell School. *Authors' collection.*

When his company laid out Rock Creek Estates along Kalmia Street in 1926, Edson Briggs had "resolved to preserve . . . not only the trees, but the brooks, hills, and dales throughout the property."[16] His highly imaginative advertisements at first evoked the dreams of homesick Bedouins and buccaneers. Then, in November 1930, he offered a new vision, promising purchasers in the Colonial Village section "the primitive beauties of Rock Creek Park" where "Pilgrim peacefulness prevails."[17] Conceived as a complement to the upcoming George Washington Bicentennial, Colonial Village was intended to have one hundred homes architecturally representative of the colonial period, complemented by "quaint stone walks such as Washington strode," picket fences, and gardens. Articles and advertisements suggested that this atmosphere, evocative of John D. Rockefeller's recently opened Colonial Williamsburg, would "rekindle sturdy traditions that distinguished American life in those early times."[18]

Unfortunately, such traditions also included racial and ethnic exclusion. Rock Creek Estates' deed covenants stipulated that for ninety-nine years the land could not be "used, occupied by, . . . sold, leased, rented, or given to . . . any negroes or . . . persons of negro blood, extraction, or descent" or "any person of the

Semitic race, blood, or origin, which racial description shall be deemed to include Armenians, Jews, Hebrews, Persians, or Syrians." Domestic servants were conveniently excepted.[19]

Even with continuous pavement, development on Sixteenth Street's northern reaches proceeded slowly. Five years after the completion of the "missing link" to North Portal, just thirteen houses stood between Alaska Avenue and the District line. Rock Creek Estates' deeds stipulated that houses had to have a high minimum value and be of a design approved by the company, and its pricey one-third-acre lots sold slowly. By 1936 only about seventy lots had been purchased within the hundred-acre subdivision.[20]

Settlement was more extensive south of Military Road, where clusters of small tract dwellings and row houses had been forming since the 1910s. Between Military Road and Colorado Avenue, Sixteenth Street bordered a section of Rock Creek Park that was being developed for mass recreation. For decades, park planning had seesawed between preserving an unspoiled wilderness traversed only by bridle paths and trails and a more populist vision of a pleasure ground for sports and socializing. An unfulfilled 1906 plan had proposed baseball diamonds and gridirons, as well as tennis courts, a golf course, and a casino near the Brightwood Reservoir (where Colorado Avenue crosses Sixteenth) to serve government clerks who could not afford country clubs.[21] In 1909 a nine-hole course had been constructed on land donated by Charles C. Glover, but it quickly reverted to nature for lack of maintenance funds. Only a few dirt tennis courts, shelters, and a picnic area had been laid out by 1918, when a plan developed by the Olmsted landscape architectural firm resurrected the idea of developing the reservoir area for intensive recreation, including a full-size golf course.[22] Buoyed by the popularity of an eighteen-hole course newly opened in Potomac Park and believing that outdoor recreation would enhance public health on the heels of the 1918 influenza pandemic, Congress commissioned a 1921 study, which recommended building a course at a more northerly site near Military Road.[23] Ex-president Wilson, despite having been an avid horseback rider and golfer before his disabling stroke in 1919, protested that the course would be "an unforgivable piece of vandalism" to Rock Creek Park.[24] Planners, speaking not entirely candidly, assured the former president that the site's trees had long been cleared for farming.

Under the guidance of noted golf architect William Flynn, a nine-hole course was completed near the terminus of Van Buren Street in 1923. A second nine-hole module opened in 1926.[25] The course drew some seventy-five thousand players in its first year and proved so popular that the Capital Traction Company added a loop across Underwood Street to its Sixteenth Street bus line to accommodate golfers.[26] Concrete and clay tennis courts were meanwhile constructed south of Kennedy Street near the reservoir and became the site for men's and women's park championship matches.[27]

After the Brightwood Reservoir was abandoned in the late 1920s, controversy seethed over repurposing its site. The Sixteenth Street Heights Civic Association opposed building a swimming pool or recreation center, arguing that crowds of children would cause too much commotion. In 1930 the association, presumably realizing that the thirst for entertainment abhors a vacuum, endorsed building a miniature golf course, thus blocking any other "undesirable enterprise."[28] Miniature golf, which required no equipment other than a rented ball and putter, had proved a perfect fad for the Great Depression. In 1930 an estimated fifty thousand such "midget," "Tom Thumb," and "pony" courses were operating nationwide, and in Washington courses opened so quickly that a *Post* reporter joked that they were "springing up like Irishmen at a fight" and might "prove a panacea for unemployment."[29]

During the spring of 1930, the Welfare and Recreation Association, a governmental entity that sponsored programs for civil servants, opened courses on the Washington Monument grounds as well as the Brightwood Reservoir site. These federal "Lilliputian links" were far more elaborate than typical vacant lot courses, which might feature tin can holes set in painted canvas putting greens. The Welfare and Recreation Association spent thirty-five thousand dollars to build Rock Creek Park's nine-hole putting course and an adjoining eighteen-hole "pitch," or short course, designed by architects Fallon and Harries of Baltimore. However, the miniature golf fad soon ran its course, and in the late summer of 1932 the Sixteenth Street course and mini-links in several other parks closed for lack of patrons. The course was soon obliterated as the National Park Service redeveloped the reservoir area with tennis courts, horseshoe pits, baseball fields, and other facilities. Like the adjacent neighborhoods, these and other Rock Creek Park facilities were segregated. Although the park's picnic grounds were open to all races by 1939, African Americans could not play the golf course until after World War II.[30]

While many side streets were lined with row houses, Sixteenth Street from Colorado Avenue south to the Piney Branch Bridge interspersed large villas like the Crandall and Himmelfarb houses (see chapter 4) with smaller dwellings that stood in clusters separated by blocks that remained nearly empty through the Depression years. Where open land met dense settlement, discontinuous spaces appeared that were neither city nor wilderness. Unlike manicured Meridian Hill Park, Rock Creek Park's uncultivated and undomesticated borders could seem like no-man's-lands where social rules were suspended and the usual order subverted. Sixteenth Street's Piney Branch Valley crossing still had such a frontier feel in the early 1930s. Here the valley was a ravine with steep, wooded slopes and a floor traversed by a dirt road that lay sixty feet below the Piney Branch Bridge.

On a sunny morning in September 1931, a woman in the apartment house at 3701 Sixteenth noticed a man lying with his arms and feet peacefully crossed beside the dirt trail beneath the bridge. Sleeping vagrants were likely a familiar sight given the times, but, when her young son said that the man's face was bloody, she called police. They identified the corpse as Patrolman Raymond Morrow, who had been missing since the previous night. The medical examiner found that Morrow held a fragment of lead between his teeth, his face was severely cut and bruised, his shirt bore a heel print above the right shoulder blade, and he had suffered a ruptured liver. The Metropolitan Police had been immersed in running scandals involving bootleggers and gambling, as well as a Justice Department inquiry into repeated claims of brutality, and rumors quickly spread that a patrolman had been "slugged" and thrown over the railing. A crowd of gawkers soon congregated on the bridge, blocking traffic on Sixteenth Street.[31] *The Evening Star* headlined the story "Suspect Murder" and suggested that Morrow's face had been bloodied by a bullet wound.[32]

Detectives, closely tracked by reporters, traced Morrow's movements during his last evening alive. They learned that, hours after telling his wife that he was calling in sick because of hay fever, a "stumbling" Morrow had left a drinking party at a friend's apartment with a mysterious brunette known only as "Sugar."[33] Sugar was soon identified as Martha Habey, the manager of the Playhouse Inn near Dupont Circle, whose "best friend in the world" was another police officer. Questioned by Assistant United States Attorney John Sirica, later of Watergate fame, Habey told a disjointed tale about trying to sober Morrow up by feeding him sauerkraut and ice cream and driving him around and around the Ellipse before sending him off in his own car during the small hours of the morning. Reversing earlier reports, police department officials testified that Morrow's car had been parked neatly by his nearby apartment, the footprint on his shirt matched his own shoe-sole, and that, despite his peaceful pose, his injuries were consistent with falling from the bridge or rolling down the steep ravine.[34] A coroner jury's verdict of death through either accident or suicide was disputed by Morrow's widow.[35] As rumors swirled, the case was reinvestigated but never reached a more definitive conclusion.

Hard Times Hit Home

Whatever Sixteenth Street's past ambitions, both its fashionable and more faded addresses mirrored the Depression's distress and upheaval. In October 1931 Adaline Greenleaf, who had lost three hundred thousand dollars in the stock market, hanged herself at the luxurious Presidential Apartments at 1026 Sixteenth.[36] In May 1932 Hugh Cramer, a real estate salesman out of work for a year, wrote his wife a note saying, "I am doing the cowardly act," and shot himself through the heart in their living room at 3126 Sixteenth.[37] In November young Val Kovacs, whose earnings at a downtown tearoom no longer covered her rent, drank poison in her room at 3701 Sixteenth.[38] Four months later, Sidney Edwards of 1823 Sixteenth, a boardinghouse keeper distraught about finances, concluded an argument about answering the door by shooting his wife in the face and then turning the gun on himself.[39]

Gangsters were a central archetype in 1930s popular culture. However, Sixteenth Street had neither notorious dives nor obvious links to the underworld, so its more genteel residents were undoubtedly shocked when a grisly murder revealed that gangland figures moved among them too. Perhaps they found it fitting that, when the former "Avenue of the Presidents" became associated with such a sordid scenario, ripples reached the White House.

A few minutes after sunrise on April 21, 1932, a Chevrolet roadster stopped behind a milk wagon that was blocking the 3400 block of Brown Street, an alley-like thoroughfare a half-block west of Sixteenth. Suddenly a black Hudson sedan pulled up behind the roadster. A man in a black coat and gray hat stepped out, shouldered a sawed-off shotgun, and fired point-blank blasts into the Chevrolet driver's head and body, hopping onto the running board to deliver the final two blasts. Yelling "Scram" at a bewildered bystander, the gunman ran to the Hudson, which backed around the corner of Meridian Terrace, and sped east toward Sixteenth Street.[40]

Despite his disfiguring wounds, the police easily identified the dead man as Milton "Milsie" Henry, a gambling impresario and reputed finger man who bankrolled gangsters preparing to pull off big jobs. Newspapers speculated whether his killers had been bookies who suspected race-fixing was behind his recent winning streak at Bowie or "sportsmen" "short-carded" at his gambling house near the Navy Yard.[41] Milsie had died with an unfired .38 in his hand while taking a back route to the Oaklawn Terrace Apartments at 3620 Sixteenth, where he lived in quiet middle-class comfort with salesmen, managers, and accountants. He had been traveling without his bodyguard, who had been shot by a police officer while holding up a rival's card game a few days earlier.

A police dragnet led to Charles Harris, a pardoned bank robber, New York gang associate, and one-time guest in Henry's home.[42] At his trial, witnesses swore Harris had been in the Bronx on the day of the killing. However, a Brown Street resident and a deliveryman placed him at the crime scene. Harris's date with the electric chair was approaching when he granted Martha Strayer of the *Washington Daily News* a death house interview. Strayer became convinced that Harris had been convicted on insufficient evidence and wrote stories advocating a stay of execution. Her regular beat was covering Eleanor Roosevelt, whom she enlisted in Harris's cause along with a star panel of civic leaders and attorneys. President Franklin D. Roosevelt stayed Harris's execution on grounds of ineffective counsel, then commuted his sentence to life in prison before ordering him paroled in 1940. Harris was later pardoned by President Harry Truman, and his story was dramatized for radio and television.[43]

The depressed economy accelerated the transformation of many of Sixteenth Street's aging mansions into rooming and boardinghouses.[44] In the 1930s rooms were available in almost every block between Scott Circle and Florida Avenue, and large boardinghouses, which often referred to themselves as clubs, advertised regularly. One flourishing establishment was the Helene Club, which occupied a Gilded Age mansion at 1730 Sixteenth. The club was named for its proprietor, Helen Meaton (1891–1949), who had opened her exclusive home for girls and women in 1928. Meaton's advertisements promised pleasing ambiance and amenities, with "beautifully furnished" rooms, "splendid" meals, a circulating library, radio and telephone access, and laundry privileges for "members."[45] In 1930 Meaton, an African American servant, and a white hostess-maid kept house for twenty-two boarders. Most were in their midtwenties, and virtually all were clerical workers, more than three-quarters of them working for the federal government. Similarly, the 1881 Carpenter mansion at 1327 Sixteenth was transformed into the College Club for Girls, while the mansion constructed by Mary Henderson and George Oakley Totten at 2620 Sixteenth became Club Meridian, a "delightful home residence for men and women" with sunrooms, lounges, and drawing rooms.[46] In 1936 the Susan Shields mansion at 1401 Sixteenth offered "desirable rooms for one, two, or three" and "selective meals." Later accounts suggest that for a time it also functioned as an exclusive bordello.[47] Oakcrest, the former Cassidy mansion at 3640 Sixteenth, became the Martha Washington Seminary in the 1920s. By 1936 it had been transformed into Fountain Court, which offered "cool, quiet, countrylike surroundings" and delicious food to a select clientele of men and women.[48]

Stormy Weather

On Meridian Hill, the tranquil atmosphere surrounding Mary Henderson's embassies became an early casualty of political and economic tumult. In January 1930 a communist party–led group with both Black and white members picketed the Mexican Embassy at 2829 Sixteenth to protest the "murder . . . of workers and peasants" by that country's government. Surrounded by police with drawn clubs, the nearly three dozen picketers "fought fiercely for their banners" in a "battle royal" followed by a mass arrest. One picketer was beaten so ferociously at the police station that he lay unconscious overnight at Freedmen's Hospital. Once incarcerated, the picketers noisily protested the segregated cell blocks at the DC Jail.[49]

Fascism cast an increasingly long shadow over Meridian Hill as the decade progressed. In 1931 the Italian Embassy at 2700 Sixteenth hosted forty cadets from Rome's Fascist Academy, on a goodwill tour to pay respects at the Tomb of the Unknown Soldier.[50] The next year police guarded the embassy after a bomb, one of a dozen thought to have been mailed by antifascists, killed three people in a Pennsylvania post office.[51]

The run-up to the Mussolini government's October 1935 attack on Ethiopia launched protests in African American communities across the country. In Washington, prominent civil rights attorney Charles Hamilton Houston urged NAACP members to picket the embassy, an effort supported by Baltimore's Ethiopian Defense Committee.[52] On the eve of the Italian invasion, the *Daily Worker* reported that, during a protest, a racially integrated team from the March Against War Committee had discovered sample boxes of shells from the Winchester Arms Company being delivered to the embassy.[53]

Tensions on Meridian Hill ratcheted up even further after civil war broke out in Spain in July 1936. The staff of the Spanish embassy at 2801 Sixteenth became polarized between supporters of the rightwing rebels and backers of the elected liberal democratic government. As rightward-leaning staff were forced out or re-signed, the embassy seemed nearly deserted.[54] Air Attaché Major Ramon Franco, brother of rebel leader Francisco Franco and a national hero known as the Spanish Lindbergh for his long-distance airplane flights, had been posted to Washington to study the American aviation industry. In September 1936 Major Franco made headlines by announcing that he was joining the rebels because Spain needed "a dictatorship for the welfare of the nation first, like those existing in Italy and Germany."[55] Although it was disrupted by hecklers, he held an auction of his personal art collection to fund his family's passage home.[56] He died flying for the fascist forces a few months before his brother's new government took possession of the embassy in April 1939.[57]

When Benito Mussolini's government supported the Spanish rebels, the Trotskyist Workers Alliance of America picketed the Italian Embassy, chanting, "Fascism means war."[58] In October 1937 the embassy hosted Vittorio Mussolini, the dictator's twenty-one-year-old son, a pilot during Italy's conquest of Ethiopia and an aspiring movie maker. Young Mussolini was in retreat from Hollywood, where newspaper advertisements had decried his declaration that "war . . . is the most beautiful and complete of sports" and his disappointment that "the splash made by his bombs dropping on Ethiopian homes did not compare" to big blasts in American movies.[59] When Mussolini visited the White House, picketers carrying signs accusing him of collective murder were dispersed by police when a brawl with the embassy's staff appeared imminent.[60] This protest, along with others at fascist powers' embassies, led to the passage of a law endorsed by isolationist congressmen that strictly limited embassy picketing. Demonstrations on Meridian Hill continued but were usually restricted to the triangular plot bounded by Harvard, Mount Pleasant, and Sixteenth Streets.[61]

Although the Depression saw a broad decline of Sixteenth Street's mansion culture, the shifting international climate bought one grand house a renaissance.

After the Kerensky government fell in 1918, sixteen years passed before the United States recognized Russia's new Soviet regime. The Russian Embassy at 1125 Sixteenth meanwhile sat as a "Brobdingnagian ghost" with boarded windows, shrouded in silence and secrecy and maintained by a former colonel of the czar's imperial guard. On a tour, a *Washington Post* reporter observed its layer of "soil made up of little pieces of rubber tire that have drifted through the closed windows" and noted that "where once was known all this opulence . . . there is now nothing but a shell of former glory."[62] Shortly after the United States recognized the Soviet Union in 1933, Stalin's government hired Eugene Schoen, a New York designer famed for his Moderne interiors, to renovate the mansion. After a tour, Schoen announced that it would be a crime to do more than restore its ornate decor.[63] Soon the embassy was again a setting for fêtes with "colossal" sturgeon and "caviar heaped up in silver bowls" said to "have in sheer lavishness surpassed anything of the kind . . . in Washington," just a few years after Stalin's genocidal Great Famine of 1932–33 had killed millions of Ukrainians.[64]

Moderne Meets Modern

As the 1930s passed their midpoint, the Great Depression was still stifling development across the nation.[65] Despite Washington's nearly 20 percent population growth since 1930, no one could blame the city's developers for approaching new projects warily. During the economic nadir, many Sixteenth Street apartment buildings had had dismal vacancy rates.[66] In 1933 older, lower-rent buildings like the Kenesaw and Northbrook Courts (see chapter 4) were about 10 percent empty. Newer buildings like Park Tower and the Ravenel were approximately a quarter vacant, while the upper-class Chastleton and Jefferson were more than one-third empty. Once-elegant Meridian Mansions was more than half vacant. Nevertheless, Sixteenth Street saw a swell of new construction as Washington's economy continued its gradual revival in 1936. During the next five years, eleven major apartment buildings were constructed on Sixteenth Street.

The building wave began modestly in January 1936, with a forty-seven-unit building at 3150 Sixteenth Street that is now known as the Park Marconi. Designed by Robert Scholz (1895–1978), one of Washington's most active apartment architects of the 1920s, it shares Park Tower's skyscraper-moderne ziggurat roofline and brick façade with limestone trim. Like most of Sixteenth Street's new generation of apartment buildings, 3150 was stylish but not luxurious, offering many studios and one-bedroom units.

In May 1937 prolific developer Morris Cafritz began constructing the Majestic, a huge 152-unit building at 3200 Sixteenth Street. Cafritz was a Deco connoisseur whose home on Foxhall Road featured a Moderne ballroom evoking those on great ocean liners like the *Normandie*. His architect was Alvin Aubinoe (1903–74), who

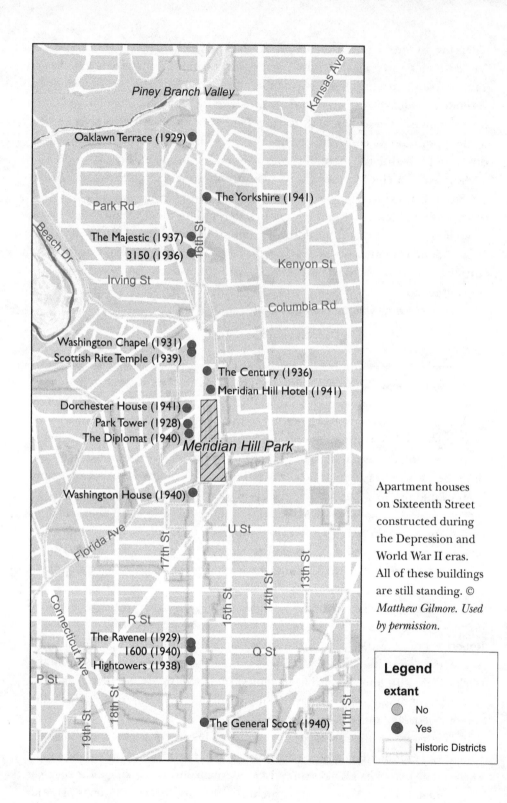

Piney Branch Valley

Oaklawn Terrace (1929) ●

The Yorkshire (1941) ●

Park Rd

The Majestic (1937) ●
3150 (1936) ●

16th St

Kenyon St

Irving St

Columbia Rd

Beach Dr

Washington Chapel (1931) ●
Scottish Rite Temple (1939) ●

The Century (1936) ●
Meridian Hill Hotel (1941) ●

Dorchester House (1941) ●
Park Tower (1928) ●
The Diplomat (1940) ●

Meridian Hill Park

Washington House (1940) ●

Florida Ave

17th St

U St

15th St

14th St

13th St

Connecticut Ave

R St

The Ravenel (1929) ●
1600 (1940) ●
Hightowers (1938) ●

Q St

P St

18th St

19th St

16th St

The General Scott (1940) ●

11th St

Apartment houses on Sixteenth Street constructed during the Depression and World War II eras. All of these buildings are still standing. © *Matthew Gilmore. Used by permission.*

Legend

extant

● No

● Yes

☐ Historic Districts

Designed by Alvin Aubinoe in 1938, Hightowers at 1530 Sixteenth Street NW features a classic Art Deco entrance. *Authors' collection.*

designed numerous Moderne apartment buildings during his dozen years with the Cafritz Company. Built in striking bright buff-colored brick, the Majestic has a set-back center section with a ziggurat roofline and flanking wings that end in semi-cylindrical towers facing Sixteenth Street. In 1938 Aubinoe created another tour de force for Cafritz. Built in light-colored brick at 1530 Sixteenth Street, Hightowers echoes the Majestic's tower-like cylindrical bays, here topped with fanciful ziggurat-shaped emblems. Its entrance is a Washington classic, with glass block surrounding polished aluminum doors that share an oculus window and aluminum canopy. It replaced several Victorian mansions and represented the first penetration of modern architectural styles in the blocks immediately north of Scott Circle.

Moderne's legacy on Sixteenth Street is indelible, but its dominance proved brief. By the early 1930s, American architects were experimenting with European modernism and the International Style, which eschewed applied ornament and emphasized a strictly rationalized, functional design approach. Its boxy architectural vocabulary consisted of flat curtain walls, horizontal window ribbons, and flat roofs. Even before the Majestic was under construction, modernism was infiltrating

Sixteenth Street with the Century at 2651 Sixteenth, designed by Louis Rouleau (1896–1937). Like Park Tower's designer William Harris, Rouleau was a successful architect before age thirty. In 1929 he had won notice for his Deco-accented Woodley Towers complex on Connecticut Avenue. A year later the Depression had rendered him bankrupt, but he soon resurrected his career, working in traditional styles before seeking a new direction with the Century in late 1936. His eight-story building included such skyscraper-moderne elements as vertical window ribbons, but it has an unadorned, relatively flat façade and other features more typical of the International Style. Rouleau could have become a leading modernist designer, but he never saw his finished creation. Construction had just gotten underway when he died of pneumonia at the age of forty-one on February 19, 1937.[67]

Despite these developments, Washington's recovery did not follow a smooth arc. When the Majestic began construction in May 1937, the nation was falling into a steep recession that largely erased the previous two years' gains and hung on through June 1938. Apartment building on Sixteenth Street stalled, regaining momentum only slowly.

Winds of War

Despite the recession-within-a-depression, by the end of 1938 Washington had begun a building boom that continued until the United States entered World War II. Between the outbreak of war in Europe in the fall of 1939 and the summer of 1942, the District's population increased by nearly one-third, driving new home sales that in 1940 more than doubled the 1937 total.[68] While Hightowers, begun in August 1938, was Sixteenth Street's last major apartment building constructed during the 1930s, the first two years of the 1940s saw the greatest wave of apartment construction in the street's history.

The first of the seven major buildings constructed during America's run-up to war was the 112-unit Pall Mall at 1112 Sixteenth, designed by Robert Scholz and begun in January 1940. Known today as the Calomiris Building, the Pall Mall has a muted Moderne façade that contrasts with the polished terrazzo floor streaked with colorful zigzag patterns that adorns the lobby. However, almost every subsequent apartment house in the class of 1940–41 fused its Moderne elements with the International Style. For example, in March 1940, construction began on the Diplomat, designed by pioneering modernists Joseph Abel (1905–85) and Julian Berla (1902–76), at 2420 Sixteenth. This beige-brick building features an asymmetrical façade whose upper stories cantilever over the lobby level, but its International Style elements are slightly leavened with horizontal bands of windows set in dark brick that suggest Moderne's streamlined speed-stripes. Situated between the Renaissance Revival Meridian Mansions and the Moderne Park Tower,

Constructed in 1940, the Diplomat is located at 2420 Sixteenth Street NW. It was the street's first true International Style apartment house. *Authors' collection.*

the Diplomat makes the 2400 block of Sixteenth a montage of three ages of apartment house architecture.

By late summer, Berla & Abel's Washington House was being built at 2120 Sixteenth. Washington House shares many of the Diplomat's International Style elements, but its cylindrical tower that turns the corner of W Street is plainly Moderne.

As construction began on the Diplomat, Alvin Aubinoe, who had left Cafritz to work on his own, began his third Sixteenth Street project. Known as 1600 Sixteenth Street, its buff brick recalls Aubinoe's Majestic, but its boldly rectilinear roofline and flat façade are characteristic of the International Style. The largest apartment house built on Sixteenth Street in 1940 was the General Scott, another International Style–Moderne hybrid whose rounded corner tower stands like a sentinel at Sixteenth Street's junction with Scott Circle. The third Sixteenth Street apartment

The Dorchester House at Sixteenth Street and Kalorama Road NW, pictured in 2020.
It radiated glamor and style from its opening in October 1941. Navy Lieutenant
John F. Kennedy stayed here briefly. *Authors' collection.*

house designed by Robert Scholz, it replaced the 1880s Cameron and Pendleton
mansions, as market forces continued to erode Sixteenth Street's Gilded Age
landscape.

Washington's economic boom continued into 1941, as department store sales
soared 20 percent in the year's first six months and one hundred new restaurants opened during its last.[69] Just before Pearl Harbor, new home sales set a ten-
month record, with 50 percent more houses sold than in the comparable period
of 1938.[70] On upper Sixteenth Street, approximately sixty more detached houses
stood between the Piney Branch Bridge and Alaska Avenue than in 1935, and
approximately thirty-five more houses had been built in the former "missing link"
to the north.[71] Some of these houses carried racially restrictive covenants, which
remained common in many Washington neighborhoods, even on the eve of a war
to preserve democracy.

That summer, construction began on two of Sixteenth Street's larger apartment houses. The Yorkshire at 3355 Sixteenth was designed by George Santmyers

Begun in early 1941 but not completed until after the attack on Pearl Harbor, the Scott Circle tunnel only briefly mitigated growing traffic woes. This 1940s photo shows the view facing south. *DC Department of Transportation.*

(1889–1960), probably the most prolific Washington architect of the twentieth century and a master of Moderne whose apprentices had included Alvin Aubinoe and Joseph Abel. Dorchester House at 2480 Sixteenth was among Washington's iconic addresses from its opening in October 1941. Designed by Francis L. Koenig (1910–93), who became a prolific apartment house designer and developer after the war, it mingled modernism with Moderne. Noted for its flashy hotel-like lobby and roof terrace, as well as the novelty of its air conditioning, the Dorchester soon became the backdrop for newspaper fashion and decoration features.[72] Its glamorous reputation has been further burnished by oft-told tales of Navy Lieutenant John F. Kennedy's romance with Danish journalist and suspected Nazi spy Ingrid Arvad while Kennedy shared a fifth-floor apartment with his sister Kathleen. Kennedy and Arvad were among the legion of young military officers, journalists, diplomats, and intriguers of all descriptions who spent wartime sojourns at the Dorchester and contributed to its romantic mystique.

As growth surged, Sixteenth Street's infrastructure lagged. After a tunnel opened in 1940 carrying Massachusetts Avenue beneath nearby Thomas Circle, Scott Circle, where Sixteenth Street intersects with Massachusetts and Rhode Island Avenues, was left as "one of the worst remaining traffic bottlenecks in the city."[73] After the National Capital Parks and Planning Commission recommended that an automobile "subway" carry more heavily trafficked Sixteenth Street under the circle, controversy flared as residents contended that the tunnel should carry Massachusetts Avenue instead.[74] By April 1941 Congress had agreed with the National Capital Planning Commission and General Scott's statue was temporarily moved so that excavation could commence. On December 29, 1941, the tunnel opened to little fanfare in a city still reeling from the attack on Pearl Harbor. The only formal observance was the district commissioners' ride in the first car through the tunnel, which was passed by a string of cars, a truck, and a bus too impatient for ceremony.[75]

The Housing Crush

No matter how many apartment buildings and houses were constructed, there was no orderly way for the housing market to absorb the hundreds of thousands of newcomers who flocked to Washington as World War II loomed. During the fall of 1941, workers were said to be streaming into the capital at the rate of three hundred per day, and the housing crisis that had gripped the city during World War I seemed destined to repeat itself.[76] Many new arrivals were women. By June 1941, 77,774 women government employees worked in the city, up from 53,038 a year earlier.[77] The supply side of the housing equation was weighted especially against them. In 1943 fully 90 percent of War Housing Center listings were offered only to men, a bias that newspapers ascribed to women's alleged reputation as difficult tenants who complained too much about living conditions.[78]

The Roosevelt administration scrambled to get ahead of the crush. In September 1941 Federal Loan Administrator Jesse Jones announced that the government would build a dormitory-like hotel for women workers at Sixteenth and Euclid Streets.[79] Construction proceeded quickly despite a backdrop of rancor. The anti-Roosevelt press sniped at the hotel as "a streamlined dream house" with overly deluxe amenities and charged that proposed rents would exclude 80 percent of women employees.[80] The Defense Homes Corporation countered that construction efficiencies had lowered costs enough for the hotel's private operator to offer affordable rents.[81]

Designed by Louis Justement, the Meridian Hill Hotel was an eight-story International Style building of blond brick, with horizontal ribbons of windows set against a dark backdrop. When it opened well ahead of schedule in July 1942, it provided 644 fully furnished rooms for single white women federal or defense

The Meridian Hill Hotel
Sixteenth at Euclid, N. W. — WASHINGTON, D. C.

Though the modernist Meridian Hill Hotel (1942) likely seemed a godsend to its white women residents, its 644 rooms took only a drop from the bucket of wartime housing needs. The building later served as housing for Howard University students and is now a commercial apartment house again. Undated postcard. *Authors' collection.*

industry employees. Some of their wartime memoirs recall its remarkable roof-top views of the cascading fountains of Meridian Hill Park, but its predominantly single-occupancy rooms with shared adjoining baths and the vast basement swimming pool must have seemed wonderful compared to cramped private market alternatives. There were also card rooms, a "soda bar," a dining room, and Emilie's Beauty Salon, which had a branch in the Mayflower Hotel, but only two public telephones for nearly 750 residents.[82] Although the hotel had no curfew, men were not allowed above its first floor.

No one expected the Meridian Hill Hotel to singlehandedly solve the housing crisis; the city's stock of rooming and boardinghouses would have to provide accommodations for most. Despite carrying a taint of unfashionability, dilapidation, and Great Depression desperation, the boarding house, as one newspaper observed, "grows livelier every day in Washington, home of the homesick." By June 1942 the *Star* calculated that as many as ten thousand rooming houses, registered or otherwise, blanketed the city, and its "Business Opportunities" classifieds offered numerous large old houses as candidates for conversion.[83] Veteran *Washington Post* reporter Scott Hart later characterized the blocks north of the Soviet Embassy as a district of "red brick dwellings, many transformed into boardinghouses" where "nocturnal traipsings about from room to room were viewed as none of the landlord's business."[84] Among them were the former Carpenter mansion at 1327 Sixteenth, the Manor at 2108 Sixteenth, Berdick's Guest House at 1914 Sixteenth, and the Bolivian Club, which offered modern baths and "unusual" meals to businesswomen in a Gilded Age house at 1633 Sixteenth. The Susan Shields House at 1401 Sixteenth became the Calvert House, offering businesspersons "selective menus" and switchboard services at reasonable rates.[85]

Living in these once-opulent houses brought little feeling of luxury. In April 1941 District Health Officer Dr. George Ruhland reported that "in some of the old mansions converted into boarding houses and rooming houses there is only one bath for every 15 occupants."[86] Throughout the war, newspapers printed feature articles and pages of letters recounting landlords' complaints about boarders and boarders' complaints about landlords. However, what memoirs of life in wartime Washington most clearly show is how a sense of adventure and shared purpose left far stronger impressions than the frustrations of shared living quarters.

Embassy Rows

By the time the United States entered the war, European adversaries were already facing off on Meridian Hill. Lithuania, whose legation was at 2622 Sixteenth Street, had been absorbed by the Soviet Union in 1940. Poland, whose embassy was two doors north, had been overrun by Germany in 1939. The United States never recognized the Third Reich's claim to the building, and the embassy provided a public presence for the Polish government in exile. In 1941 the body of Jan Paderewski, concert pianist and former premier, lay in state in the embassy's parlor before temporary interment in Arlington Cemetery.[87]

The Italian Embassy, across Fuller Street from the Polish Embassy, had stopped publishing party guest lists even before Mussolini signed the Axis pact in June 1940. However, its fêtes remained well attended even as its staff was scrutinized for fifth-column activities that included the sabotage of ships embargoed in American ports.[88] In July 1941, shortly after Mussolini charged the United States with fighting an undeclared war against Italy, a counter-note sounded with the dedication of the Marconi Memorial at Sixteenth and Lamont Streets, five blocks to the embassy's north. Sculpted by Italian immigrant and Frank Lloyd Wright collaborator Attilio Piccirilli, the memorial was donated by an organization of Italian Americans to demonstrate their loyalty to the United States and its democratic institutions. At a dedicatory dinner, Italian language newspaper publisher Generoso Pope launched a blistering attack on fascism while leaders of both political parties extolled the solidarity of Americans of all backgrounds.[89]

Two days after the attack on Pearl Harbor, two five-gallon cans of gasoline were carried through the Italian Embassy's front doors, and dense clouds of smoke mixed with charred paper billowed from its chimney. The Polish Embassy staff

The Majestic apartment building provides a backdrop for the Guglielmo Marconi Memorial at Sixteenth and Lamont Streets NW. Sculpted by Attilio Piccirilli and dedicated in 1941, the monument was donated to the city by an organization of Italian Americans opposed to fascism. *Authors' collection.*

thoughtfully provided scotch to the knot of reporters keeping watch. On December 12 the embassy closed, leaving its affairs to be administered by the Swiss Legation and its building to be tended by longtime caretaker Tony Celotto.[90]

While fascist Spain remained officially neutral, its embassy staff was widely assumed to be advancing Nazi interests. During the summer of 1942, the Office of Strategic Services burglarized the embassy with the aid of a mole disguised as a secretary, a paroled safecracker posing as a locksmith, and a Philadelphia couple who threw a party to keep the diplomats out late. The agents photographed a rich lode of documents without detection. However, Strategic Services Director General William Donovan and FBI Director J. Edgar Hoover were locked in a turf war over domestic intelligence gathering. A second Office of Strategic Services foray was interrupted by the blaring sirens of Metropolitan Police cars, and the agents were fortunate to escape arrest. Donovan accused Hoover of arranging the raid; Hoover maintained that a suspicious neighbor had called the police. President Franklin D. Roosevelt resolved the standoff in Hoover's favor by placing such espionage operations under the control of the FBI.[91]

Lodgings by the Night

Even before wartime transience made such needs acute, Washington's aging hotels lacked conference spaces and modern accommodations. The Statler, Washington's first new hostelry since the 1920s, was conceived in late 1940 when then–Commerce secretary Jesse Jones and Arthur Douglas, brother of Supreme Court Justice William O. Douglas, commiserated about crowded accommodations at a Gridiron Club dinner.[92] Douglas, a Statler Hotels vice president, quickly convinced his fellow executives that the capital was in dire need of an up-to-date hotel, and construction began in the spring of 1941. Clearing the northeast corner of Sixteenth and K Streets claimed five Gilded Age mansions, creating the melancholy spectacle of the Chandler-Hale House's Doric columns lying on its front lawn and the nearby Frelinghuysen-Couzens House "stand[ing] shell-like around a fast-dissolving pattern of marble staircase, dining hall, and ballroom."[93]

Architects Holabird & Root of Chicago and local partner Angelo Clas designed the hotel for business travelers, providing amenities that included an interior driveway to alleviate curbside traffic jams, guest rooms that transformed into meeting spaces in minutes, and a ballroom that could seat a gathering of 3,500. Two nightclubs, the rooftop Veranda bar, and a men's club paneled in wood and pigskin ensured that no one went to bed thirsty. Space-hungry federal agencies had been taking over apartment buildings and hotels wholesale, but when Statler officials offered the building to the government in 1942, they reportedly were told the need for hotel space was more critical.[94] Despite wartime shortages that curtailed construction everywhere, the Statler received timely allocations of

Overcoming wartime materials shortages, the Statler, on the northeast corner of Sixteenth and K Streets NW, was completed in January 1943. Now the Capitol Hilton, it was Washington's first modern business hotel. *Authors' collection.*

everything from steel to elevator machinery, and it opened on January 18, 1943, as the world's largest air-conditioned hotel. The *Post*'s Scott Hart called the Statler wartime Washington's "rallying place for lobbyists and contract seekers," but its government ties and location on what advertisements nicknamed Washington's "famous Embassy Street" fostered a reputation for intrigue.[95] Rumors persistently suggested that it was a secret home away from home for Eleanor Roosevelt or that the navy was using much of its space for clandestine purposes.

After Dark

Washington nightclub life reached its apogee during the war years. A common souvenir of the times is a flashbulb photograph of a bleary couple, the man in uniform, perhaps the woman too, seated at a table in a crowded restaurant with two full glasses, two empty bottles, and an over-full ash tray. The photo is tucked into a gaily colored folio embossed with the name of the café, perhaps with a scrawled date that marks the scene as either a momentous occasion or a moment randomly snatched from the rush of events. The times were full of both.

While Sixteenth Street had never been a center of revelry, its hotels had enlivened the city's nightlife since repeal. When the posh Carlton opened in 1926 (see chapter 4), it featured a secure and richly decorated basement hideaway for cabinet officers, high-ranking diplomats, and the like, with admission by cards issued by a membership committee.[96] After prohibition ended in 1933, the hotel hit full swing with the Carlton Club, a spectacular Moderne bar designed by Nat Eastman, creator of Miami Beach's famed Surf Club. The Carlton Club was noted for its murals and fireplace with neon faux flames, but it became even more famous for its "Servidor," a seemingly automated bar whose three tiers of rounded green glass panels were topped by a fountain and figure of Diana with her stag. The cocktails that magically appeared in metal cylinders that rotated across the middle tier were actually mixed by a bartender who crawled through a sliding panel at the beginning of his shift.[97]

In September 1936 the Carlton opened El Patio, a dance room and fantasy environment that evoked a romantic night under the stars in a cantina. Its waiters' costumes imitated traditional Mexican dress and its wall and ceiling murals were said to be so realistic that *Post* columnist "Chanticleer" quipped "you'll almost feel that gay senoritas are gazing down from the balconies."[98] El Patio functioned like a private club, even turning away Cornelius Vanderbilt Jr. for lack of a membership card, and it soon faltered.[99] In December 1937 the Carlton replaced it with Shar-Zad, a supper club whose so-called Egyptian and "futuristic or modernistic decorative motif" included leopard-skin chairs and a ceiling traversed by an electric moon amid 502 twinkling stars.[100] When the Mayflower's competing Sapphire Room opened in September 1940, Shar-Zad was renamed the Cosmos Room, for the "dawn and moon goddesses roaming among [the] assortment of comets and constellations" on its walls. It continued to purvey polite dance music by hotel-circuit bands throughout the war years.[101]

Fittingly, Sixteenth Street's next nightclub opened on that former citadel of temperance, Meridian Hill. In 1936 the once-elegant Meridian Mansions (see chapter 4) closed for remodeling and reopened as the Hotel 2400, offering apartments for both transients and long-term residents. In 1938 the hotel announced plans for the Lounge Riviera, a cocktail room designed by Elsie de Wolfe of New York. De Wolfe (1859?–1950) had been America's leading society decorator in the early twentieth century, but her vogue was long past. The septuagenarian seemed a quixotic choice to decorate a nightclub, and when the Lounge Riviera opened, *Post* columnist Mary Harris suggested that she had "reveled with four shades of brown." However, a subsequent *Post* article suggested that de Wolfe's purpose was to subtly flatter women guests by "faithfully . . . duplicat[ing] the latest powder tints, eye shadow tones, and lipstick shades." Her draperies especially complimented the "deep Mediterranean blue" eyeshadow favored by blondes, while her "flesh-colored mirrors gleam . . . back the cameo tones of the fragile new powder shades," and "cardinal colored floats . . . repeat the dusky lipstick colors of this vintage ridden season."[102] Whatever its color scheme, the Lounge Riviera was successful. In 1942 it was doubled in size and repainted deep blue and oyster white.[103]

Each Sixteenth Street nightclub had its own personality. The Lounge Riviera, often described as an outpost for the social register young, was long identified with its bandleader, pianist Pete Macias (1899–1947). Macias, whose sound was called "sugar and dynamite" by the *Post*'s Mary Harris, was the son of a Cuban diplomat.[104] A fixture at Connecticut Avenue's Heigh-Ho Club, he came to the Lounge Riviera shortly after its opening and stayed until his final illness. Rather than playing jazz or swing, the Macias band specialized in tunes from Broadway and the movies that had opened at the F Street picture palaces that week. Cynically humorous and expansive, its leader was beloved by newspaper columnists, who considered it tragic that he never wrote a promised book recounting the bizarre events he witnessed during his decades on Washington bandstands.

One Sixteenth Street nightclub generated true star wattage. In October 1941 Maria and Max Kramer, owners of the Edison and Lincoln Hotels in Times Square, purchased the Roosevelt Hotel. Max Kramer was a major Manhattan real estate developer, but Maria Kramer's life could have played on Broadway. Born outside Tucson in 1883, Maria, who claimed to be part Aztec, had escaped to Paris after winning a beauty and talent contest at age sixteen. Although her operatic career never took flight, she settled in France, married a British millionaire, and served as a front-line ambulance driver in World War I before turning to fashion design. After her first husband died, she moved to New York and presided over a successful Fifth Avenue salon before marrying Max and becoming chief executive of the Lincoln and Edison Hotels Corporation. Her acumen soon became legendary; the *Post* called her a "feminine hotel genius," while a *New York Times* profile hailed her as "the first lady of American hotels . . . who has time and time again flabbergasted the men who rule over nation-wide hotel chains with her financial and business ability to turn money-losing 'white elephants' into going concerns."[105] Music was both a lifetime love and part of Maria Kramer's business arsenal. An occasional lyricist and full-time friend to musicians, she was an important Manhattan jazz impresario, presenting major acts in the Edison's Blue and the Lincoln's Green Room. When she died in 1986 at age 103, obituaries noted how she had leveraged her clubs' success into live jazz broadcasts that publicized her hotels nationwide at no cost.

It was no surprise that the Roosevelt's renovation included a nightclub, which opened a month after Pearl Harbor as the Victory Room.[106] Maria Kramer vaulted her club to entertainment's major leagues by flying in the Glenn Miller Orchestra, probably the country's most popular band, to play opening night. She followed with a parade of stellar acts whose appearances were often broadcast on network radio. After the Miller band came Columbia Records' popular Tony Pastor Orchestra,

Opening shortly after the attack on Pearl Harbor, the Hotel Roosevelt's Victory Room brought star swing bands and much-needed diversion to a city at war. Menu cover. *Authors' collection.*

succeeded by trumpet superstar Harry James, whose "Sleepy Lagoon" would be the nation's number-one record a month later. Louis Prima's New Orleans–inflected band appeared next, and "King of Swing" Benny Goodman followed on the night of April 9. Among his successors were singer-dancer-bandleader Ina Ray Hutton, who "brought out the zoot suit crowd," trombonist Will Bradley, whose "Beat Me Daddy, Eight to the Bar" was a major hit of 1941, and Les Brown and His Band of Renown, whom superstar bandleader-clarinetist Artie Shaw joined on stage for a birthday celebration.

Like restaurants and theaters, Washington nightclubs were segregated; African Americans were not welcome at the Victory Room or any other white nightclubs. Black entertainers, no matter how famous, rarely, if ever, played at white venues. However, in March 1942 Mary Harris's column suggested a revolutionary prospect. The list of "topflighters" that Maria Kramer intended to feature at the Victory Room included the Duke Ellington and Count Basie orchestras.[107] However, while the Victory Room's lineup arguably represented the greatest aggregation of white jazz musicians in the city's history, these African American masters came no closer to its bandstand than U Street, Washington's "Black Broadway," just a few blocks to the south, where they played to equal or greater renown to audiences that could include white patrons.[108]

Of course, not everyone in Washington was a swing fan. In June 1942 several dozen residents of Washington House, located across the street from the Roosevelt, signed a petition complaining about the noise spilling from the nightclub's windows after midnight. Their protest was effectively countered by three congressmen—one of whom argued that half the men patrons were in uniform and deserved a good time—and about sixty Roosevelt residents who appreciated the free music.[109] Although bands were increasingly decimated by the draft, the Victory Room continued to present entertainment for the war's captured duration. It remained open until the hotel closed in the early 1950s.

From the Statler's debut in 1943, its nightclubs appealed to a crowd with cosmopolitan tastes. Its Embassy Room opened on January 30, 1943, with a birthday ball for President Roosevelt to the music of radio star and Waldorf-Astoria bandleader Xavier Cugat.[110] "The Rumba King" was succeeded by Dolores and Her Orchestra and other purveyors of satiny sounds, as well as a long residency by comedian-pianist Victor Borge, a refugee from German-occupied Denmark. Columnist Harris somewhat unflatteringly captured the Statler's "peacock alley" ambiance by noting that, "between its Embassy Room and the cocktail lounge, the Statler looks like a set out of a Joan Crawford movie. So chi-chi that it's overpowering."[111]

The War Comes Home

Even before war broke out, looming conflict wrought innumerable changes in the city's daily life. Sidewalks and buses were full of newcomers, whose numbers swelled steadily. When war came, families on Sixteenth Street volunteered for committees that allocated tires, gasoline, and automobiles, collected scrap metal and lard, bought war bonds, and prepared to send their children off to battle. But some things remained the same. While many blocks south of Meridian Hill were bordered by African American neighborhoods, nearly every Sixteenth Street resident was white. According to the 1940 Census, the street's few African American residents were either live-in servants or the superintendents of apartment buildings who lived on-premises with their families. On upper Sixteenth Street, much of the newer housing would be sold under racially restrictive covenants until the late 1940s.

The war brought new anxieties. By 1941 massive bombing of European cities had become a newsreel staple. Eyewitness testimony made the prospect of such destruction coming to Sixteenth Street, so close to the prize target of the White House, even more real. During a June YWCA meeting at 1201 Sixteenth, English relief worker Winifred Galbraith told interviewers of seeing a flash while sitting in her parents' London drawing room and finding herself staring at the sky beneath a blanket of bricks.[112] Just after Pearl Harbor, Meg Carlson, a former American consular official in Copenhagen, circulated a mimeographed air raid survival handbook to her neighbors at the General Scott. Carlson advised taping windows as a precaution against being flayed by flying glass. Her shopping list included a blue-light flashlight and heavy accordion-style paper lamp shades for blackouts, as well as a warm outfit that could be donned in the dark in two minutes or less and a bag large enough to hold one's valuables but small enough to be quickly grabbed when sirens blew.[113]

Washington officials had begun preparing for air raids months before Pearl Harbor. At 8 p.m. on October 25, 1941, a radio broadcast kicked off citywide civic association meetings to organize a District Civil Defense Council. Besides watching the skies and patrolling the streets during blackouts, Defense Council volunteers were to coordinate dealing with conventional and incendiary bombs and rendering first aid. Split among several zones, Sixteenth Street became deeply involved in Home Front defense. The Dupont Circle Defense Area established its command center in the Chastleton, while Deputy Chief Warden William Kruglack of Park Tower supervised sixteen subordinates in the Kalorama area. The oft-publicized Sixteenth Street Heights Defense Area covered the street's northern reaches. By the war's second month, its volunteers had set up a chain of first aid centers along Kalmia Street. Soon afterward, the *Post* interviewed William T. Kirk, the extraordinarily energetic warden for its Sector 8, Zone B. Behind a double set of blackout doors, Kirk's basement command post was packed with shovels, axes, lanterns, and military-grade first aid kits. He also had arranged for fifteen tons of sand to be dumped at strategic locations, enough to provide each household six buckets' worth for fighting fires.[114]

Although most wardens were men, women were also essential to the civil defense effort. In January 1942, a public meeting of more than two hundred Sixteenth Street Heights women set up a network of women wardens to watch the skies while men were at work downtown.[115] Led by committee chair Elizabeth Pine, the Sixteenth Street Heights Council conducted first aid classes for women, as did the Kalorama Area Council at the Dorchester.

Despite public enthusiasm, the District's early blackout drills did not exemplify civic competence. Cars abandoned in the middle of the street frequently blocked emergency vehicles, and because each siren had to be switched on individually by a police officer, alerts never sounded in some neighborhoods. However, the volunteers persevered. On the evening of October 28, 1942, a chillingly realistic scenario was staged at the Dorchester. Its script had a bomb from an undetected plane fall at the corner of Sixteenth and Euclid Streets, sending a dense column of smoke and the "odor of garlic or horseradish," associated with poison gas, throughout the neighborhood. Hard on its heels, the script had an incendiary bomb set the Dorchester aflame. In response, a meticulously organized team of thirty-five wardens, fire monitors, and first aid workers successfully evacuated almost four hundred residents. The first aid squad was headed by a woman, and almost all the volunteers depicted in newspaper photos were women.[116] Soon afterward, a centralized citywide alert system finally debuted, and later in the war Washington's air raid and fire wardens were described as the best trained in the country.[117]

The war truly came home to Sixteenth Street as news about loved ones began to arrive. Helen Newman had moved from Pittsburgh to her sister's Park Tower apartment when her husband was dispatched to Guam. Just weeks after Pearl Harbor, the island fell to the Japanese and Ensign Samuel Newman disappeared, along with William Lee Owen, a legal advisor to the island's military governor whose parents lived at the Chastleton. In early 1942 a cryptic radio message from Newman claimed that he was being treated well but advised his wife by implication that he had lost thirty pounds in just a few months.[118]

Both Newman and Owen endured years of privations. After being liberated, Newman returned to Japan to testify at war crimes trials and later authored a memoir entitled *How to Survive in a Prison Camp*. Major Carl Baehr Jr. was less fortunate. Baehr, a West Point graduate and son of a brigadier general who lived at 1750 Sixteenth Street, was captured when the Philippines fell in 1942. After surviving two years in prison camps, he is believed to have died when a ship transferring American POWs to Japan was sunk on December 15, 1944. Marine Second Lieutenant Harry M. Hobbins, whose wife lived at 1801 Sixteenth, died when the transport USS *Henry R. Mallory* was torpedoed off Iceland in February 1943. Army Lieutenant Thomas V. Burke, whose family lived at the Washington House, was killed on January 9, 1945, during the Battle of the Bulge.[119]

Aviators represented a high proportion of Sixteenth Street's casualties. Bunyan Cooner, a navy pilot and the son of a Chastleton resident, had been seriously wounded during the attack on Pearl Harbor. After six weeks in hospitals, he returned to duty and at the Battle of Midway scored torpedo hits on two Japanese cruisers and an aircraft carrier. Ten days later, his plane struck a construction derrick, killing him. Ensign Cooner was posthumously awarded the Navy Cross and had a destroyer-escort named for him. Franklin Chaimson, whose mother lived at 1635 Sixteenth, had starred in football at Central High School and worked his way up from delivery boy to *Washington Post* district circulation manager before becoming a policeman. On April 27, 1944, on his first mission over Germany, Army Air Corps Lieutenant Chaimson's Flying Fortress was hit by flack. The crew parachuted from the flaming aircraft, but Chaimson was found dead under his parachute, apparently shot while floating to earth.[120]

The war fell especially heavily on the Hartney family of 3120 Sixteenth. During World War I, Colonel Harold E. Hartney had downed six German planes while commanding Eddie Rickenbacker, America's leading air ace.[121] He later held important aviation industry posts and wrote a best-selling war memoir called *Up and At 'Em*. In 1943 Hartney gave a well-publicized and highly inflammatory speech predicting that Nazi planes from secret bases in the American South and huge fortress aircraft flying across the North Pole would drop poison gas on Washington.[122] At the war's outbreak, Colonel Hartney and his wife lived in Washington with their daughter, June, whose husband, former West Point end Frederick Yeager, was stationed in the Philippines. After Corregidor fell in 1942, Lieutenant Yeager's fate was unknown.

June's younger brother Harold Hartney Jr. was as enamored of airplanes as his father was. After high school, he went to work at Republic Aviation before enlisting in the Army Air Corps. In the spring of 1944, he was stationed in Europe as pilot of one of the Republic P-47 Thunderbolts he had helped build and soon became wingman of Captain Robert S. Johnson, the leading American ace in the European Theater. On May 13, 1944, twenty-two-year-old Harold breakfasted with June, then serving as a Red Cross nurse near his base in England and took off on his ninth mission. That afternoon his Thunderbolt was shot down over Germany. His body was reinterred at Arlington National Cemetery in 1949, some forty years before the remains of his younger brother James, shot down over North Vietnam in 1968, were repatriated.

Yeager's story had a happier, if harrowing, outcome. During more than three years of near starvation, he endured the Bataan Death March and five prison camps, where he organized an I Like It Here club to raise his fellow POWs' spirits. Yeager learned Russian from a fellow prisoner, and, after reuniting with his wife in Washington in October 1945, he embarked on a distinguished career as a professor of Russian.[123]

Sanctuary

Sixteenth Street's churches delivered more than spiritual solace to those buffeted by the Depression and world war. Many sustained their congregation's spirits with special services and musical programs while functioning as community centers and systems of mutual aid. Despite the intense need, few houses of worship were constructed on the "great avenue of churches" during the Depression and none during the war.[124] As late as 1940, the Sixteenth Street Heights Civic Association was advancing congregations money to build churches in its environs.[125]

Among the exceptions is the Moderne-accented Sixth Presbyterian Church at Sixteenth and Kennedy Streets, clad in rubblestone from quarries on upper Connecticut Avenue. A year after its dedication in 1930, the Washington Board of Trade commended its architect, Joseph Younger, for the church as well as his iconic Kennedy-Warren Apartments on Connecticut Avenue. Less than a year later, Sixth Presbyterian was the scene of Younger's funeral. On a May night, the

Even as suburbanization loomed after World War II, boulevard-like Sixteenth Street still ended just beyond North Portal (Sixteenth Street and Eastern Avenue NW) in Maryland, as seen in this 1948 south-facing view. *DC Department of Transportation.*

forty-year-old architect, who had been suffering financial reverses, awakened his wife and announced, "I have washed the spot," before shooting himself through the heart.[126] A few blocks to the south, Christ Lutheran Church, constructed at 5101 Sixteenth in 1931, has beautiful stonework by the Perna Brothers Company, a firm of Italian American master masons with a stone yard in Tenleytown whose work graced Washington buildings, bridges, and abutments for more than seventy-five years.[127]

In her later years, Mary Henderson sold undeveloped tracts on Meridian Hill for causes she thought worthy. In 1922 she was solicited by Utah Senator Reed Smoot and a delegation from the Church of Jesus Christ of Latter-Day Saints. Mormons faced widespread hostility, but Henderson had high regard for Senator Smoot and presumably appreciated the church's opposition to alcohol and tobacco. Resisting protests from George Oakley Totten and a group of Protestant clergymen, she sold the LDS Church a plot at Columbia Road.[128] After years of fund-raising, the Washington Chapel was dedicated on the site in 1933. Designed in eye-catching Utah birdseye marble by Young & Hansen of Salt Lake City, its form recalled that city's Mormon Tabernacle.[129] The chapel was noted for its musical programs; its original organist, Edgar Kimball, played its five-thousand-pipe organ six nights each week for walk-in audiences, and it long hosted weekly classical concerts. In times of crisis, it presented special programs, including a 120-concert Music for Defense series that began in September 1941.[130] Throughout the war servicemen on leave were given free meals and slept on cots in its basement gymnasium.[131]

Peace

Census Bureau estimates of Washington's population immediately after the war ranged as high as 920,000 residents.[132] Fifteen years of depression and war had transformed the city's landscape. South of Scott Circle, the street's Gilded Age legacy was fast disappearing before the onslaught of hotels and commercial buildings. The Victorian brick blocks above Scott Circle and Beaux-Arts Meridian Hill had new skylines punctuated with sleek apartment buildings, and the street's once-empty northern squares were filling in with houses. The postwar world would continue to reshape these patterns in ways that few could have predicted.

SIX

Midcentury Upheaval

FOR MANY WASHINGTONIANS, the end of World War II brought a welcome respite from a wide array of everyday deprivations. Temporary war workers, including the dollar-a-year men who had volunteered for public service, went back to their hometowns. DC residents who had offered rooms to these workers were able to take back their privacy. Government workers, who had been required to work Saturdays during the war, had full weekends to themselves again. Rationing—for food, gasoline, and tires—gradually eased. Automobile production ramped back up, inviting more residents to become motorists for the first time.[1]

It was time for the fresh ambitions of the postwar era to find expression. From Lafayette Park to the Maryland line, dramatic changes took place on Sixteenth Street, changes that mirrored the profound upheaval in the fabric of urban life across the city. African Americans fought for and worked for better lives and better living quarters. Latinos staked their claim to the area north of Meridian Hill, and an increasingly diverse array of religious institutions and embassies broadened the cosmopolitan character of the street. Among the most dramatic changes was the disappearance of residential living in the downtown area, south of Scott Circle.

Office Buildings Take Over Downtown

Propelled by an optimism about the future expressed in the sleekness of modern office construction, developers and city planners alike embraced demolition of old buildings as a prerequisite for progress in the postwar years. Lower Sixteenth Street—the segment from Lafayette Square to Scott Circle—became one of many targets across the city for wholesale reconstruction. Zoned exclusively for residential use in the 1920s, by the 1940s Sixteenth Street was a slender housing oasis amid a grid of downtown blocks devoted to office and commercial use. Thus, it was perhaps inevitable that in January 1947 Sixteenth Street property owners petitioned the city's board of zoning to permit commercial uses. At the board's hearing, opponents objected that commercial zoning would result in a garish and unattractive strip replete with "neon lights, barber poles, and liquor stores." Vestrymen of the venerable Saint John's Episcopal Church, by far the street's longest continuous resident, worried about increased traffic and congestion. Nevertheless, there was broad support for allowing office buildings. The American Federation of Labor and the Motion Picture Association of America were eyeing properties on Sixteenth where they hoped to move into or replace old houses to create new headquarters. Proponents of the change hoped to eliminate the remaining boarding houses on lower Sixteenth—old mansions that they characterized as "ramshackle skeletons of former splendor."[2] While turning down the original proposal for full commercialization, the board ruled in April that banks and office buildings would be permitted, as long as they didn't include commercial display windows, neon signs, or anything else that would have an adverse effect on the neighborhood.[3]

The zoning change opened the door for extensive office redevelopment, finishing the job of remaking Sixteenth Street that had begun with the construction of large hotels such as the Carlton, Hay-Adams, and Statler. The prominent intersection of Sixteenth and K Streets, for example, already featured the Statler Hotel, a limestone behemoth that had replaced the exquisite Chandler-Hale mansion on its northeast corner—originally Cook Corner (see chapter 1)—in 1941. Likewise, the Carlton Hotel, on the southeast corner, had in 1926 taken the place of the Nicholas Longworth mansion, designed by Henry Hobson Richardson. In 1949 the vacant southeast corner was transformed with the construction of the sleek eight-story World Center Building, clad in modernist limestone and echoing the look of the Statler Hotel. Last to develop was the northwest corner. In 1955 the Bakery and Confectionary Workers International Union of America purchased a cluster of four old mansions on this corner—including the former home of Admiral George Dewey (1837–1917), the celebrated hero of the Battle of Manila Bay during the Spanish-American War—and replaced them with a modernist office box called the Solar Building.[4]

Unions and trade associations were the predominant drivers of much of the office construction on lower Sixteenth Street in the 1950s. The increasing dominance of the federal government as a labor-force regulator, coupled with the postwar rise in the power and influence of unions, made a move to Washington essential. Locating on Sixteenth Street near the White House created instant prestige for unions that moved here both from other parts of the city as well as from around the country. Forty-seven national or international unions were located in Washington in 1953, according to the *Washington Post*.[5]

The American Federation of Labor purchased property just north of Saint John's Church in 1948 for its new headquarters. In 1955 President Eisenhower laid the cornerstone for the buttoned-down, limestone-clad building, and it opened the following year as headquarters of the newly merged American Federation of Labor and Congress of Industrial Organizations (AFL-CIO).[6] In 1971 the union purchased and razed the old Hotel Lafayette, which stood next to its building on the southeast corner of Sixteenth and I Streets. The Lafayette, originally conceived as a residential hotel for bachelors and completed in 1915, had grown old and unfashionable.[7] The union's headquarters building was soon expanded to fill the northern half of the block.

Meanwhile, the American Chemical Society, which had acquired the elegant Warder Apartment House at Sixteenth and M Streets (see chapter 2) in 1941, deemed it "highly inefficient" as an office building and tore it down in 1958.[8] The society's new headquarters, clad in an intricate array of metal brise-soleil shades, opened the following year. In 1960 the International Hod Carriers and Common Laborers Union moved into its own new building, a dignified structure with a grand two-story entrance portal clad in red granite, located opposite the AFL-CIO site on the northeast corner of Sixteenth and I.

Another large-scale transformation took place on the east side of Sixteenth Street above M Street, where the National Education Association (NEA) similarly felt the urge to level motley old structures and replace them with something big. Like the chemical society, the NEA had started out in one of Sixteenth Street's grand residences, the Cecilia Howard mansion on the northeast corner of Sixteenth and M, opposite the Warder Apartments. Simon Guggenheim had lived in the mansion from 1907 to 1913, while he was senator from Colorado, and the NEA had taken it over in 1920. In 1953 the NEA began a program to tear it down along with several adjoining buildings, replacing them with a mammoth eight-story headquarters. Starting with an addition on M Street, the association built the giant box in three stages, culminating with the demolition of the Howard House as well as the next-door Hotel Martinique, a 1920s residential hotel that, like the Hotel Lafayette, had seen better days. Also lost was the elegant Beaux-Arts-style Williams House, built in 1908 for Caroline Williams, a wealthy socialite and benefactor, and subsequently used as a headquarters for the Sons of the American Revolution. The new NEA headquarters, faced in Vermont granite, aluminum, and green-tinted glass, was completed in 1959.[9]

Perhaps most emblematic of the passing of the old order was the demolition in 1959 of the Gordon Hotel, on the west side of the street between I and K Streets. As we saw in chapter 2, this venerable building had started out as the Hotel Arno, one of the city's most fashionable residential hotels in the late nineteenth century. Renamed the Gordon Hotel by owner Gordon McKay in 1898, the dark Victorian labyrinth, extended when adjoining structures were annexed, grew more and more antiquated as the twentieth century progressed. As late as 1944, three elderly sisters—daughters of William E. Prall, the original builder of the hotel—had clung to their long-gone way of life in two five-story townhouses adjoining the hotel. A

The Hotel Martinique (*left*), the Cecilia Howard Mansion (*center*), and an apartment house (*rear*) on the northeast corner of Sixteenth and M Streets NW. All three were replaced by the National Education Association headquarters building in 1959. Postcard, 1950s. *Authors' collection.*

newspaper reporter found them carrying on without running water or electricity in the wisteria-covered mansions. The boiler in one was long broken, so the sister who lived in that house came over to join her siblings during the winter when her house was too cold to occupy. Embroiled in a decades-long dispute over the title to their homes, the sisters finally were evicted by the District government, which discovered that they had not paid any property taxes since 1887.[10]

The sisters' townhouses were torn down as part of the World Center office building project in 1949, but the adjoining Gordon Hotel survived through the 1950s, occupied by about two hundred elderly residents. Most were retired government workers who clung to the slow, homey pace of life in the old hotel. Author Tom Wolfe, working as a city reporter for the *Washington Post*, witnessed the hotel's last days in 1959. One resident told him, "The day I moved out I burst into tears as soon as I reached the lobby. And I wasn't the only one."[11]

By the 1960s, just three of the great freestanding mansions of the Gilded Age were left on Sixteenth Street below Scott Circle, and two would not survive the decade. These two sat across from each other at Sixteenth and I Streets:

the Justice Horace Gray House was on the northwest corner and the Lucius Tuckerman House on the southwest corner. (The third, still-standing mansion is the Pullman House, now the Russian ambassador's residence.) The Horace Gray House had been owned since 1947 by the mother church of the First Church of Christ, Scientist in Boston, which also owned the adjacent Hotel Gordon site. The church had been using the old house as a Christian Science Reading Room, but always had in mind tearing it down to build a new church. The house came down in May 1967.[12] The church that replaced it in 1971 was the Brutalist-style Third Church of Christ, Scientist (see epilogue).

It was only a few months later, in September 1967, that the Tuckerman House was demolished. The Joint Committee on Landmarks, organized by the National Capital Planning Commission and the Commission of Fine Arts, had designated the structure a historic landmark when it put together its first list of such landmarks in 1964. However, historic preservation was in its infancy in those days, and designation merely highlighted the building's significance; it did not confer the same level of legal protection from demolition that landmark designation generally provides today.[13] The Motion Picture Association of America wanted to capitalize on its prime location a block from Lafayette Square and succeeded in getting a permit to demolish the landmark mansion. Once it was razed, the association built an eight-story office block in its place. Dismissed by *Washington Post* architecture critic Wolf Von Eckardt as a "bronze-tinted glass box on stilts enclosed by a bold screen of tan concrete," it was designed by modernist architect Vlastimil Koubek (1927–2003) and completed in 1969.[14]

Progress or Decay?

For many reasons, urban living across the nation went into steep decline in the decades after World War II. The suburbs had become an irresistible draw for white families. Seemingly everyone wanted a spacious and affordable new home with a big yard, not a relic of an older age like the row houses that lined DC's urban streets. New highways made it practical—easy, even—to live further and further away from the city's center and still commute by automobile to work downtown. Perhaps most importantly, the suburbs seemed clean and safe, at least to whites. They were certainly designed to be white only: no Blacks or immigrants, no impoverished or disadvantaged. Government housing policies and commercial lending practices made sure of that. Meanwhile, African Americans were migrating to Washington from the south in large numbers to take government jobs and seek out other opportunities unavailable back home. In 1940 Black Washingtonians numbered 187,266, just 28 percent of the population. By 1970 that total had nearly tripled, to 537,712, and accounted for 71 percent of the population.[15]

As white flight to the suburbs proceeded apace, little or no investment was made to keep up the city's old neighborhoods. The residential blocks north of Scott Circle, like many other parts of Washington, lost their earlier luster. In 1952 *Washington Post* reporter Chalmers Roberts penned an incendiary series of articles titled "Progress or Decay?" in which he instilled fear in readers' hearts that the District would be ruined if drastic urban renewal projects were not quickly given the go-ahead to clear away old buildings and replace them with new ones. Accompanying one of his articles was a color-coded map of the L'Enfant city that used red lines to designate vast sections as "blighted." On Sixteenth Street, O Street to Q Street as well as R Street to T Street were all in the red zone.[16]

This section of Sixteenth, between Scott Circle and Florida Avenue, was and still is a quiet, tree-lined stretch featuring blocks of distinguished row houses interspersed with Victorian mansions and early twentieth century apartment buildings. Though little altered in outward appearance from earlier in the century, the character of this neighborhood had changed dramatically. An influx of Black residents is what ultimately earned the neighborhood Roberts's "blighted" label.

The historic heart of the Black community in Washington was within easy walking distance, just a few blocks to the east. The famous U Street entertainment district, nicknamed "Black Broadway," was here, hosting Duke Ellington, Cab Calloway, Louis Armstrong, Miles Davis, Sarah Vaughan, Billie Holiday, and Jelly Roll Morton, among many others. By the 1910s, Blacks increasingly moved into the neat rowhouses in the blocks around Sixteenth. Charles Robertson, a resident of the 1500 block of T Street, notes that his block was solidly African American in the 1920s and remained so until the 1970s.[17]

The cream of African American artistic talent was all around this neighborhood. At nearby 1461 S Street NW, renowned African American poet and playwright Georgia Douglas Johnson (1880–1966) hosted a celebrated literary salon which she called Half-Way House because "I'm half-way between everybody and everything and I bring them together."[18] Poet Langston Hughes frequented Half-Way House, as did many other Black intellectuals, artists, and educators. Another celebrated African American artist, singer and Howard University professor Todd Duncan (1903–98), lived on the southwest corner of Sixteenth and T Streets beginning about 1935. Famous for creating the role of Porgy in George Gershwin's opera *Porgy and Bess*, Duncan taught voice in his studio at Sixteenth and T in later years.

This area had been known in the 1920s as a Strivers' Section—a spot where ambitious middle-income Blacks owned homes alongside whites as they "strove" for a better lot.[19] As early as 1929, a Black-owned enterprise, the National Benefit Life Insurance Company, had even purchased the elegant Balfour apartment building at Sixteenth and U Streets NW. Facing financial setbacks, it was forced to sell the property a few years later. Nevertheless, with Blacks from all walks of life living on either side of Sixteenth, the street that Mary Henderson had envisioned as an exclusive white residential enclave became one of the most integrated spots in the city.

In 1949 African American businesswoman Geneva K. Valentine, an ardent promoter of equal access to housing, purchased the modest 1920s apartment house at 2008 Sixteenth Street, just north of the Balfour. Valentine's Equitable Realty Company converted the building to a cooperative, offering units for sale "without regard to religious belief, race, color or national origin." Soon, Black homeowners were living in the building side by side with whites, an alarming development for some longtime white residents of the neighborhood, who began to think about moving, while others welcomed the greater diversity.[20]

By the 1960s African Americans as well as Blacks from around the world would make their home on Sixteenth Street, turning older apartment houses like Meridian Mansions (at that time called the Envoy) and the Chastleton into remarkable enclaves of diversity. Acclaimed Marxist historian and philosopher C.L.R. James (1901–89), a native of Trinidad, moved into the Chastleton in 1969 when he came to Washington to teach at Federal City College, a predecessor to the University of the District of Columbia. James, who held Friday afternoon teas with notable intellectuals in his modest, book-cluttered apartment, told the *Washington Post* that he chose the building when he "saw the people who lived here and felt here was a chance to live as a worker in a city of blacks."[21]

All the while, real estate agents on the other side of the racial divide had been accelerating the trend of white flight by actively encouraging white residents in "transitional" neighborhoods such as this one to think of themselves as being under siege. Some agents gladly bought houses at a discount from fleeing whites and then sold them to African Americans at inflated prices. With the courts no longer enforcing racially restrictive covenants that had previously prevented Blacks from entering white neighborhoods, many whites nursed racist fears that their neighborhoods would decline rapidly as Blacks moved in.

While whites were fleeing, African Americans were pushing for equality. Nationwide, the decades following World War II marked the height of the modern civil rights era, a period of landmark legal advances in education, housing, jobs, commerce, and recreation, all gained through a range of mainly nonviolent protests and acts of civil disobedience. Step by step, the Jim Crow era of discrimination and segregation came to an end. Turning points included the Supreme Court's ban on the enforcement of racially restrictive housing covenants in 1948, its upholding of Reconstruction-era laws banning discrimination in restaurants and other public places in 1953, and its overturning of segregation in DC public schools in 1954. The Civil Rights Act of 1964, which ended segregation in public places and banned employment discrimination nationwide, and the Fair Housing Act of 1968, which prohibited discrimination in the sale, rental, and financing of housing, cemented these gains.

Of course, legal gains did not change lives overnight, and frustration over the persistent lack of opportunities for African Americans in Washington continued to grow. Urban unrest led to civil disturbances in several large American cities in the mid-1960s, and officials feared the same kind of violence could hit DC. It finally did in April 1968, following the assassination of Martin Luther King Jr. The uprising began at Fourteenth and U Streets NW, just two blocks east of Sixteenth, and was concentrated primarily along three corridors: Fourteenth Street from U Street to Park Road, Seventh Street NW from Mount Vernon Square to Florida Avenue, and H Street NE from Second Street to Benning Road.[22] Many businesses along these commercial arteries were looted and burned, and many homes—where the businesses were located as well as nearby houses—were destroyed. The impact of the uprising of 1968 would hang over the District for decades, accelerating disinvestment and leaving Black communities seriously underserved.

Just the year before, future mayor Marion Barry Jr. and several associates founded Pride, Incorporated, a self-help organization supported by grants from the US Labor Department. The unique organization took shape when Barry learned of the Lyndon B. Johnson administration's willingness to spend money to keep restless Black youths gainfully employed and off of inner-city streets. Barry realized that he could leverage federal funding to develop an organization that would not only help bridge the divide between inner-city Blacks and white liberals seeking to assuage their concerns but also begin to build his own political power base from a grassroots level. Pride, Inc., initially offered summer jobs targeted to the most disadvantaged African American youths. In agreeing to fund the enterprise, US Labor Secretary Willard Wirtz hoped to avoid in Washington the kind of social disturbances that had plagued other cities.[23]

After it had been in operation for several months, Barry told the *Evening Star*, "the guys are not what society calls 'disciplined' or 'very nice,' but if you look at some of them and see the change—it's what I'd call a miracle."[24] Government officials and politicians alike were amazed and more than happy to celebrate the program's early success, which led to increased federal funding. Pride, Inc., soon set up its headquarters in a former automobile showroom on the southeast corner of Sixteenth and U Street and began expanding its operations to help incubate future Black businesses. While the goal of avoiding social disturbances was not to be achieved, Pride nevertheless gave a start to many young Black men and women through its five-year existence. Though crippled by financial misdeeds that ultimately forced it to shut down, Pride served as an important element in Barry's strategy to assert African American control over the affairs of the District of Columbia. The organization continued to be based at Sixteenth and U until it closed in 1981.[25]

Meanwhile, crime continued to plague the city. Richard Nixon, running for president in 1968 on a conservative, law-and-order platform, called DC "one of the

Marion Barry (*second from left*), Mayor Walter Washington, and others stand in front of the Sixteenth and U Streets NW headquarters of Pride, Inc., at its opening in 1968. *DC Public Library, Star Collection,* © *The Washington Post.*

crime capitals of the Nation" and "an often hostile and sometime frightening city for its people."[26] Even the venerable houses of worship on Sixteenth Street were not immune. All Souls Unitarian formed a safety committee, which recommended that congregants come to church in groups and not carry valuables. The National Baptist Church began locking its doors when services were not being held, something it had never before found necessary. In one brazen incident, a gunman stole the contents of the collection plate from a nighttime service at Saint Stephen and the Incarnation Church, near Sixteenth and Newton Streets.[27] The activist group Jews for Urban Justice met to discuss the Vietnam War at Saint Stephen's in 1969, but it wasn't easy for participants to attend. "One girl arrived in tears, nearly hysterical, after having a gun jabbed into her ribs and her purse taken by two youths on 16th Street," the *Star* reported.[28]

Remarkably, Saint Stephen's did not respond to these events with animosity toward the local community. In 1969 the congregation was taken aback, however, when the Black United Front, a militant organization cofounded by activist leader Stokely Carmichael shortly before the 1968 uprising, demanded that Saint

Stephen's pay reparations to the Black community for its "collusive white racism." The well-integrated church was 60 percent African American at the time, having been in 1957 the first Episcopal church in the city to become integrated. Its rector, Reverend William A. Wendt, was an activist who had been passionately involved in the civil rights movement in the District. Wendt, who would serve on the DC school board and was always vigorously involved in the local community, would go on in 1974 to defy church authorities by allowing Reverend Alison Cheek, one of the first women ordained a priest in the Episcopal church, to celebrate the eucharist for the first time at a public service.[29]

Wendt and his congregation recognized that the Black United Font's demands reflected a real need for housing in the wake of the riots and urban renewal, and they responded by donating the land surrounding their building for the construction of affordable housing.[30] The seventy-two-unit Urban Village, a community of low- and moderate-income apartments, opened on the property in 1978.

Magnanimous as it was, this gesture did not help address the problem of crime, which distressed Black residents as much as whites, or the role of police brutality in aggravating the issue. Instead, the Roosevelt Hotel at Sixteenth and V Streets became an unlikely focal point for an attempt at a community-based solution for these issues. By the 1960s the Roosevelt had been converted into a retirement home, and it stood as a wary bastion of calm in an uneasy neighborhood. "The risky world of Washington's 13th Precinct has a tranquil heart where crime is no problem," the Star reported in 1969.[31] In the basement of this building, the Pilot District Project, an ambitious effort to improve relations between police and the local community, was headquartered from 1969 until the project disbanded in 1973.[32]

The Pilot District Project was conceived by a white government official as a potential solution to the problem of police brutality; it would attempt to bring police and African American community members together to better understand each other and work together. Over its five-year history, the project spearheaded establishment of twenty-four-hour police stations, citizen ride-alongs, and police sensitivity training. In recognition of the growing presence of Latino immigrants, the program also included Spanish language courses for police officers.

The project, however, was not well received by key Black community leaders, who felt it was being imposed on them by white bureaucrats and offered little opportunity for real control over police activities.[33] Marion Barry, whose Pride, Inc., was headquartered just two blocks south on Sixteenth Street, led the charge against the project. Barry and Dick Jones of the Concerned Citizens of Central Cardozo held a news conference on the lawn of the Roosevelt in September 1969 to denounce the project, which had sidestepped them in seeking community approval. They then moved inside to the project's basement offices to hold an impromptu "people's court," where they condemned the project's director for "conspiracy to

Pilot District
Project protester on
Sixteenth Street in
1969. *Thomas L. Lalley
Pilot District Project
files, DC History Center.*

defraud the black people."[34] Barry eventually gained control of the citizens' board that advised the project but quickly grew frustrated by the board's limited authority. Ultimately, the project ended having failed to significantly reduce tensions between police and local residents.[35]

The Two Faces of Malcolm X Park

Stately Meridian Hill Park, envisioned by its City Beautiful designers as a peaceful enclave, evolved along with its changing neighborhood through the 1950s, 1960s, and 1970s. While it too gained a reputation as an unsafe urban space, the park simultaneously became a symbol of hope for social equality and reconciliation.

A key milestone occurred in June 1949, when the Washington Theater Festival opened a temporary summer amphitheater on the park's southern terrace, with seating for more than nine hundred. The festival, funded by contributions from some sixty local supporters, was a response to the decision by the National

Building the temporary theater at the southern end of Meridian Hill Park in June 1949.
DC Public Library, Star Collection, © *The Washington Post.*

Theatre—Washington's only live theater at the time—to close in 1948 rather than allow Blacks to attend its performances.[36] Renowned African American activist Mary McLeod Bethune was among the guests of honor when the festival opened, and she wrote enthusiastically of the integrated event as a "logical and natural step to put democracy in action in the Capital of the World."[37] While the 1949 season would be the only one for the Washington Theater Festival, the park's role as a symbol of social equality had been established.

Public concerts had been held in the park during World War II, but fewer events were staged there in the 1950s and early 1960s. While nannies and young mothers still brought children to play in the park during the day, at night it became a very different place. Poor lighting had always been a problem, and the seclusion created by the walls and thick shrubbery invited crime. Muggings and robberies became common. Statues and sculptures were vandalized as well. One summer night in 1967, five men accosted a woman in the park, raping and beating her until she was unconscious.[38] Neighbors complained that the park was derelict and dangerous, and everyone learned to stay away from it after dark.

Meanwhile, almost as if in a parallel universe, the park's role as a symbol of equality and social connection was enhanced in 1968 when the National Park Service orchestrated a massive celebration to inaugurate its Summer in the Parks program, designed to draw the city's residents to its public parks during the warmer months. Cohosted by Perle Mesta—one of the city's best-known society hostesses—and famed actor and singer Pearl Bailey, the event featured entertainment by Bailey, jazz bandleader Cab Calloway, cabaret singer Hildegarde, Melvin Deal's African Heritage Dancers and Drummers, and others. The park's lighting had been greatly improved by famed industrial designer Russel Wright (1904–76), transforming it into a venue that comfortably facilitated the crowd of some twenty thousand. Bailey, who had grown up in Washington, joked that "out of the 20,000 people here I think I know 19,000."[39]

The Summer in the Parks event took place only a few months after the April 1968 uprising. Nerves were still raw in the African American community, and demonstrators took the opportunity to continue their protest against police brutality, handing out flyers and chanting "no more murders" during some of the performances.[40] Numerous other demonstrations in the park would follow, including several rallies by the Black United Front against police brutality. In 1969 the front unofficially renamed the park Malcolm X Park, after the famed civil rights leader who had been assassinated in 1965.[41] The new name resonated with the local community and by the 1970s was used more regularly than the park's official name (and continues to be used at least as often). In 1972 some twenty thousand demonstrators massed in the park and marched from there to the Mall to support liberation movements in Africa.[42] African Liberation Day events would continue in the park for years to come.

Meanwhile, the park's day-to-day existence continued to fluctuate between daytime tranquility and nighttime disorder. In connection with the nation's bicentennial celebration in 1976, the National Park Service spruced up the park, clearing away broken bottles and other debris, sodding the upper terrace, fixing broken benches, and restoring the grand cascade.[43] The improvements were short-lived, however. In 1977 the *Evening Star*'s Earl Caldwell interviewed a policeman patrolling the park. "The way I see it," the cop told him, "the park changes four times a day. From sunrise until 3 in the afternoon, it is the best park in the world. After 3, we get the school kids and the evening people. After dark the criminal element comes in. About 10 or 11 o'clock it changes again. Then the morally undesirable element comes along—you know, the guys and the women come here to be picked up and they are here until 6 in the morning."

The overall decline persisted for many more years. The delicate armillary sphere at the southern end, a graceful symbol of intellectual curiosity, was so damaged that it was removed by the park service sometime after 1977 and is now lost.[44] An August 1981 article in the *Post* noted that five police officers had been assaulted

Reverend Walter Fauntroy speaks in Malcolm X Park (Meridian Hill Park) at a July 1968 Black United Front rally against police brutality. *DC Public Library, Star Collection, © The Washington Post.*

while on patrol in the park in that year alone. "This is a sad park, a very sad park," one officer told the *Post*'s reporter.[45] In the late 1980s and early 1990s, as DC weathered the devastating crack cocaine epidemic, the park was overrun by drug dealers.

After a teenager was murdered just outside the park in 1990, neighborhood volunteers, businesses, and associations formed a group to try to take the park back as a safe haven for the community. Originally known as the Friends of Meridian Hill, the group began working with the park service and the park police to refurbish and reclaim the park.[46] By the mid-1990s, a remarkable transformation had occurred. President Bill Clinton stopped by on Earth Day in 1994 to publicly thank the Friends of Meridian Hill and to note that crime in the park had dropped 90 percent.[47] While crime at night has never been eradicated, the park generally has not been considered a dangerous place since that time. Meanwhile, the Friends of Meridian Hill—now called Washington Parks and People—has moved on to reclaim other neglected parks across the city.

Friction between Blacks and whites was not the only source of social upheaval along Sixteenth Street in the mid-twentieth century. Newcomers from Latin America also struggled to find their place. The Latino community in Washington had its beginnings in the 1950s in the Adams Morgan neighborhood just to the west of Sixteenth Street. The fact that a local Italian grocery store stocked Latin American foods may have been a small spark that encouraged Latino workers from nearby embassies as well as students from Latin America to congregate in and around the neighborhood. By the 1960s immigrants from Central and South America fleeing poverty and upheaval in their native countries began to arrive in significant numbers, settling in Adams Morgan and Mount Pleasant, just to the north. The newcomers often found homes in older apartment buildings that had originally housed middle-class whites. Soon restaurants, bodegas, and other Latino-operated shops arose on Eighteenth Street, Columbia Road, and Mount Pleasant Street, and a vibrant new community began to take shape.[48]

Social services agencies responded to the community's needs. In 1962 the Barney Neighborhood House moved into the large, three-story house at 3118 Sixteenth Street over objections from some white neighbors who feared its presence would signal the neighborhood was declining. Founded by progressive activist Charles Weller in 1901, Barney Neighborhood House had provided educational and social services to children and youths at Weller's former home on N Street SW. Forced out of Southwest by urban renewal, the agency found a second life on upper Sixteenth Street and would offer youth services there for almost four more decades.[49]

Many more social service organizations began offering help to immigrants, most notably the Catholic church, which was closely attuned to the growing Latin presence through its Shrine of the Sacred Heart, located at Sixteenth Street and Park Road.[50] However, another city institution—the DC public school system—seemed to be taken by surprise. In the 1960s, the school system had embarked on a program to build "model schools" in underserved parts of the city. At Sixteenth and Irving Streets, the Abraham Lincoln Junior High School was intended to be one such school. When the gleaming new building opened in September 1967, it immediately encountered problems. It was overcrowded by more than two hundred students on opening day. The low, suspended ceilings in some hallways proved too much of a temptation for some students, who could easily jump up and punch out ceiling panels. Vandalism quickly got out of hand.[51]

Notably, the student body included some seventy Spanish-speaking students who had difficulty with the English-only curriculum and were harassed by other students. To their credit, school officials moved quickly to add English language classes for the Latino students, but discipline and order would remain a problem for years to come.[52] The Reverend Gino Baroni, director of the Catholic church's Office of Urban Affairs, remarked in 1969 that "Lincoln Junior High School, a $4 million building, was plunked down without any thought of what the community wanted to do with it. The kids were simply told where to go. The result—they don't feel as though it's their school, and an expensive building is being wasted."[53]

Tensions at school were only compounded by struggles at home. Beginning in the 1970s, the struggle to find and maintain affordable housing for low-income residents became a defining issue for Sixteenth Street and the city as a whole. The Kenesaw Apartments, catty-corner from Lincoln Junior High at Sixteenth and Irving Streets, epitomized the issue. The Kenesaw had been the first large apartment building above Florida Avenue on Sixteenth Street when it opened in 1906 (see chapter 4) and catered to white professionals. By midcentury, however, the owners could no longer charge high rents. Upkeep was deferred, and the building spiraled into decline. Impoverished families, including immigrants from Latin America, were happy to get apartments in the Kenesaw, even if the building was a bit shabby.

To meet their needs, the Catholic church opened the Centro Católico Hispano in the Kenesaw's former dining room in 1967. It was one of the first social support agencies for Spanish-speaking residents in the District, offering such services as employment assistance, medical and dental care, and literacy programs.[54] By this time, many of the Kenesaw's tenants were immigrants from Latin America and their families. They worked as domestics, janitors, health aides, and dishwashers.

The Antioch Law School, long an advocate for the city's impoverished in tenant-landlord disputes, received the Kenesaw as a gift in 1975, but it soon became a financial albatross around the neck of the struggling school. By August 1977 the school had lost an estimated $150,000 on the building, which was in such poor condition that dead rodents and garbage could be found in the hallways, and more than six hundred housing code violations went unaddressed. Antioch offered to sell the building to the tenants, who wanted to convert it into a low-income housing cooperative, but the eight-hundred-thousand-dollar price tag was beyond their reach.[55] Antioch tried instead to sell the building to a developer, but that deal fell through.[56] Meanwhile, many tenants left, and the building nearly fell into ruin. Drug addicts got high in abandoned apartments, while vandals wrecked others. The building's ancient boilers failed, leaving it with no heat when winter set in.

Finally, under the leadership of Reverend Sean O'Malley, director of the Centro Católico Hispano, a group of mostly Latino tenants formed a cooperative and vowed to remain in the building that was their home. While fighting a protracted legal battle with the Antioch Law School, the cooperative took upon itself to maintain the desolate structure, cleaning up the halls, mowing the lawn, and closing and securing empty apartment units. In June 1978 they finally prevailed upon Antioch to allow them to buy the building, through the intercession of the DC Development Corporation, a quasi-independent city agency devoted to rehabilitating low-income housing.[57] Under the agreement worked out with Antioch, the DC Development Corporation would take over ownership of the building and would sell it to the cooperative after it was renovated.

The struggle did not end there, however. A settlement had to be reached with a competing bidder, draining some of the tenants' savings. The DC government began to renovate the building in 1979 but halted the project when it was found that the contractor's work was shoddy. Much of the rehab work had to be redone, delaying the project and adding to its cost. When the renovated building, rechristened La Renaissance, opened in 1984, it was not the cooperative that the tenants had tried so hard to attain. The cooperative simply did not have the money to buy back the building in its entirety.[58] Instead, most (fifty-one) of the units were sold as market-priced condominiums, with only the units occupied by the cooperatives' members—thirty-two households—reserved as a low-cost cooperative for the period those residents remained in their units. While the Latino and African American tenants had achieved a modest victory, they had not stemmed the tide of gentrification. In fact, they had relied on condo purchases by wealthy newcomers to finance their ability to stay in the building.[59] Nevertheless, the Latino presence has remained strong on Sixteenth Street, especially on the stretch between Columbia Road and Piney Branch, with low-income housing units available in multiple other buildings.

Testing the Limits

Apartment house construction had picked up during the 1950s along this section of Sixteenth Street, as large, boxy structures, typically clad in blond brick, began to appear. Richman Towers, across the street from the Kenesaw, is an example. The eight-story building, designed by modernist architect Edwin Weihe, was constructed in 1954.[60] In another case, one of the grand residences on Meridian Hill designed by George Oakley Totten for Mary Henderson—at 2620 Sixteenth Street—was unceremoniously demolished and replaced with an ungainly apartment box in 1965.[61]

Further north, two large-scale apartment house projects near Piney Branch served in the early 1950s to test the limits of high-density residential development on the avenue. The most glamorous residential building to be constructed on Sixteenth Street in the 1950s was undoubtedly the Woodner Hotel at 3636 Sixteenth, just south of the Tiger Bridge over Piney Branch. The hotel's picturesque eight-acre site had previously hosted real estate developer John I. Cassidy's large, Spanish Revival estate house, Oakcrest, which had been sold to the Martha Washington

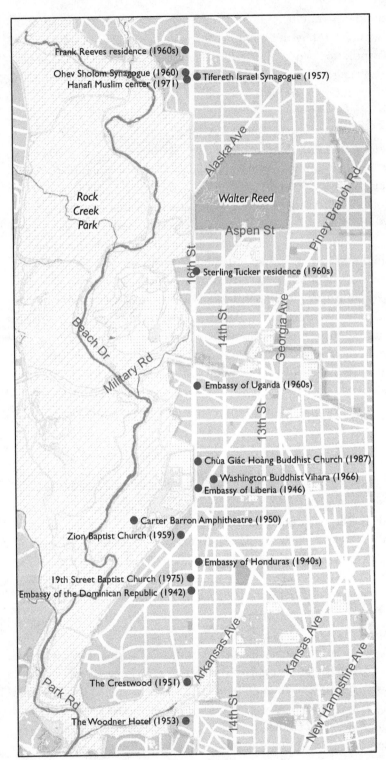

Frank Reeves residence (1960s) ●

Ohev Sholom Synagogue (1960) ●
Hanafi Muslim center (1971) ●   ● Tifereth Israel Synagogue (1957)

*Rock
Creek
Park*

Walter Reed

Aspen St

16th St

14th St

● Sterling Tucker residence (1960s)

Georgia Ave

13th St

● Embassy of Uganda (1960s)

● Chùa Giác Hoàng Buddhist Church (1987)
● Washington Buddhist Vihara (1966)
● Embassy of Liberia (1946)

● Carter Barron Amphitheatre (1950)

Zion Baptist Church (1959) ●

● Embassy of Honduras (1940s)

19th Street Baptist Church (1975) ●
Embassy of the Dominican Republic (1942) ●

The Crestwood (1951) ●

The Woodner Hotel (1953) ●

Churches, houses, embassies, and other structures from the 1950s and 1960s are marked on this map, which traces upper Sixteenth Street from Oak Street NW to the Maryland border. © *Matthew Gilmore. Used by permission.*

The Woodner apartment house, at 3636 Sixteenth Street NW, was among the city's largest when it was constructed in 1953. *Authors' collection.*

Seminary for girls in the 1920s.[62] The old mansion and other school buildings were torn down in 1949 to make way for the sprawling hotel and apartment complex. Designed by Wallace F. Holladay (1920–2012), whose wife, Wilhelmina Cole Holladay (1922–2021), would found the National Museum of Women in the Arts in 1981, the new hotel took more than three years to complete. Opened in phases between 1951 and 1953, the Woodner was reported to be the largest residential structure in the District at the time, with 1,142 units to accommodate some three thousand residents.[63]

Originally to be called Rock Creek Plaza, the project was the brainchild of jet-set developer Ian Woodner (1903–90), who ultimately named the massive complex after himself. Woodner was an architect and real estate developer who had grown wealthy building housing developments in New York. The Woodner was so large—it was said to be the largest air-conditioned building in the world at the time—that it was almost a small city unto itself. In addition to an elegant, first-class restaurant called the Golden Steer, the Woodner featured a rooftop party room and decks for concerts and starlight dancing, a large swimming pool, a three-hundred-car garage, drugstore, valet, barbershop, travel bureau, and grocery store. Mail was even delivered to each apartment.

For a time in the 1950s, the Woodner was as fashionable as Meridian Mansions or the Chastleton had been in the 1920s. Jimmy Hoffa was one of the powerful people who rented an apartment at the Woodner, while celebrities such as Duke Ellington, Bob Hope, Louis Armstrong, and Jayne Mansfield all booked stays in the hotel section at the front of the building. The go-go living at the Woodner was not always on the up-and-up, however. Senators and congressmen were rumored to secretly put up their mistresses in stylish Woodner apartments. And not long after it opened, police raided the hotel and arrested two men for operating a large-scale gambling business there. Using a sledgehammer to break open the door of Jack Kiatta's apartment, the cops seized numbers slips and $6,500 in cash.[64] Meanwhile, Ian Woodner faced a protracted fight with the federal government over the status of the building. Woodner had obtained close to $10 million in loans from the Federal Housing Administration, but the loans were meant to be used for two residential apartment buildings, not the single hybrid apartment-hotel complex that Woodner had built.[65] By the 1970s the building was converted entirely to apartments.

Just north of the Woodner, on the opposite side of Piney Branch, another large apartment building also went up around the same time. Developer Harry Poretsky had proposed building the Crestwood apartments, at 3900 Sixteenth Street, as early as 1941. The structure would mark the first time a high-rise apartment building was constructed on Sixteenth Street north of Piney Branch. Born in Poland, Poretsky had come to Washington in 1923 and had built apartment buildings across the area before he purchased the lot on Sixteenth Street.[66] He was determined to build there, but the well-to-do residents of the adjoining Crestwood neighborhood were adamantly opposed to the project.

The neighbors formed the Crestwood Citizens Association expressly to combat the threat of the new building. "An apartment on this site would be like placing a pig in a parlor—pigs may be all right in their place, but not in a parlor," association member Harold W. Breining told the District Zoning Commission at a 1941 hearing. Law professor John R. Fitzpatrick, another member of the group, warned that if the building were permitted, it would open up a flood of similar applications on other parts of Sixteenth Street north of Piney Branch.[67] After considering the case for several months, the zoning commission sided with the neighbors, touching off a ten-year court battle that twice went to the US Supreme Court. While the legal challenges were underway, the neighbors also hedged their bets by appealing directly to Congress, which in 1945 considered purchasing the property from Poretsky and adding it to Rock Creek Park.[68] But the government purchase was never authorized, and the neighbors eventually lost the protracted court battle as well.[69]

The swank, 224-unit apartment building, originally to be called Park Plaza, was completed in 1951.[70] Designed by the modernist firm of Joseph H. Abel and Julian E. Berla, the Crestwood sported a dramatic midcentury modern lobby that embodied the exuberance of the postwar era. Though the neighbors were disappointed

Present-day view of the Crestwood Apartments, built in 1951 at 3900 Sixteenth Street NW. *Authors' collection.*

by the new structure's presence, Harry Poretsky was certainly pleased. He moved in with his family and lived at the Crestwood until his death in 1966.

When he finally had the chance to build the Crestwood, Poretsky partnered with the construction firm of Morris Pollin (1898–1977) and his sons Jack (1921–1973) and Abe (1923–2009). Morris Pollin had immigrated with his wife, Jennie, and first son, Jack, in 1922 to escape the persecution of Jews in Russia. He became a plumber, moving his family to DC in 1933 and growing his plumbing firm to be among the largest in the city. Then, in 1945, Morris quit the plumbing business and formed a family construction firm with sons Abe and Jack.[71] Originally building homes for returning GIs in Southeast, Morris Pollin and Sons, Inc., went on to construct apartment buildings, including the Crestwood and many others. After Morris retired in 1958, Abe Pollin took over. Abe would go on to be best known of the three as the owner of the Washington Wizards and Washington Mystics basketball teams and the Washington Capitals hockey team. He would build first the Capital Centre in Landover, Maryland, and later the MCI Center (now the Capital One Arena), in downtown Washington to house his teams, helping to spur the revival of the downtown business district in the 1990s.

Among the apartment buildings constructed by Morris Pollin and Sons was the only other large apartment building built north of the Crestwood on Sixteenth Street. The Rittenhouse at 6101 Sixteenth was designed by Abel and Berla, like the Crestwood, and completed in 1956.[72] That building, which won the Washington Board of Trade's architectural award in 1957, was set 150 feet back from the street, in deference to the low-rise, residential character of upper Sixteenth Street.

Embassies Come and Go

Luring and keeping embassies on Sixteenth Street was always a highly competitive sport. For years Mary Henderson's Meridian Hill had vied with enclaves promoted by other developers—including Dupont Circle, Kalorama, and Sheridan Circle—for the most important foreign legations. Large Beaux-Arts mansions around the city in need of new owners were frequently eyed for embassy use. A major setback to Meridian Hill's preeminence came with the decision of the British government to move from its old embassy on Connecticut Avenue near Dupont Circle to a large new complex on Massachusetts Avenue in 1931, the same year Mary Henderson died. After that tipping point, Meridian Hill lost its appeal for many foreign legations. In addition to a healthy stock of existing mansions, Massachusetts Avenue and other areas further west of Rock Creek Park, such as Foxhall Road NW, offered more spacious plots for building large, modern diplomatic compounds as well as, at midcentury, a crucial sense of enhanced safety and security.

"Foreign embassies are leaving Sixteenth Street in search of considerably more peace and quiet and lots less traffic and crime," the *Post* reported in 1973. Most of the embassies that Henderson had enticed to Sixteenth Street eventually moved to other locations, although turnover did not happen as quickly as the *Post* implied.[73] One of the largest moves was not from Meridian Hill but from the downtown segment of Sixteenth Street. The government of the Soviet Union had been wanting a larger embassy for some time, and in 1969 and 1972 it signed treaties with the United States to allow it to build a new complex on a former veterans' hospital site on Wisconsin Avenue above Glover Park. As these negotiations were underway, the Russian Embassy in the former Pullman House on Sixteenth Street became a site for frequent protests about the mistreatment of Jews and other minorities in the Soviet Union, echoing the social tensions that had spread along much of the street and the city at large.

In reaction to the 1968 uprising as well as a growing need for more office space, officials at both the Italian and Mexican embassies began exploring options for new sites, but neither found it easy to relocate. Both waited many years to leave their historic homes.[74] After Italian Ambassador Egidio Ortona was mugged while walking one evening through Meridian Hill Park in April 1969, he began looking for a safer neighborhood for the embassy.[75] In 1976

Italy bought the elegant Firenze House mansion on Albemarle Street NW to be its new ambassador's residence, but its chancery remained on Sixteenth Street. Italy would eventually construct a striking new modernist chancery building at Massachusetts Avenue and Whitehaven Streets NW, but it wouldn't fully move to that location until 2000.

The Embassy of Mexico likewise stayed on Sixteenth Street for many years, finally moving its chancery to a new building on Pennsylvania Avenue in 1986 and its ambassador's residence to a 1930s mansion on Loughboro Road in 1990. The Embassy of Spain also stayed, albeit not always with a feeling of security. By 1970 the Spanish ambassador was so concerned about the safety of Sixteenth Street at night that he chose to ride in his limousine to a dinner party at the Italian Embassy—directly across the street—rather than walk there with his wife.[76] Nevertheless, the Spanish government did not purchase a new site for their ambassador's home until 1989 and didn't move its chancery until 1994, when it occupied a new building on Washington Circle.

The French delegation had never considered their Sixteenth Street building, which they rented from Mary Henderson, to be a permanent embassy. The French government had planned a new embassy, designed by noted architect Paul Cret, to be built just north of Meridian Hill Park, on the site that was eventually occupied by the Meridian Hill Hotel (see chapter 5). However, after Mary Henderson's death, that site was sold, and the embassy moved in 1936 to a palatial French Renaissance mansion on Kalorama Road that had been designed by Jules Henri de Sibour and constructed in 1910.[77] The grand Sixteenth Street residence built by Mary Henderson then served in the 1940s and 1950s in the decidedly less distinguished role of a rooming house. For a while, a branch of the Church of the Healing Christ used the old ambassador's office on the ground floor for religious services and instruction.[78] The Embassy of Ghana purchased the building in 1962 to use as a chancery, staying there until 1990. Since that time, it has been home to the Council for Professional Recognition.

Not all of the diplomatic missions moved away; the Cuban Embassy continues at its original Sixteenth Street address, as does the Lithuanian Embassy. And even as many of Meridian Hill's prestigious diplomatic residents left, new embassies were being established among the many large and elegant 1920s and 1930s residences on upper Sixteenth Street. The former residence of theater mogul Harry Crandall (see chapter 4) was one example. In 1942 the Dominican Republic purchased the mansion from Crandall's heirs for use as their embassy. With a stern portrait of repressive dictator General Rafael Trujillo mounted over the fireplace in the library, the embassy hosted many gracious fêtes that belied the suffering that was going on in the Dominican Republic under Trujillo's rule.[79] The Dominicans moved to an Embassy Row site near Massachusetts Avenue in 1954, selling the old building to the Kingdom of Cambodia, which still uses it as its chancery.

Other upper Sixteenth Street embassies included Haiti, which had its embassy at 4842 Sixteenth in the 1940s and 1950s, and Honduras, which purchased the former home of real estate investor Paul Himmelfarb at 4715 Sixteenth in the late 1940s. Like the Dominican embassy nearby, the Honduran embassy was known within diplomatic circles for its especially frequent parties in the 1950s.[80] The Hondurans stayed in the house until the early 1960s; it now houses a school.

As African nations achieved independence in the forties, fifties, and sixties, several chose to establish their embassies on upper Sixteenth Street. Examples include 5201, purchased by Liberia for its embassy in 1946; the Embassy of Upper Volta (Burkina Faso) at 5500, now owned by the Embassy of Egypt; the Embassy of the Congo, at the intersection of Sixteenth and Colorado Avenue, now in private hands; the Gambian Embassy at 5630; and the Ugandan Embassy at 5909, where exiles gathered in April 1979 to hear news of the fall of dictator Idi Amin.[81]

Churches Evolve and Adapt

Many houses of worship tend to move as their congregations move; their physical locations are less important than the congregants that support them. Several of the more established houses of worship on Sixteenth Street, having moved once from a downtown location earlier in the twentieth century, wrestled with whether to move again to the suburbs in the decades after World War II. The alternative was to try to draw new members from the local community to replace those who had moved away. In practical terms, this usually meant African Americans taking the places of whites as congregants. Ultimately, integration occurred at least to a partial degree, and departures of entire churches were few. The total stock of Sixteenth Street houses of worship didn't significantly decrease, although some formerly white churches were replaced with Black institutions.

The white Gunton Temple Memorial Presbyterian congregation, which had built a striking Romanesque Revival church at Sixteenth and Newton Streets in 1924, initially resisted pressure to move. In fact, in 1955 the congregation installed behind their altar a new twenty-foot-tall mosaic cross of Venetian marble, an ornament that was supposed to last for one thousand years. "We hope to remain here and outlast the cross," the church's minister declared.[82] That did not happen, however. Struggling to maintain membership, the congregation moved to suburban Bethesda, Maryland, just eight years later, in 1963.

Gunton sold its building to the Canaan Baptist Church, an African American congregation that brought new energy and life to the staid Sixteenth Street site. M. Cecil Mills, pastor of Canaan Baptist, had dreamed of leading the first African American church on Sixteenth Street and hosted a month-long celebration when that dream came true.[83] Reverend Walter Fauntroy spoke at the church's dedication and five years later attended a Black United Front meeting at the church with

August 1968 meeting of the United Black Front at Canaan Baptist Church, attended by Reverend Walter Fauntroy and Stokely Carmichael. *DC Public Library, Star Collection,* © *The Washington Post.*

Stokely Carmichael, Sterling Tucker, and other Black leaders. As the attendees discussed the pros and cons of the Pilot District Project proposal, militants among them insisted on ejecting whites from the gathering.[84] The friction did not last, however. Pastor Mills insisted on a policy of welcoming all comers to his church, and Canaan Baptist has maintained an active and nurturing presence in the community to this day.

Woodrow Wilson's Central Presbyterian Church, at Fifteenth and Irving Streets (see chapter 4), lost so many of its predominantly white congregants in the 1960s that it was unable to continue as an independent entity. It held its last service in January 1973. "Fragile old ladies, white-haired couples from the suburbs and grandmothers leaning on the arms of their grandchildren braved the drizzle to be present at the last services of the 104-year-old church," the *Washington Post* reported.[85]

While the congregation had been unsuccessful in recruiting a new generation of worshipers to its services, its church and school building nevertheless became an invaluable resource for the local community. The church's Sunday School building, built in 1930 directly behind the church at 1470 Irving Street NW, was used in the 1960s as an informal community center. In 1971 the church agreed to provide use of the building, along with financial support, to establish the Wilson International Center, also known as the Centro Wilson, to serve the local Latino community.[86] The center offered vocational training, recreational activities, and social events and soon became a vital social center. "Words cannot describe what goes on here and how important it is to the community," said program coordinator Maria Estella Squella in 1979, when the center was briefly under threat of eviction.[87] The center grew in importance in the 1980s, when it hosted live performances of Latin American theatrical productions as well as punk rock concerts by local bands. The church was extensively remodeled for educational use in 2004 and in 2020 housed the Next Step Public Charter School. The former Wilson Center continued to house a children's center that had moved there in 1973.

Just down the street at Columbia Road, the Mormon Chapel also underwent a significant transition in the 1970s. Like other long-standing houses of worship, the Mormon Chapel experienced declining attendance as congregants, especially families, moved to the suburbs. The only Mormon house of worship inside the District, the chapel had developed a reputation as a singles congregation. In 1975 church officials in Utah, overruling the wishes of the chapel's remaining congregants, decided to sell the building and assign its members to suburban congregations. "Because of our strong beliefs in the importance of the family, we want these single young people to get a feel for what it's really like, so they will have more of a desire to marry and to have families," one church official explained to the *Star*.[88] Another, more practical concern was that the building's beautiful but porous birdseye marble, from Utah, was deteriorating in the humid DC climate and needed prohibitively expensive repairs.[89] After taking down the gilded statue of the angel Moroni that had been perched atop the church's tall spire and removing the contents of the cornerstone, the Mormons decamped, and in their place, Sun Myung Moon's controversial Unification Church moved in.[90] The Unification Church has remained in the building and, over time, has undertaken badly needed restoration work on the exterior.

Other congregations actively adapted to remain engaged with their changing communities. Notably, the All Souls Unitarian Church, located across the street from the Mormon Chapel, became a pivotal force for social justice and integration, beginning with the leadership of Reverend A. Powell Davies (1902–57) who came to the church in 1943. Davies gained a national reputation as an advocate for civil rights, welcoming the first African American members to the All Souls congregation in 1950. Under Davies, All Souls members boycotted segregated restaurants and places of entertainment and organized one of Washington's first desegregated youth clubs. Davies's successor, Reverend Duncan Howlett, led more than one thousand people from All Souls Church to the Lincoln Memorial as part of the March on Washington for Jobs and Freedom on August 28, 1963, where they heard Reverend Dr. Martin Luther King Jr. deliver his famous "I Have a Dream" speech.[91] Reverend James J. Reeb (1927–65), a young civil rights advocate who was killed while participating in a protest at Selma, Alabama, served as an associate minister at All Souls during Howlett's tenure.[92]

The church opened its doors for a wide range of civic engagements in the 1960s. For example, in February 1962, the church's Pierce Hall auditorium was the site where jazz musicians Charlie Byrd and Stan Getz recorded their groundbreaking album, *Jazz Samba*, which introduced the bossa nova style of jazz to Americans and became popular across the country.[93] Pierce Hall had previously served as one of the city's first integrated movie theaters.

Of the church's pastors, the best known in the wider community was Reverend David H. Eaton (1932–92), All Souls' first African American pastor, who was called to lead the congregation in 1969. A native Washingtonian who had attended Dunbar High School and Howard University, Eaton was a charismatic leader and a powerful orator known for his booming voice and commanding presence. He gained notoriety in May 1970 after delivering a sermon on a crime bill the Nixon administration had proposed that included a provision allowing police under certain circumstances to forcibly enter houses without a warrant and without announcing themselves. The "no-knock" provision was widely denounced in the African American community, and Eaton flatly advised his parishioners that "any time persons break into your house unannounced, shoot them!" Though some parishioners were uneasy with Eaton's stance, the church's board supported him and his role as a community leader was ultimately strengthened.[94] Under Eaton's leadership, All Souls formed a corporation with city funding to build new housing for low- and middle-income residents along the riot-torn Fourteenth Street corridor. Eaton later became head of the DC School Board and even considered running for mayor, all while leading the congregation at All Souls.

All Souls, along with Central Presbyterian, the National Baptist Church, Canaan Baptist, and the Shrine of the Sacred Heart, formed the Columbia Heights Church Community Project in April 1968 to provide emergency assistance to those who were displaced by the destruction of homes on Fourteenth Street. In May the project offered food and temporary shelter to participants in the Poor People's March on Washington.[95] The social turmoil seemed to bring new power and relevance to the missions of these community institutions.

As the churches in Columbia Heights responded to pressing needs, a variety of smaller religious groups representing a wide range of faiths began taking up quarters farther to the north. In 1949 a faction of the Russian Orthodox Church split away from the main branch because it did not recognize the authority of the patriarch of Moscow under Soviet rule. This faction, the Russian Orthodox Church Outside of Russia, built a small cathedral at Seventeenth and Shepherd Streets

The Russian Orthodox Cathedral of Saint John the Baptist, at Seventeenth and Shepherd Streets NW, was built in 1958. Its gold onion domes date to a 1980s expansion. *Authors' Collection.*

The Chùa Giác Hoàng Buddhist Temple at 5401 Sixteenth Street NW. *George F. Landegger Collection of District of Columbia Photographs in Carol M. Highsmith's America, Library of Congress.*

NW, just a block west of Sixteenth Street, in 1958. With modifications in the early 1980s, the church reflects the Seventeenth-century Muscovite-Yaroslav style and features a distinctive gilt onion-dome cupola. Little more than a block away, at Sixteenth and Upshur Streets, the Greek Orthodox Church of Saints Constantine and Helen was built in 1952. Though built of brick rather than marble for cost reasons, the church clearly reflects the Byzantine style, with round-arched windows and two domed turrets, adding another Eastern Orthodox cultural reference point to Sixteenth Street.[96] The church is now the Washington chapel of Iglesia Ni Cristo.

From Colorado Avenue to Military Road, quiet upper Sixteenth Street attracted followers of religious faiths brought to the area largely by immigrants in the 1960s and 1970s. Among the first such groups to settle in the large houses of upper Sixteenth Street were Sri Lankan Buddhists, who formed the Washington Buddhist Vihara (Society) in 1966, converting a canary yellow house at 5017 Sixteenth Street into their meeting space. They were joined by native-born Americans who converted to Buddhism.[97] In contrast, the members of the Chùa Giác Hoàng Buddhist Congregational Church of America at 5401 Sixteenth are almost entirely Vietnamese. After the fall of Saigon in 1975, thousands of Vietnamese immigrants settled in the Washington area, creating a demand for a Vietnamese Buddhist temple. The temple's organizers began services in 1976 in the house at 5333 Sixteenth but quickly found they needed more space. They moved to a larger house at 5401 Sixteenth and in 1987 built a colorful three-story temple next to it with an elaborate ceremonial gate.[98] Other religious groups that have had upper Sixteenth Street addresses include Saint Andrew's Ukrainian Orthodox Church (4842), Saint Luke's Serbian Orthodox Church (5917), and the Nipponzan Myohoji Japanese Buddhist Temple, which began services at 4900 Sixteenth in 1974.[99]

One of the more unusual houses of worship, if it can be called that, was the Washington Ethical Society, which moved to a new meeting house at 7750 Sixteenth Street in 1966. Founded in 1944, the society espouses "ethics as a religion," promoting humanistic goals and ideals. Integrated from its inception, the society chose the Brightwood area for its permanent home because the neighborhood was committed to integration. The society's modernist meeting house, designed by the Washington firm of Cooper and Auerbach, featured alternating floor-to-ceiling panels of frosted and clear glass that expressed the society's transparent viewpoint into the world from a perspective of religious freedom.[100]

Rise of the Gold Coast

The eminently restful neighborhoods on the upper reaches of Sixteenth Street, looking a lot like nearby suburban Maryland, were far removed from the devalued lower portions of the street in the 1950s and 1960s. Well-to-do African Americans were increasingly drawn to this swath of suburban DC. From Crestwood to Sixteenth Street Heights, this area came to be known as the District's "Gold Coast," an attractive and safe place for Blacks who could afford to move there. One resident told an *Evening Star* reporter in 1961, "Yes, I know that the other Negroes call this the Gold Coast. There are some who call this the Negro's Spring Valley. Well, since this is the best area that's the reason we guard it just as jealously as they do in Spring Valley or Wesley Heights. We're not snobbish. That's not it. But look at it this way: Why put a big price on a home if you're going to allow the neighborhood to deteriorate?"[101]

Successful African American doctors, lawyers, businessmen, and government officials all made their homes in the Gold Coast. Famed Georgetown University basketball coach John Thompson lived here.[102] Sterling Tucker, the prominent civil rights organizer and first elected chair of the DC City Council in 1974, lived at 6505.[103] Likewise, Frank D. Reeves, another prominent civil rights activist and legal counsel for the Southern Christian Leadership Conference, lived at 7760, while Frank Nabrit, president of Howard University, lived at 7211. Even Stokely Carmichael, the controversial head of the Black United Front, lived for a brief time on Blagden Avenue, just off of Sixteenth, in the late 1960s.

Within the Gold Coast, the exclusive community of North Portal Estates, just south of the Maryland border on the western side of Sixteenth Street, was the most elite, earning the nickname "Platinum Coast" in the 1970s. Being as far north as it was, this area was not developed until the 1950s, when Leo M. Bernstein and others began building luxury homes here. "Some of the most distinctive, speculatively built homes in the area are located in North Portal Estates, an unusual home development located just to the left of 16th st. nw, and adjacent to Rock Creek Park," the *Washington Post* reported in 1955.[104] While the area was originally a largely Jewish enclave, by the 1970s Black doctors, lawyers, and politicians had moved in, eager to live well and exert their influence on the city.[105] They were impressed when mayoral candidate Marion Barry, with a reputation as a volatile activist, arrived at a Platinum Coast cocktail party in 1978 to sell himself to influential voters. Instead of causing friction, as some feared, Barry blended in smoothly. Asked about his new image, Barry insisted, "I am polished."[106]

The rise of the Gold and Platinum Coasts followed the same pattern of displacement that had previously changed the character of older DC neighborhoods. Wealthy whites who had built homes here in the 1920s through the 1950s moved further west across Rock Creek Park or to the Maryland suburbs, and African Americans largely took their places. Several prominent African American congregations moved here as well, including the Zion Baptist Church, which had been organized during the Civil War at 337 F Street SW. Founded by formerly enslaved men from Fredericksburg, Virginia, who were brought to Southwest Washington by Union soldiers, the church had grown to be one of the most influential in the city, with more than two thousand members, in the early decades of the twentieth century.[107] In 1956 the congregation learned that it was to be evicted from its historic 1891 church building, which was leveled along with most of the surrounding neighborhoods for the vast Southwest urban renewal project that displaced thousands of residents. The church found its new home on Blagden Avenue in 1959. Harold L. Biddiex (1918–96), an architect and planning engineer for the district's public school system who was parishioner at Zion Baptist, designed a striking modernist church building with a sweeping, tent-like roof for his congregation. It was completed in 1962.[108]

Another, even older African American congregation also chose to move to upper Sixteenth. The Nineteenth Street Baptist Church began in the 1830s as an offshoot of the white First Baptist Church of Washington, which had been founded in 1802. Eventually landing at its own Sixteenth Street home (see chapter 2), First Baptist had begun at Nineteenth and I Streets, where it built its first church building. By 1833 some forty Blacks were members of the congregation, and when First Baptist moved to a new location, it donated the old building to the Black congregants, who officially established an independent First Colored Baptist Church in 1839. In 1871 the congregation replaced the original building

The Nineteenth Street Baptist Church took over the former B'nai Israel synagogue building at Sixteenth and Crittenden Streets NW in 1975 after moving from its original home at Nineteenth and I Streets NW. *Authors' collection.*

with a pressed red brick structure and changed its name to the Nineteenth Street Baptist Church.[109]

By the 1970s the church had outgrown its historic home and had seen many of its members move to other parts of the city. As luck would have it, the B'nai Israel Congregation was at the same time reluctantly looking to sell its Sixteenth Street synagogue and move to Maryland. The Nineteenth Street church took the opportunity to buy the beautiful former synagogue at Sixteenth and Crittenden in 1975 and sell its old Nineteenth Street building to Pepco, which tore it down and replaced it with a power substation.[110] In a special departure service, Jerry Moore Jr., pastor of the church and a member of the DC Council, led congregants out of the old church and into their cars for a ride to the new one. "I'm sure my sentiments will spill out later," he told a reporter, as his eyes welled with tears.[111] The Nineteenth Street Baptist Church kept its historic but now anachronistic name as it settled into its Sixteenth Street home. It has remained there ever since, its prestige acknowledged by the fact that President-Elect Barack Obama and his family attended service there two days before his inauguration in January 2009.

While the grand houses of the Gold Coast overwhelmingly projected an abiding sense of peace and tranquility along the upper stretches of Sixteenth Street, one house was a tragic exception to the rule. The handsome stone-and-brick mansion at 7700 Sixteenth Street, constructed in 1929, was the former residence of restaurateur Thomas Cannon. Situated on a large corner lot, it became the site of a horrific mass killing in 1973 that stunned the neighborhood and the entire city.

In 1971 basketball star Kareem Abdul-Jabbar, a Gold Coast resident, purchased this house for use by an African American religious group known as the Hanafi Muslims. The Hanafi leader, Hamaas Abdul Khaalis, had recruited Abdul-Jabbar as a supporter when the two were in New York City. Khaalis formed the Hanafi group as a breakaway from the much larger Nation of Islam, headed by Elijah Muhammad. Khaalis had once served as one of Elijah Muhammad's trusted lieutenants but disagreed with key tenets of the Nation of Islam, including the exclusion of whites and the belief that Elijah Muhammad was a messenger of Allah. Khaalis formed his own group and moved from New York to Washington after Abdul-Jabbar bought the Sixteenth Street house for the group.[112] About a dozen Hanafis lived at the Sixteenth Street house; they were quiet and peaceful, keeping to themselves and maintaining a meticulously groomed yard. But their peaceful existence was short-lived. Khaalis had not been satisfied simply to split from the Black Muslims. He went a fateful step further, writing letters to the leaders of Black Muslim mosques, denouncing Elijah Muhammad and urging them to leave the Nation of Islam.[113]

The letters, Khaalis believed, were why a group of some eight out-of-town men descended on the Sixteenth Street house on January 18, 1973, when Khaalis was away. Forcing their way into the house, the intruders murdered two adults and five children, brutally shooting some and drowning others. Khaalis's daughter Amina, who was shot five times but miraculously survived the ordeal, later said that one of the attackers had told her, "You know your father wrote those letters, don't you? Don't you know he can't do anything like that?"[114]

The *Washington Post* quickly asserted that the grisly crime was the largest mass murder that had ever occurred in the District.[115] As shockwaves of alarm spread through the local community, the formerly peaceful Hanafis grew defensive and belligerent. The *Post* reported that "the azaleas [in front of the house] were cut down and cleared away. Hedges, shrubbery—anything that might hide an intruder—were leveled until a bare expanse of gravel had replaced the garden. The windows were barred; a spotlight shone on the front steps. And Hanafi guards, armed with machetes and long Japanese swords, began a night-and-day vigil outside the Khaalis house."[116] The armed camp at the corner of Sixteenth and Juniper Streets NW had become a strange and sad danger zone.

The police mounted an intensive investigation. Based on evidence left behind and eyewitness accounts, seven men from Philadelphia were charged with the crime, and five went to prison.[117] But this was not enough to quiet Khaalis's simmering rage, which finally boiled over in March 1977, when the Hanafis launched a coordinated attack on three downtown sites: the District Building, where the mayor and city council had their offices; the headquarters of B'nai B'rith, a Jewish service organization on Rhode Island Avenue (the Hanafis were deeply anti-semitic); and the Islamic Center of Washington on Massachusetts Avenue, where the Hanafis hoped to gain the attention of other Muslims. The group took 134 hostages in the sensational, headline-grabbing raid. Khaalis's primary demand at the time was that the seven men accused of the 1973 murders be turned over to him so he could exact revenge. After more than two days of tense negotiations, the Hanafis surrendered to police, but not before gunshots in the District Building killed a reporter, Maurice Williams, and wounded councilman Marion Barry in the chest. Several B'nai B'rith staff were injured as well. When the drama was finally over, Barry may have ended up a benefactor from the chilling act of terror. The outpouring of sympathy he received from being shot contributed to his decision to run—successfully—for DC mayor in 1978.[118]

Sixteenth Street Synagogues

Another element of Sixteenth Street's diversity is the thriving Jewish community that has lived on and around the upper stretches of Sixteenth Street since World War II. While restrictive covenants kept some of this housing off limits to Jews before 1948, when the Supreme Court ruled the enforcement of such practices unconstitutional, other homes never had such covenants. The area offered modern houses and a suburban residential feel that was still within the District of Columbia. In the 1950s and early 1960s, several prominent synagogues were constructed here.

As in many American cities, Washington's first Jews arrived in the nineteenth century as immigrants, mainly from Germany and Eastern Europe. Many came to Washington to make a living running small businesses, and after the Civil War they often made their homes near their businesses in the Seventh Street NW commercial corridor, in what is now called Penn Quarter and Mount Vernon Triangle. Others settled in Southwest, where housing was inexpensive. In the 1920s and 1930s Jews began moving from these downtown locations to "suburban" neighborhoods within the District, like Columbia Heights and Petworth. Moving to upper Sixteenth Street, sometimes in advance of their congregants, was a logical next step.

One of Sixteenth Street's most striking synagogues is the gleaming white building at Sixteenth and Crittenden Streets NW that eventually became the

Nineteenth Street Baptist Church. It was constructed in 1951 by B'nai Israel, a conservative Jewish congregation. Formed in 1925 largely by federal government workers, B'nai Israel worshiped for over two decades in a former Methodist church at Fourteenth and Emerson Streets NW. When it decided to build a new, larger synagogue, the congregation moved just a few blocks west to Sixteenth Street. The elegant, modernist building it built, reminiscent of the Moderne style of the 1930s and 1940s, was designed by Harry A. Brandt (1890–1955). Faced in Alabama limestone, it includes a copper-covered dome over the main seating area, which can accommodate 1,350.[119]

By the 1950s, when the synagogue was built, white flight into the Maryland suburbs was already well underway, and much of the Jewish community was beginning to move to Montgomery County. B'nai Israel, one of the largest congregations in the city, saw its membership begin to decline in the early 1960s, something that had never happened before. Whereas half of all area Jews lived in the District in the mid-1950s, by 1969 half lived instead in Montgomery County. Even the Jewish Community Center at Sixteenth and Q (see chapter 4) finally moved to Rockville in 1969.[120] Despite the trend, Rabbi Henry Segal told the *Washington Post* that the B'nai Israel congregation had wanted to stay in its Sixteenth Street home: "We tried. We tried very, very hard. But we became a completely depopulated area." With most of its members in Maryland, the synagogue decided to move to Rockville in 1970 and sold its twenty-year-old building to the Nineteenth Street Baptist Church. Having to leave behind their handsome Sixteenth Street home was "one of the most wrenching experiences of my life," according to Rabbi Segal.[121]

Two other congregations that built synagogues further north on Sixteenth Street faced similar pressures to move to the suburbs but ultimately decided to stay where they were. Tifereth Israel, a conservative congregation, built its synagogue at 7701 Sixteenth Street in 1957. Ohev Sholom, an Orthodox congregation, built another across the street, in 1960. The two institutions would serve as anchors for the Jewish community in the 1960s and 1970s.

Tifereth Israel, founded in 1916 by a handful of Eastern European immigrants, began, like B'nai Israel, in Columbia Heights. For some thirty-six years, its synagogue was the former home of Supreme Court Justice John Marshal Harlan at Fourteenth and Euclid Streets NW, which had been converted to a school and could accommodate six hundred worshipers.[122] As its congregants moved away from Columbia Heights, Tifereth followed them to a new location, at Sixteenth and Juniper Streets NW, in 1957.[123] The handsome, streamlined synagogue was dedicated in a solemn ceremony that featured a motorcade carrying the congregation's holy scrolls from the old building to the new. The adjoining auditorium was named in honor of Joseph "Uncle Joe" Cherner, an automobile dealer and benefactor who had died the previous year.[124]

The Tifereth Israel Synagogue, completed in 1957 at Sixteenth and Juniper Streets NW, pictured in 2020. *Authors' collection.*

Tifereth had been nominally an Orthodox congregation, like Ohev Sholom, but construction of its new synagogue sparked a shift in affiliation. Orthodox synagogues are designed with separate seating areas for men and women, but Tifereth Israel adopted mixed seating and changed its affiliation from Orthodox to Conservative. The congregation also chose a Conservative rabbi, Nathan Abramowitz, who brought a new sense of social activism to the congregation.

By the late 1960s, as nearby B'nai Israel was contemplating its move to the suburbs, Tifereth Israel's leadership became convinced the congregation would also have to move or merge with another one. The issue came to a head in 1969, after synagogue trustees fired Rabbi Abramowitz and began planning to merge the synagogue's school with a suburban temple as a first step to a possible move to the suburbs. But younger members of the synagogue objected, arguing that with better management the synagogue could be revitalized and could flourish once again without moving and turning its back on the local community. In that

Members of Neighbors, Inc., meet in 1965. *DC Public Library, Star Collection,*
© *The Washington Post.*

year's annual election, the younger group ousted the older board members and
brought back Rabbi Abramowitz. Tifereth Israel adopted a distinctly progressive
course, committed to staying in and advancing causes that mattered most to the
local community.[125]

Rather than fearing the arrival of large numbers of African Americans to the
community, the new leaders of Tifereth Israel embraced the resulting social diversity. In 1958 Marvin Caplan, a journalist and activist member of Tifereth, cofounded Neighbors, Inc., with Warren Van Hook, a Black pharmacist. The group's
goal was to fight the destructive "block-busting" techniques that real estate agents
were using to clear whites out of DC neighborhoods and resell their homes to
African Americans at inflated prices.[126] Other neighborhoods to the south had
been flipped from white to Black by these tactics, which destroyed neighborhood
cohesion in the interest of lining the pockets of brokers and investors. The pur-
view of Neighbors, Inc., was the neighborhoods of Shepherd Park, Manor Park,
Takoma, and Brightwood; Rock Creek Park was the western border, with Sixteenth
Street tracing part of that border north of Colorado Avenue.

Neighbors, Inc., attracted Blacks and whites from all denominations who believed in integrated communities. The organization hosted information-sharing
events, met with real estate agents to try to limit predatory behavior, and organized "block spotters" who kept on the alert for signs of instability on individual

blocks.[127] One of its early successes in 1960 was in working with other groups to convince the local newspapers to stop categorizing real estate listings by race.[128]

The group gained a lot of good publicity for its noble intentions, but its success would be limited, in no small part because it was fighting a deep-rooted social problem. "Students of the problem point out that whites and Negroes generally do not know how to live with each other," the *Post* suggested in 1962.[129] Whites—especially families with school-age children—continued to leave the Neighbors, Inc., neighborhoods and be replaced by Black families. "There are many people in this area who want their children to go to integrated schools," one white house-wife told the *Star* in 1965, "but when the school gets to be all Negro it's a problem. There's no denying it."[130] Further, some African Americans found it difficult to work with Neighbors, Inc., because it focused so heavily on luring whites to move in or stay and much less on addressing the needs of Black residents.[131] Perhaps the group's greatest achievement was simply to demonstrate the viability and desirabil-ity of an integrated community. A school official told the *Star*, "I honestly think that Neighbors is doing one of the most important things in the country today. They are showing that urban living doesn't have to be faceless."[132] The Shepherd Park neighborhood has remained a stable, integrated neighborhood in the de-cades following the establishment of Neighbors, Inc.

Fairyland

By midcentury, the aspirations of earlier generations for a grand Sixteenth Street had long been superseded, but at least one more project with lofty ambitions was on its way. It would be undertaken in 1950 just to the west of Sixteenth Street at Colorado Avenue, close to where the ponies had once raced at the Brightwood track and where tennis tournaments were an established attraction. The new project was an amphitheater to commemorate the 1950 sesquicentennial of the District of Columbia, complete with a commissioned pageant about the early his-tory of the country called *Faith of Our Fathers*.

As early as 1918, John Charles and Frederick Law Olmsted Jr., sons of the famed landscape architect of Central Park and the US Capitol grounds, prepared a land-scape study for Rock Creek Park that suggested "band concerts" might be held on parkland west of Sixteenth Street as part of an enclave devoted to sports and recreation.[133] Having added sports facilities, in the 1940s the National Park Service developed a plan for an open-air amphitheater on a site approved by Frederick Olmsted Jr. The opportunity to turn the idea into reality came when Congress char-tered the National Capital Sesquicentennial Commission in 1947. Carter T. "Red" Barron, a former college football star who represented Metro-Goldwyn-Mayer stu-dios and served as the head of the Loew's theater chain in DC, was selected to lead

The Carter Barron amphitheater, completed in 1950, aerial view, 1954. *DC Public Library, Star Collection, © The Washington Post.*

the effort. Among other initiatives, Barron decided to build the amphitheater and to commission playwright Paul Green to write a historical and patriotic drama to be produced for it.[134] Green inspected the site in April 1949 and was delighted, declaring that the new four-thousand-seat venue "would look like Fairyland," when it hosted his play. He vowed that in writing it he would "try to interpret the meaning and destiny of this country, as well as we can do it."[135]

National Park Service architect William Haussmann and engineer Robert C. Horne designed the amphitheater, which originally had no curtain separating stage from audience. Finished in rough-faced, local limestone, the minimalist structure was meant to strike a balance between the rustic look typical of other Park Service structures and the formal monumentality of Washington's federal buildings.[136] Construction took about seven months and was completed in July 1950.[137] After Carter T. Barron died from cancer that November at age forty-five, President Truman decided to name the amphitheater in his honor.

Playwright Green had hoped his *Faith of Our Fathers* would run for forty years, but the patriotic spectacle drew only a tepid response from the public and was soon cancelled. Lofty pageantry didn't work. That left Carter Barron rudderless for several years, as its park service managers mulled what performances to host. Neighbors disliked the traffic, noise, and dust from the graveled parking lot and publicly objected to new productions. Nevertheless, by 1954 the park service had contracted with a private company led by impresarios Irvin and Israel Feld to produce a variety of high-profile stage acts that began drawing large crowds. Danny Kaye, Ella Fitzgerald, Louis Armstrong, Diana Ross and the Supremes, Harry Belafonte, and Ray Charles were among the performers who packed in audiences over the next ten years or so, turning a handsome profit for the venue during its golden age. "Prestige was synonymous with the CB," wrote *Star-News* reporter Jacqueline Trescott. "Like the Hollywood Bowl, it enjoyed an international reputation and performers clamored for booking there."[138]

Then things changed again. After the 1968 uprising, many potential attendees, both white and Black, assumed that an open-air arena like Carter Barron would be unsafe, especially at night, and they stopped attending events there. New, larger suburban venues, including Wolf Trap Farm Park in Virginia and Merriweather Post Pavilion in Maryland, drew patrons away, as did the John F. Kennedy Center for the Performing Arts. The mostly Black youths who still came to Carter Barron to see pop music concerts could not cover the costs of producing the shows they attended. In 1975 a valiant effort was made to attract a broader spectrum of viewers by hosting general interest shows—including the rock group Blood, Sweat and Tears, singers Bruce Springsteen and Joan Baez, and comedian Richard Pryor.[139] The shows were popular, but nevertheless the season was again a money-loser.

Though originally disliked by some of its neighbors, Carter Barron over the years has come to be appreciated for its memorable performances, its up-and-down pattern of success reflecting fickle levels of support from the National Park Service and local institutions. The Shakespeare Theatre Company, for example, offered free summer productions of Shakespeare's plays at the amphitheater from 1991 to 2008 that were very popular. However, at the time of this writing, Carter Barron was closed indefinitely due to structural deterioration.

EPILOGUE

A WASHINGTONIAN OF 1980 might find today's city disorienting. During the early twenty-first century, the city's population curve sharply reversed its slope after a half century of decline. By 2018, Washington had seven hundred thousand residents—its population on the eve of World War II—for the first time since 1975.[1] The influx of new residents, who tended to be young, affluent, and white, fueled a real estate boom that accelerated a dramatic demographic shift. African Americans, 60 percent of city residents in 2000, constituted just 47 percent in 2017. While rising rents and housing prices, glossy blocks of restaurants, and a forest of downtown cranes reflected a new wave of prosperity, they also spot lit issues of racism, gentrification, and economic inequality that remain a citywide focus of concern.[2]

Many current Sixteenth Street trends came to the fore as the street's economic renaissance gathered momentum in the 1980s and 1990s. At that time the District's population was still dropping, as the city continued to be buffeted by high crime rates and municipal scandal as well as disinvestment and economic stagnation. However, some close-to-downtown neighborhoods with older but well-built housing had been attracting increasing numbers of affluent residents since the 1970s. Among the most prominent were areas on Capitol Hill, near Dupont Circle, in Adams Morgan, and along Sixteenth Street. This new wave of residents readily paid higher prices for housing, thus restricting opportunities for working-class renters, who disproportionately included African Americans suffering the effects of long-term economic and social discrimination. Such racially linked displacement was not a new phenomenon on Sixteenth Street.[3] However, earlier instances—like the displacement of the working-class African American community south of Scott Circle—had been marked by the wholesale redevelopment of the community's buildings. The late twentieth century phenomenon was characterized by the refurbishment and readaptation of historic building stock, with infill construction predominantly catering to affluent residents. By the late 1970s, the term "gentrification," coined by British sociologist Ruth Glass in 1964, was commonly applied to this citywide displacement process.

In 1985 the *Washington Post* noted that a "wave of gentrification [had] surged east from Adams Morgan to Sixteenth Street since the late 1970s."[4] One manifestation was the conversion of older apartment buildings from rentals to condominiums with refurbished living spaces and common areas, often marketed to small households with upper-middle-class incomes. One of Sixteenth Street's earliest condo conversions was Harry Wardman's Northbrook Courts (chapter 4), which began marketing units in May 1979. Northbrook Courts' advertising suggested that its "restoration" would bring back Sixteenth Street's past elegance, though the new units were much smaller than the originals.[5] Northbrook Courts was quickly followed by the Brittany (chapter 4) in 1980, the Alturas at 1509 Sixteenth in 1981, and the General Scott (chapter 5) in 1982. Although hyperinflation and high interest rates caused the real estate market to crash in the early 1980s, condo conversions responded to pent-up demand by accelerating when the economy recovered, further diminishing Sixteenth Street's stock of affordable units.

Renovation was not limited to condominiums. The Balfour (chapter 4) at 2000 Sixteenth was refurbished after several years' vacancy and reopened as rental apartments in 1986. Perhaps no building could match the phoenix-like rebirth of the once-opulent and oft-troubled Meridian Mansions (chapters 4 and 5). During the 1960s, the venerable building, then known as Envoy Towers, had been renovated with a HUD-backed mortgage, but then endured a series of defaults, foreclosures, and resales. By the late 1970s, its 190 original apartments had been subdivided into 334 units where "roaches, rats, and leaky ceilings proliferated," leading to bitter rent strikes. The *Post* reported that by 1979, Envoy Towers had become a "high rise ghost town" where three out of four apartments were vacant. A tenant-sponsored condominium conversion, which included an innovative plan to help low-income tenants buy their units at below-market prices, failed, and the building was purchased and refurbished by New York investors in 1983.[6] Renamed the Envoy, its renovation was hailed in a 2000 *Washington Post* article for retaining the building's stunning architectural features and achieving full occupancy. Its tenants were predominantly well-to-do students and young professionals, with a dozen-odd holdovers from the pre-renovation era.[7]

Although gentrification's negative effects on some neighborhoods were lamented by everyone from *Washington Post* architecture critic Wolf Von Eckardt to Mayor Marion Barry, few effective measures were taken to remedy the problem. On Sixteenth Street and elsewhere, initiatives such as the Kenesaw condominiums (chapter 6) or the Envoy's ownership plan were rare and generally limited. While legal requirements facilitating purchase of their units at reduced rates helped some moderate-income residents, by and large market forces prevailed. Dozens of Sixteenth

Street row houses and small apartment buildings were transformed into multi-unit condominiums. At the same time, housing discrimination remained a fact of life. In 1988 the owners of the Ravenel (chapter 5), whose tenants had been 85 percent Black or Latino in 1985, agreed to pay a record $325,000 settlement to an African American woman who had been told no apartments were vacant at a time when units were available to whites.[8]

By the 1970s, dissatisfaction with the wanton destruction of historic structures in Washington and in other cities had led to the rise of historic preservation activism, as exemplified by the founding of Don't Tear It Down (now the DC Preservation League) in 1971. Don't Tear It Down lobbied to save iconic structures such as the Old Post Office on Pennsylvania Avenue and the Franklin School on Franklin Square. Preservationists' efforts also led to enactment of the District of Columbia Historic Landmark and Historic District Protection Act of 1978, one of the country's strongest preservation laws.[9] The Sixteenth Street Historic District, established just months after the law's passage, offered the first legal protection to some of the street's most historic blocks. The new district, originally encompassing 119 buildings, bounded Sixteenth Street between Scott Circle and the old city boundary at Florida Avenue. It was designated for its sense of place as well as its catalogue of eclectic architectural styles and works by outstanding local architects.

Through the 1980s, political battles raged over historic districts' effects on gentrification. The Sixteenth Street District had grown out of a 1977 proposal to expand the Dupont Circle Historic District north to Florida Avenue and east beyond Fifteenth Street. After the DC government protested that the proposal lumped together neighborhoods with differing histories and degrees of connection as Dupont Circle, the expanded district's eastern boundary was redrawn to run west of Seventeenth Street, and buildings directly bounding Sixteenth Street became a separate district. In 1982 a new plan to enfold the Sixteenth Street District by expanding the Dupont Circle district beyond its proposed 1977 boundaries became intensely controversial. Opposition was centered in a coalition of African American business owners and activists who resided east of Sixteenth Street. They charged that a historic district would increase rents and property taxes, lead to increased gentrification and displacement, and extend white political and economic control over an area they regarded as an extension of the historically African American Shaw neighborhood. One leading opponent spoke of her fears of seeing real estate flyers advertising condominiums in Dupont Circle East on her block.[10] Supporters argued that landmarking would benefit all communities by preserving their heritages and contended that historic designation was not tantamount to displacement.

After years of discussion and negotiation, the expansion effort was abandoned. However, by the early 2000s, the blocks it included had been incorporated into multiple new historic districts, which each celebrated its own history and pattern

Sixteenth Street is included in several historic districts as well as Cultural Tourism DC's Neighborhood Heritage Trails. The site of Mary Henderson's Boundary Castle is marked by a signpost on Roads to Diversity, the Adams Morgan Neighborhood Heritage Trail. *Authors' collection.*

of significance.[11] In 2007 the Sixteenth Street District was extended south to Lafayette Square, and its period of significance, which originally covered buildings constructed between 1875 and 1930, was brought forward to 1959. This expansion provided protection to midcentury office buildings as well as apartment houses like the General Scott and Washington House, which the original nomination had identified as "intrusions" that were said at the time to distract from the district's historic character.[12] In 2013 the Mount Pleasant Historic District, which had been designated in 1986, was joined by the Meridian Hill Historic District, covering the west side of Sixteenth Street between Florida Avenue and the Piney Branch valley. The Meridian Hill district protected blocks on the street's east side as far north as Irving Street.

With few open lots and many historically protected buildings, new infill construction on Sixteenth Street was limited. Although some had hoped the former Henderson castle tract would be used for affordable housing, it instead became the site of Beekman Place, a gated community of 108 duplex condominium townhouses, with no affordable units, in 1976. These relatively pricey dwellings, whose security was a selling point, drew much attention in an area where upscale residential construction had been rare for decades.[13] In 1978 they were joined by a row of similar, market-rate townhouses near the corner of Irving Street.

After long stagnation, major apartment building construction was rekindled in response to the city's turn-of-the-twenty-first-century population boom. The Regent, which opened at 1640 Sixteenth in 2001, was Sixteenth Street's largest apartment construction project in decades. It was built on a parking lot once occupied by the home of Mary Spackman (chapter 2) and three other Civil War–era houses, whose residents had picketed against plans to clear them in 1965.[14] The new fifty-three-unit building recalled the street's heritage of elegant apartment living, with a Deco-influenced façade in red and cream brick that evoked the nearby Park Tower and vast apartments with marble baths and ten-foot ceilings that suggested the glory days of Meridian Mansions. Every apartment had a gas fireplace and at least two bedrooms; penthouses renting for seven thousand dollars per month were said to be among the city's most expensive units at its opening. Soon after its opening, the *Washington Post* noted that no children lived in the new building, whose tenants were mostly empty nesters or young professionals.[15]

The Tapies, completed in 2005 at 1612 Sixteenth, has been called Sixteenth Street's sliver building. Containing four stacked 2,000-square-foot condominiums and a smaller basement unit, the eight-story building stands between the massive Ravenel and Barclay apartment houses on a former rowhouse lot just twenty-one feet wide[16] This site presented such challenges that construction continued for more than three years after the demolition of its predecessor, one of Sixteenth Street's most curious survivors. 1612 Sixteenth had been a composite structure consisting of a one-story storefront attached to the front of an 1870s frame Italianate house standing deep in the shadowy canyon between two apartment buildings. The storefront predated Sixteenth Street's 1920 zoning restrictions; in the 1930s it had housed a delicatessen named Stella's after the proprietor's wife, then a café called the Garden Restaurant for its dining patio. It later served Chinese food.

Designed by Bonstra Haresign, the Tapies has a Postmodernist façade whose gold masonry frame surrounds glass-walled bays with balconies wrapped in tiers of steel bows. It was envisioned that greenery from the balconies' planters would reach above a cornice with steel hoops to a tangled-wire rooftop sculpture evoking the work of its namesake, Catalan sculptor Antonio Tàpies. With the addition of the Tapies to the Beaux-Arts Barclay (1924), the Moderne Ravenel (1929), and International Style 1600 (1940), the north side of the block between Q and Corcoran Streets became a gallery of the evolution of Washington apartment house design.

The Tapies, completed in 2005 at 1612 Sixteenth Street NW, brought twenty-first-century design motifs to one of Sixteenth Street's most venerable Victorian blocks. *Authors' collection.*

The north side of Sixteenth Street's 1600 block is a notable gallery of the ages of the Washington apartment house. *Authors' collection.*

Changing Spaces

Sixteenth Street's shifting demographic patterns were reflected in community and religious institutions. In 1984 Federal City College moved out of the former Jewish Community Center (chapter 4), which the city had purchased in 1968 after its founding organization had followed much of its membership to the suburbs. In 1990 a group headquartered near Dupont Circle purchased the boarded-up building. After seven more years of fund-raising and renovation, a new Jewish Community Center opened in the refurbished building. It offered an art gallery and theater as well as athletic, social, and cultural activities to Jewish and non-Jewish members.[17]

Upper Sixteenth Street continued to gain houses of worship. By 1992 when the Sixteenth Street Civic Association sought zoning changes to limit further conversions of residential structures to institutional uses, almost fifty houses in the area bounded by Hamilton Street, Colorado Avenue, and Rock Creek Park had been repurposed, for religious use as well as day care and social service centers.[18] New houses of worship were constructed as well. In addition to Chùa Giác Hoàng Buddhist Temple (chapter 6), new structures on upper Sixteenth Street included the post-modern Iglesia Adventista Del Séptimo Día de la Capital (1984) at 4800, the Fourth Church of Christ, Scientist (1990) at 5510, and the Mormon Chapel (2014), which replaced a Dominican Sisters' convent at 4901.

A few years into the twenty-first century, Sixteenth Street's Modernist buildings no longer seemed modern, and, in rapidly changing times, some already had outlived their owner's needs. From its completion in 1971, the Third Church of Christ, Scientist complex at Sixteenth and I Streets had been among the city's most polarizing architectural works. I. M. Pei and Associates' brutalist composition included an octagonal, virtually windowless raw concrete church, likely inspired by the form of the eleventh-century Florentine Baptistry, and a slender, glass-banded office tower across a triangular, paved plaza. Critic Wolf Von Eckardt had captured the contrary emotions the complex provoked, calling it "rude, brutal, military, and uncivilized," but also "ingenious" and "perhaps even quite beautiful."[19] To some, the complex was an unalloyed masterpiece. In the 1970s it won the Washington Board of Trade's Award for Excellence in Architecture and a craftsmanship award from the Washington Building Congress. The 1974 *AIA Guide to the Architecture of Washington, D.C.* stated that "the tension of tower, wall and octagon make this, perhaps, the most satisfying new complex in the city." In 1988 the US Commission of Fine Arts pronounced it "a tour de force," and a 1992 *Architecture* magazine article called it "an essay in bold urbanism and austere geometry."[20] However, the church's uncompromising architecture remained challenging to many others. In the 2000s, online blog commenters assailed it as "ugly" and "cold," misapplied the term "brutalism" to its intended effect on the beholder, and complained that "somehow this building makes me think of Stalin and Russia and the KGB."[21]

In 2007 the land beneath the complex and the office building were sold to a developer, with the Third Church congregation retaining title to the church building only.[22] In December 2007 the complex was listed on the DC Inventory of Historic Sites as a notable work of master architects, embodying the distinguishing characteristics of a significant architectural style and possessing high artistic and aesthetic values.[23] However, in October 2009, the congregation sued the District government, contending that the designation violated federal laws guaranteeing freedom of religious practice, and filed an appeal of its landmark listing with the mayor's agent for historic preservation. The mayor's agent subsequently ruled that denial of a demolition permit would create an undue economic hardship for the congregation, which had cited declining membership and high maintenance expenses, and allowed plans for demolition to proceed, provided that the congregation obtained a permit to build a new church on the site.[24] The complex was

From its completion in 1971 to its demolition in 2014, Pei and Associates'
Third Church of Christ, Scientist and Christian Science Monitor complex on the
northwest corner of Sixteenth and I Streets NW was among Washington's most
controversial buildings. *Authors' collection.*

demolished and replaced by a building that incorporated both office space and
the new church. Conservatively designed by the prestigious firm of Robert A. M.
Stern Architects, the boxy new building seemed to again proclaim the indomita-
bility of commercial interests in shaping the city's skyline.

Whose Street Is It?

On Sixteenth Street, the drive to obliterate old buildings and replace them with
completely different structures has been largely tempered by historic district designations. Here historic preservation serves as an extension of the early twentieth-
century desire, encoded in zoning regulations, to preserve the street's residential
character. The Adele, at 1108 Sixteenth near the corner of L Street, exemplifies
currents that continue to shape Sixteenth Street. Its core is an amalgam of three
nineteenth-century bay-front townhouses, which were structurally combined into
a medical and professional building in the early 1920s. In 2018, the longtime

commercial structure was transformed again, into an eight-story luxury condominium that retains the two lower stories of the 1920s façade.[25] This switch back to residential use reflects a new trend away from the late twentieth-century practice of converting residential buildings to office space, exemplified by the adjoining William Calomiris Building, an office building created from the repurposed Pall Mall Apartments of 1940 (chapter 5).

The adaptive repurposing of Sixteenth Street's historic buildings is further illustrated by the Modera Sedici complex at 2700 Sixteenth. This luxurious development incorporates the old Italian Embassy building, which has been subdivided into 22 units, with a 112-unit, 9-story high-rise at the rear of the former embassy's grounds. The project's completion in 2019 marked the end of more than a dozen years of regulatory proceedings and negotiations that pitted the goals of increasing residential density and maintaining historic character against each other. The visually appealing result attracts those who can afford rent of more than three thousand dollars per month but adds no new affordable housing.

In the more than two hundred years since Andrew Ellicott first ran his surveyor's chains across the woods and fields that would become the District of Columbia, Sixteenth Street has embodied both the capital's great ambitions and its more mundane realizations. To Peter L'Enfant, plotting the street's route as a grand avenue that ran to no particularly notable spot expressed the hope that the nation's capital city would one day require such a majestic thoroughfare. To the African Americans who flocked to the city after the Civil War, the street was the center of a community that sought the benefits of freedom despite severe economic and social oppression. During the Gilded Age, it reflected increasing social stratification and hierarchical politics. Mary Henderson and other early twentieth-century City Beautiful visionaries wanted Sixteenth Street to surpass L'Enfant's imaginings and become a ceremonial Beaux-Arts boulevard populated by elite residents. Though Henderson's vision endured in the beautiful Meridian Hill Park, the years from the beginning of the automobile era through World War II represented a much more complex dynamic in which zeal for progress and modernism collided with economic upheaval. From mid-century, suburbanization and reurbanization reshaped Sixteenth Street, the rest of Washington, and other cities across the United States. All the while, thousands of ordinary residents lived their lives on Sixteenth Street, striving to navigate the changing times regardless of where they might take them.

Today Sixteenth Street shines with a well-burnished luster. Its buildings are among the city's best tended and most carefully curated. Despite cycles of construction, demolition, and redevelopment, an hour's walk from Scott Circle up Meridian Hill to the Piney Branch Bridge is a trip through time. Buildings like the brick-corbelled house at 1536 Sixteenth, which may date to President Ulysses

Grant's first term, stand in the same block as the red brick Victorian bulk of the Shields mansion, Hightowers' twin Deco ziggurats, and the sleek glass and steel façade of the Tapies. Like the currents of the nineteenth and twentieth centuries, social change as well as new conceptions of the ideal cityscape will continue to change Sixteenth Street. But its historic character and ambiance place it among the city's civic treasures. With any luck, Sixteenth may someday evolve to truly serve as an emblem of democracy, providing opportunities for Washingtonians from all walks of life to live and thrive along its majestic length.

Notes

Introduction

1. A Sixteenth Street NE and Sixteenth Street SE also exist in the District of Columbia; the city is divided into four quadrants, centered on the Capitol building. In this book, whenever the term "Sixteenth Street" is used, it refers to the street in the northwest quadrant. The locations of other streets that are not in the northwest quadrant are noted when mentioned in the text.
2. Kohler and Carson, *Sixteenth Street Architecture*.
3. The grand embassies and other houses of Massachusetts Avenue are thoroughly documented in Carson et al., *Massachusetts Avenue Architecture*.

Chapter 1

1. Scott W. Berg's *Grand Avenues* offers an excellent biography of L'Enfant and a useful overview of his plan for Washington. See also Kenneth R. Bowling's *Peter Charles L'Enfant*.
2. Ellicott, "Plan of the City of Washington."
3. Harmon, "Historical Map of the City of Washington in the Year 1801–1802."
4. Luria, *Capital Speculations*, 3–34; Gutheim and Lee, *Worthy of the Nation*, 21–28; Costanzo, *George Washington's Washington*, 21–26.
5. Gutheim and Lee, *Worthy of the Nation*, 23.
6. Elkins and McKitrick, *The Age of Federalism*, 180; Federal Writers' Project, *Washington*, 44.
7. Quoted in Costanzo, *George Washington's Washington*, 19; Kite, *L'Enfant and Washington*, 34.
8. Seale, *To Live on Lafayette Square*, 1–2, 12.
9. Quoted in Arnebeck, *Through a Fiery Trial*, 594–95.
10. Quoted in "The City of Washington," *Daily National Intelligencer*, Dec. 12, 1853.
11. Holland, *Black Men Built the Capitol*, 3–4.

12. Green, *The Church on Lafayette Square*, 4–8.

13. *Daily National Intelligencer*, Nov. 7, 1816.

14. Baker, *Building America*, 27.

15. For Latrobe's views on the design of the Federal city, see Carter, "Benjamin Henry Latrobe," 128–39.

16. "St. John's Church," Historic American Buildings Survey DC-19 (1961); Eberlein and Hubbard, *Historic Houses of George-Town and Washington City*, 248–51; Maddex, *Historic Buildings of Washington, D.C.*, 48–52; Scott and Lee, *Buildings of the District of Columbia*, 162–63.

17. Baker, *Building America*, 177; Green, *The Church on Lafayette Square*, 7.

18. Grimmett, *St. John's Church, Lafayette Square*, 18ff.

19. Quoted in Maddex, *Historic Buildings of Washington, D.C.*, 48.

20. Grimmett, *St. John's Church, Lafayette Square*, 26–36.

21. Tank, "Dedicated to Art," 27–29.

22. Robertson, *American Louvre*, 21; Goode, *Capital Losses*, 64–65; "Mr. Corcoran Dead," *Washington Post*, Feb. 25, 1888; Seale, *The Imperial Season*, 78.

23. Kim Williams's *Lost Farms and Estates of Washington, D.C.* offers a thorough survey of the early farms and estates of Washington County, with an emphasis on those with surviving remnants.

24. Long, *Nothing Too Daring*, 39ff.

25. Long, 142.

26. McKevitt, *Meridian Hill*, 22–24.

27. Hadfield's obituary notes the house as one of his major accomplishments (*Daily National Journal*, Feb. 7, 1826). Hadfield biographer Julia King also attributes the house to him (King, *George Hadfield*, 130–31). See also Eberlein and Hubbard, *Historic Houses of George-Town and Washington City*, 450; Hinton, *History and Topography of the United States of North America*, 429.

28. Quoted in King, *George Hadfield*. King states that a very faint drawing by John Trumbull from March 1817 exists in the collection of the New York Historical Society that may depict the house (King, *George Hadfield*, 216).

29. Porter, *Memoir of Commodore David Porter*, 265.

30. Long, *Nothing Too Daring*, 181; 1820 US Decennial Census, District of Columbia, Washington County.

31. Porter, *Memoir of Commodore David Porter*, 269.

32. Long, *Nothing Too Daring*, 274.

33. Adams, *Memoirs of John Quincy Adams*, vol. 8, 102–4; Long, *Nothing Too Daring*, 285.

34. "A Scene at Washington," *United States Telegraph*, Aug. 22, 1829.

35. Quoted in Bryan, *A History of the National Capital*, 610.

36. Kayser, *Bricks without Straw*, 1–37.

37. "Historic Rock Creek," *Washington Post*, Aug. 18, 1889; "Fad of an Old Hunter," *Washington Post*, Jan. 29, 1899. See also Swerdloff, *Crestwood*, 15–19, for a summary of Bodisco's life in Washington.

38. "Equipages of the Past," *Washington Post*, Jul. 23, 1893.

39. "Russian Minister's Residence Burnt," *Baltimore Sun*, Jan. 6, 1849.

40. 1850 US Decennial Census, District of Columbia, Washington County. Blagden filed for compensation for freeing the Boyd brothers in 1862, as provided for by the DC Compensated Emancipation Act. The act made DC the only jurisdiction where former slaveholders were compensated.

41. James F. Duhamel, "Our Eyes Are Dimmed," letter to the editor, *Washington Post*, Sep. 18, 1934.

42. Lessoff, *The Nation and Its City*, 18.

43. Stevens, *Three Years in the Sixth Corps*, 7.

44. It was not until 1869 that Corcoran was able to get the damaged gallery building back from the government. The Corcoran Gallery of Art finally opened to the public in 1874. Robertson, *American Louvre*, 51–60.

45. "The Female Prison at Washington," *New York Times*, Jan. 17, 1862. The intriguing "cake affair" remains a mystery for further research.

46. Ann Blackman's *Wild Rose* is an excellent source for information about Greenhow.

47. Goode, *Capital Losses*, 42.

48. Stevens, *Three Years in the Sixth Corps*, 8–9.

49. Matthew Baird to Maggie Bowker, Dec. 23, 1862, *Historic Charlton Park's Blog*, https://charltonpark.wordpress.com/2012/12/23/matthew-baird-dotted-with-tents/.

50. *Evening Star*, Mar. 20, 1862.

51. "A Military Execution," *Evening Star*, Jan. 6, 1862.

52. "Fire at Meridian Hill," *Evening Union*, Mar. 26, 1866; *Evening Star*, Mar. 26, 1866.

53. *Evening Star*, Sep. 7, 1871.

54. John Clagett Proctor, "Brightwood Is Linked with Memories of Crystal Spring Track," *Evening Star*, Apr. 7, 1929.

55. "Ho! For the Grand Pic Nic at Crystal Spring," *Evening Star*, May 27, 1862.

56. "Crystal Springs," *Evening Star*, May 28, 1863.

57. "Coaches for Crystal Spring and the Race Course," *Evening Star*, Jun. 27, 1863.

58. "Locked Up," *Evening Star*, Aug. 13, 1862.

59. "Brightwood No More," *Washington Post*, Nov. 14, 1909.

60. "Trotting at Washington," *New York Times*, May 12, 1876.

61. "Sports in the District," *Washington Post*, May 27, 1878.

62. "Three Bakers and Their Horses," *Washington Post*, Nov. 28, 1884.

63. James Croggon, "Course of Slash Run," *Evening Star*, Jun. 3, 1906.

64. *Daily National Republican*, Aug. 6, 1861.

65. *Daily National Intelligencer*, Aug. 29, 1845.

66. Harrison, *Washington during Civil War and Reconstruction*, 156–58.

67. *Daily National Republican*, May 8, 1866; *Daily National Intelligencer*, May 6, 1867; *Evening Star*, Dec. 24, 1868; *Evening Star*, Jun. 18, 1870; *Evening Star*, Nov. 19, 1870.

68. "District Investigation," *Daily National Republican*, May 5 and May 13, 1874; "Dust! Dust! Dust!," *Evening Star*, Mar. 23, 1870.

69. Letter to the editor, *Washington Post*, Mar. 18, 1926. Emma Knorr was one of the three Prall sisters who in the 1940s would cling resolutely to their decaying townhouses on

Sixteenth Street as development transformed the neighborhood around them. See chapter 6.

70. "Call to the Health Officer," *Evening Star*, Apr. 27, 1886.

71. Benson, *Ballparks of North America*, 406.

72. "The Great Baseball Match," *Evening Star*, Aug. 26, 1867. Some sources state that the diamond was at Sixteenth and S Streets.

73. "Baseball—Olympics Versus Nationals," *National Republican*, Sep. 24, 1868.

74. "Baseball—Formal Opening of the Olympic Grounds," *National Republican*, Apr. 30, 1870. Some sources state that the Olympics field was slightly north of the National Grounds. See "Original Nats Clouted 'Em Out at 16th and S," *Washington Post*, Oct. 1, 1933, SM6.

75. "Baseball," *Evening Star*, Jun. 21, 1869, 1.

76. All statistics are drawn from Baseball Reference, baseball-reference.com.

77. "Muldoon's Home-Run," *Washington Post*, Sep. 24, 1879, 1; "Senators' New Name," *Washington Post*, Mar. 26, 1905, S1.

78. W. J. Dwyer, "Washington's History as a Major League Baseball Town," *Washington Post*, Apr. 6, 1930, 17. Biographical data from Baseball Reference, baseball-reference. com; Batesel, *Players and Teams of the National Association*.

79. "Baseball—A Novel Game," *National Republican*, Sep. 21, 1869.

80. William Henry Jones, *The Housing of Negroes in Washington, D.C.*, 28.

81. Croggon, "Course of Slash Run."

82. Green, *Washington*, Vol. 1, 272–77.

83. Calbert, *From Strength to Strength*, 27.

84. Asch and Musgrove, *Chocolate City*, 122–23.

85. The congregation subsequently moved to Ninth and P Streets NW in 1924. Calbert, *From Strength to Strength*, 25ff.

86. William Henry Jones, *The Housing of Negroes in Washington, D.C.*, 57–58.

87. "The Freedman Cleansing Their Quarters," *Daily National Republican*, Apr. 18, 1866.

88. Gatewood, *Aristocrats of Color*, 39–40; Waite, *Washington Directory and Congressional and Executive Register*, 20.

89. Gatewood, "John Francis Cook," 221.

90. *Special Report of the Commissioner of Education*, 200ff.

91. Asch and Musgrove, *Chocolate City*, 76–78. The civil disturbance of 1835 came to be known as the Snow Riot because the rioters also sacked and destroyed the restaurant of Beverly Snow, a free Black citizen. See Morley, *Snow-Storm in August*, for a detailed account of the Snow Riot and its aftermath.

92. *Daily National Intelligencer*, Mar. 23, 1855.

93. "John F. Cook Dead," *Evening Star*, Jan. 21, 1910.

94. David Taft Terry, "A Brief Moment in the Sun: The Aftermath of Emancipation in Washington, D.C., 1862–1869," in Clark-Lewis, *First Freed*, 84.

95. Green, *Secret City*, 25; Cromwell, "The First Negro Churches," 64–65.

96. Cromwell, "The First Negro Churches," 73; *The Washingtonian*, Jun. 21, 1845.

97. Kohler and Carson, *Sixteenth Street Architecture*, Vol. 2, 220.

98. Cromwell, "The First Negro Churches," 73–76; Jacqueline Moore, *Leading the Race*, 18–20.

99. "Identified with Capital's Growth," *Washington Post*, May 8, 1905.

100. Logan, *Reminiscences of a Soldier's Wife*, 522.

101. Jacqueline Moore, *Leading the Race*, 3ff.

102. Kohler and Carson, *Sixteenth Street Architecture*, Vol. 2, 222.

103. Fitzpatrick and Goodwin, *The Guide to Black Washington*, 191–92; Roberts, "The Bethel Literary and Historical Society."

104. Green, *Secret City*, 127.

105. "Building the Capital," *Daily National Republican*, Jul. 12, 1873.

Chapter 2

1. The period from October 1873 to March 1879 was the longest economic contraction in US history. See "Business Cycle Expansions and Contractions," *National Bureau of Economic Research*, https://www.nber.org/cycles/cyclesmain.html.

2. "The Louise Home in Washington," *Baltimore Sun*, Apr. 25, 1871, 4.

3. "Louise Home," *Chicago Tribune*, Jan. 27, 1872, 2; "Letter from Washington," *Baltimore Sun*, Apr. 26, 1871, 4.

4. "Letter from Washington."

5. *Chicago Tribune*, Jan. 27, 1872, 2.

6. "Life in Washington," *Chicago Tribune*, Jan. 1, 1879, 10.

7. Subhead from Page, *The World's Work*, 199.

8. "Death of Lieut. General Scott," *New York Herald*, May 30, 1866, 5.

9. "News of the Day," *Alexandria Gazette*, Jul. 26, 1870; "Washington News and Gossip," *Evening Star*, Feb. 11, 1872, 1.

10. "The Hero of Lundy's Lane," *National Republican*, Jan. 24, 1874.

11. "Condensed Locals," *Evening Star*, Jan. 2, 1874; "Improvement of the Public Grounds," *Evening Star*, Apr. 2, 1873, 1.

12. "The Scott Statue," *National Republican*, Dec. 10, 1873.

13. "Statue of General Scott," *Alexandria Gazette*, Jan. 12, 1874.

14. "Scott Statue Not Dedicated," *National Republican*, Feb. 24, 1874, 1.

15. "Gadabout's Column," *Evening Star*, Jan. 31, 1874, 1.

16. *National Republican*, Jan. 24, 1874; Jacob, *Testimony to Union*, 101.

17. *National Republican*, Jan. 24, 1874.

18. "New Statuary," *Evening Star*, Jul. 5, 1872, 1.

19. "New Scott Statue," *National Republican*, Jan. 29, 1874.

20. "Launt Thompson Scott," *National Republican*, Mar. 23, 1874.

21. "Grotesque Statues That Make Nation's Heroes Ridiculous," *Washington Post*, Feb. 25, 1917, SM6.

22. Clark, "The Horseless Age," 27.

23. The commissioners first formalized the tracking of building permits in 1877.

24. "Improvements in Washington and Vicinity," *Baltimore Sun*, Nov. 13, 1880, 6. Construction level estimates from the DC Building Permits Database, https://dcra .dc.gov/page/permit-records.

25. "Our Winter Saratoga," *Washington Post*, May 2, 1880, 7.

26. "Our Winter Saratoga."

27. "A Fresh Start," *National Republican*, Apr. 16, 1881; "A Real Estate Revival," *Washington Post*, Apr. 9, 1881, 4.

28. Greene and Bruff, *City of Washington, Statistical Maps*.

29. "Founding Fathers: Thomas S. Huntley."

30. Mullendore, "The Mullan Road."

31. "C.C. Huntley and the Mail Contracts," *Helena Herald*, Mar. 12, 1874.

32. "Virginia City Items," *New Northwest* (Deer Lodge, MT), Nov. 7, 1874; "Brevities," *Helena Weekly Herald*, Oct. 18, 1877, 7.

33. "Mail Contracts," *Helena Weekly Herald*, Dec. 23, 1880, 7.

34. "The Notorious Star Mail Route Scandal," *Evening Star*, Dec. 9, 1880, 3; "The Virginia Political Cases," *Baltimore Sun*, Dec. 10, 1880, 1.

35. "The Star Route Ring," *Chicago Tribune*, Nov. 10, 1881, 4.

36. "Mr. C. C. Huntley's Death," *Washington Post*, Oct. 13, 1883, 2.

37. "Interior of an Ideal Home," *Washington Post*, Dec. 12, 1905, SM12.

38. James, *The American Scene*, 331–32, 343–44.

39. Kohler and Carson, *Massachusetts Avenue Architecture*, Vol. 2, 119–21.

40. "Don Cameron's New Home," *Washington Post*, Sep. 24, 1880, 4.

41. "Replacing Rotten Roadways," *Washington Post*, Apr. 21, 1881, 4.

42. O'Toole, *The Five of Hearts*, 326–31.

43. "Carp's Letter," *Cleveland Leader*, Nov. 27, 1885, 4.

44. Though born and raised in Ohio, Benjamin Harrison made his political career in Indiana.

45. Carpenter, *Carp's Washington*, 81.

46. "Carp: A Glance at the Past," *Cleveland Leader*, Dec. 31, 1883, 4.

47. "Senator Pendleton's New House," *Washington Post*, Jan. 16, 1882, 4.

48. "Capital Jottings," *National Republican*, Feb. 7, 1882, 1; E.W. Lightner, "A Glimpse of Some Washington Homes," *Harper's New Monthly Magazine*, May 1885, 523; Kohler and Carson, *Sixteenth Street Architecture*, Vol. 2, 254–63.

49. Grant, *The Papers of Ulysses S. Grant*, 63.

50. "The Robeson Case," *Washington Post*, Feb. 17, 1879, 2.

51. "The Robeson House Sold," *Washington Post*, Aug. 12, 1897, 7.

52. Logan, *Reminiscences of A Soldier's Wife*, 271.

53. "Elegant Residences Now Building," *Evening Star*, Dec. 17, 1881, 3.

54. Frank Carpenter, "Public Men's Palaces," *Saint Paul Globe*, Feb. 27, 1898, 16.

55. Carpenter, 16.

56. *Guide to Washington, DC*, 153–54.

57. "Real Estate Gossip," *Evening Star*, June 8, 1880, 6; "Social and Personal," *Washington Post*, Mar. 10, 1891, 5.

58. "Real Estate Gossip," *Evening Star*, May 16, 1891, 11.

59. Winchcole, "The First Baptist Church in Washington, D.C.," 4.
60. "First Baptist Church," *Washington Critic*, Dec. 3, 1887, 1; "A New Church to Be Built," *Evening Star*, Feb. 29, 1888, 6. "An Imposing Edifice," *Evening Star*, Mar. 23, 1889, 8.
61. "A New Baptist Church, *Washington Post*, Jan. 11, 1890, 7; *Evening Star*, Mar. 23, 1889, 8.
62. "Real Estate Features," *Washington Post*, Jan. 8, 1883, 4.
63. Friedlander, "Henry Hobson Richardson, Henry Adams, and John Hay," 146–47; O'Toole, *The Five of Hearts*, 4; O'Gorman and Richardson, *Living Architecture*, xx.
64. O'Toole, *The Five of Hearts*, 56.
65. O'Toole, 60.
66. Friedlander, "Henry Hobson Richardson, Henry Adams, and John Hay," 145–46; O'Toole, *The Five of Hearts*, 56–66.
67. Friedlander, "Henry Hobson Richardson, Henry Adams, and John Hay," 146–47; "The Real Estate Boom," *Evening Star*, Mar. 26, 1881; Ochsner, *H. H. Richardson*, 256.
68. Lewis, *The Opulent Interiors of the Gilded Age*, 383–85.
69. Nicholas Anderson to Larz Anderson, Oct. 31, 1883, letter in possession of the Society of the Cincinnati Library, Washington, DC.
70. Goode, *Best Addresses*, 108.
71. Lightner, "A Glimpse of Some Washington Homes," 523; O'Gorman and Richardson, *Living Architecture*, 126.
72. Van Rensselaer, *Henry Hobson Richardson*, 105.
73. Lewis, *The Opulent Interiors of the Gilded Age*, 136.
74. Nicholas Anderson to Larz Anderson, Oct. 18, 1882, letter in possession of the Society of the Cincinnati Library, Washington, DC.
75. O'Gorman and Richardson, *Living Architecture*, 126.
76. O'Toole, *The Five of Hearts*, 141.
77. Friedlander, "Henry Hobson Richardson, Henry Adams, and John Hay," 150; Luria, *Capital Speculations*, 128.
78. O'Toole, *The Five of Hearts*, 180; Friedlander, "Henry Hobson Richardson, Henry Adams, and John Hay," 138.
79. Shackleton, *The Book of Washington*, 123–24.
80. Luria, *Capital Speculations*, 134.
81. O'Toole, *The Five of Hearts*, 196–206; Friedlander, "Henry Hobson Richardson, Henry Adams, and John Hay," 138. The affair is widely described as a long-standing emotional involvement, though it is unknown whether it was physically consummated.
82. Cater, *Henry Adams and His Friends*, 168.
83. Shackleton, *The Book of Washington*, 123.
84. "Carp's Letter," *Cleveland Leader*, Nov. 16, 1885, 4.
85. "The Coming Season," *Evening Star*, Oct. 29, 1887, 2.
86. "Washington's Colored People," *Evening Star*, Dec. 19, 1883.
87. "Real Estate Gossip," *Evening Star*, Apr. 20, 1889, 6.
88. "Defeat of Senator Chandler," *New York Herald*, Jan. 22, 1875, 4.
89. Kohler and Carson, *Sixteenth Street Architecture*, Vol. 2, 148 and 149.

90. "Interior of an Ideal Home," *Washington Post*, Dec. 10, 1905, SM12.

91. "A Park with Houses in It," *New York Times*, Oct. 5, 1890, 17.

92. Kohler and Carson, *Sixteenth Street Architecture*, Vol. 2, 265, 268.

93. 1880 Census, Enumeration District 17, p. 4.

94. Moldow, *Women Doctors in Gilded-Age Washington*, 94, 104–7.

95. "A Clinic for Women," *Washington Post*, Oct. 18, 1890, 8.

96. "Pioneer Woman Physician," *Washington Post*, Jun. 26, 1904, 11.

97. Kohler and Carson, *Sixteenth Street Architecture*, Vol. 1, 196–97; Coolidge, "Herbert Langford Warren," 690.

98. "The New Church," *Evening Star*, Dec. 8, 1894, 12; Kohler and Carson, *Sixteenth Street Architecture*, Vol. 1, 205–8.

99. Kohler and Carson, *Sixteenth Street Architecture*, Vol. 1, 201–5; "Memorial Window Unveiled," *Washington Post*, Apr. 19, 1897, 7.

100. Brain, "Discipline and Style," 810.

101. Fogelsong, *Planning the Capitalist City*, 163.

102. Franklin Webster Smith, *The Aggrandizement of Washington*, 73.

103. "4th of July Avenue," *Washington Post*, Sep. 1, 1907.

104. Kohler and Carson, *Sixteenth Street Architecture*, Vol. 1, 157.

105. Goode, *Best Addresses*, 72–73.

106. "Real Estate Gossip," *Evening Star*, Jun. 3, 1905.

107. Liana Paredes, "Private Homes, Public Lives," in Field and Gournay, *Paris on the Potomac*, 100.

108. Leon, "The Life of American Workers in 1915"; Brudnick and Dwyer, "Salaries of Members of Congress."

109. "Nathan Wyeth Will Become City Architect," *Washington Post*, Jan. 12, 1934, 15; "More Room for President," *Washington Post*, May 20, 1909, 3; Sefton, *National Register Nomination for the District of Columbia Municipal Center*, documents Wyeth's biography.

110. Kohler and Carson, *Sixteenth Street Architecture*, Vol. 1, 178–80; "Russia's Stately New Embassy Marvel of Architectural Skill," *Washington Post*, Nov. 8, 1913, 4.

111. Kohler and Carson, *Sixteenth Street Architecture*, Vol. 1, 165–66.

112. "Embassy Buys Home," *Washington Post*, Nov. 4, 1913, 4.

113. Kohler and Carson, *Sixteenth Street Architecture*, Vol. 2, 186.

114. Kohler and Carson, 180–81.

115. "Public Buildings and Bridges Add Much to the City Beautiful," *Evening Star*, Sep. 12, 1908, 4.

116. Kohler and Carson, *Sixteenth Street Architecture*, Vol. 2, 290.

117. "Will Erect a Temple," *Washington Post*, Dec. 12, 1909, CA 8.

118. "Million Put in Deals," *Washington Post*, Jun. 21, 1914, 31.

119. Kohler and Carson, *Sixteenth Street Architecture*, Vol. 2, 279; "Mausoleum at Halicarnassus."

120. Walker, *Guidebook to the House of the Temple*, 39.

121. Walker, 36–37.

122. Walker, 48–58, 79.

123. Walker, 71, 80.

Chapter 3

1. McKevitt, *Meridian Hill*, 46–47.

2. Francis, "BLOCK 8," 16.

3. Roberts, oral history interview, Mar. 14, 1984.

4. Details about Meridian Hill residents come from Mara Cherkasky, Sarah Jane Shoenfield, and Brian Kraft, *Mapping Segregation in Washington, DC,* https://www.arcgis .com/apps/MapSeries/index.html?appid=825617c96aff4db59f2f216e83b9d713, accessed Feb. 22, 2020. Cherkasky, Shoenfeld, and Kraft have studied and mapped the African Americans on Meridian Hill in great depth and detail.

5. "To Build Up Wayland," *Washington Post,* Oct. 7, 1896; "Will Move Wayland Seminary," *Washington Post,* Feb. 16, 1897; "Mission Board's Deception," *Washington Post,* Jul. 16, 1897; John Clagett Proctor, "Swimmers of Old Washington," *Sunday Star,* Jul. 10, 1938.

6. "For Destitute Colored Girls," *Washington Post,* Oct. 16, 1888; "Mrs. Cleveland a Patroness," *Washington Post,* Feb. 3, 1896; "Doing Good Work Quietly," *Evening Star,* May 4, 1897.

7. "Neck Broken by a Fall," *Evening Star,* Sep. 6, 1897.

8. Foote, "Circumstances Affecting the Heat of the Sun's Rays," 382–83. Eunice Foote's recently rediscovered paper has been the subject of magazine articles and a scientific symposium. McNeill, "This Lady Scientist Defined the Greenhouse Effect."

9. "The Marriage of Senator Henderson," *Evening Star,* Jun. 25, 1868; "Wedding at the National," *Daily National Intelligencer,* Jun. 26, 1868.

10. *Saint Louis Globe-Democrat,* Jun. 7, 1877, 8; "The World of Art," *Saint Louis Globe-Democrat,* Jan. 7, 1878, 5; "Art Notes," *Saint Louis Globe-Democrat,* Nov. 21, 1880, 11.

11. *Chicago Inter Ocean,* Feb. 17, 1875.

12. "Personalities," *National Republican,* Mar. 19, 1887.

13. "Ex-Senator Henderson's New House on Meridian Hill," *The Republic* (Saint Louis), Aug. 5, 1888.

14. "Personalities," *National Republican,* Mar. 19, 1887; "City and District," *Evening Star,* Jan. 14, 1888, 2.

15. Harrison, *Washington during Civil War and Reconstruction,* 302–10.

16. Kohler and Carson, *Sixteenth Street Architecture,* Vol. 1, 340.

17. "Beautiful Cotillion at Castle Henderson," *Washington Times,* May 2, 1902, 7.

18. "A Gay House-Warming," *Washington Post,* Feb. 11, 1890.

19. Henderson, *The Aristocracy of Health.*

20. "Feast without Meat," *Washington Post,* May 19, 1905.

21. "Ex-Senator's Old Wine Poured into Gutters," *New York Times,* May 18, 1906. See also "Runs Red with Wine," *Evening Star,* May 17, 1906; "Wine without Stint from Boundary Castle," *Washington Post,* May 18, 1906.

22. "J.B. Henderson Dead," *Washington Post*, Apr. 13, 1913.

23. See Charles Moore, *The Improvement of the Park System*; Gutheim and Lee, *Worthy of the Nation*, 119–43; Kohler and Scott, *Designing the Nation's Capital*.

24. Henderson, *The Aristocracy of Health*, 21–22.

25. Mayme Ober Peak, "Gentlewoman Who Is Landlady to the Nations," *Seattle Daily Times*, Oct. 1, 1922.

26. Bushong et al., *A Centennial History*, 168.

27. Peak, "Gentlewoman Who Is Landlady to the Nations."

28. Tragically, the balconies were hacked off in the late 1980s after balusters had come loose on one of them, posing a limited safety hazard that could have been remedied with far less drastic repairs. See Kohler and Carson, *Sixteenth Street Architecture*, Vol. 2, 456, 463.

29. Kohler and Carson, 451.

30. Kohler and Carson, 452.

31. Selwa Roosevelt, "'Edwardian' Mrs. Marshall Field Once Lived in the Pink Palace," *Evening Star*, Feb. 5, 1955.

32. Peak, "Gentlewoman Who Is Landlady to the Nations."

33. Kohler and Carson, *Sixteenth Street Architecture*, Vol. 2, 424.

34. "French Embassy's Beautiful Home to Be Ready for Use in November," *Washington Times*, Aug. 4, 1907.

35. "First Formal Dinner in New French Embassy," *Washington Post*, Jan. 14, 1908.

36. "Houses in Spanish Style Are Planned by Hendersons," *Washington Times*, Oct. 13, 1907; "Houses Near Completion," *Washington Post*, Jun. 7, 1908.

37. "New Diplomatic Home," *Washington Post*, Jan. 24, 1909; "Hendersons Build Embassy," *Evening Star*, Jun. 16, 1909.

38. "Home for a Diplomat," *Washington Post*, Apr. 11, 1909.

39. Kim Prothro Williams, "Meridian Hill Historic District," registration form for the National Register of Historic Places, 2014.

40. "Cuban Legation Bids Opened," *Washington Post*, Nov. 16, 1916.

41. Neil Henry, "The Cuban Embassy: A Tale of Lost Dignity," *Washington Post*, Aug. 21, 1977, 35.

42. "Noted Landmark Now On New Site," *Evening Star*, Nov. 21, 1925.

43. "Restoring Warder Home," *Evening Star*, Dec. 8, 1924. The office building that replaced the Warder mansion was the Investment Building, designed by Jules Henri de Sibour, which stands on the northwest corner of Fifteenth and K Streets NW.

44. "Apartment to Contain Frame of Famed Home," *Evening Star*, Nov. 29, 1924; Kohler and Carson, *Sixteenth Street Architecture*, Vol. 1, 120–43.

45. Kohler and Carson, *Sixteenth Street Architecture*, Vol. 1, 466.

46. "Offers Home for Vice Presidents," *Evening Star*, Jan. 25, 1923.

47. Wallace, "No Palace for Cal." At the time, the Coolidges were living in an apartment at the Willard Hotel.

48. "Senators Decline Offer of Mansion to Vice President," *Evening Star*, Feb. 19, 1923.

49. "Henderson House, Which US Rejected, Is Bought by Spain," *Washington Post*, Apr. 3, 1927.

50. Kohler and Carson, *Sixteenth Street Architecture*, Vol. 1, 485–509.

51. "Gift for Mr. MacVeagh," *Washington Post*, Sep. 27, 1910.

52. "Embassy to Be Converted into Model Mexican Salon," *Washington Post*, Mar. 29, 1925; "Mexican Embassy Newly Decorated with Brilliant Series of Murals," *Washington Post*, Oct. 12, 1941.

53. "Site for a New Executive Mansion," *Evening Star*, Dec. 18, 1868.

54. Mary F. Henderson, "Avenue and White House," *Evening Star*, Mar. 19, 1900.

55. "Proposed New White House," *New York Times*, Dec. 11, 1898.

56. Franklin Webster Smith, *The Aggrandizement of Washington*, 40–46.

57. Savage, *Monument Wars*, 183–85, 213–15.

58. William S. Odlin, "Washington's Hill of Diplomats Rises," *New York Times*, Jul. 19, 1925. Note that Mary's ex-post-facto characterization of the Hendersons' predicament contrasts with their earlier optimism about the neighborhood's development potential, which had led them to invest in it substantially.

59. Francis, "BLOCK 8," 14–15.

60. "Say It Is a Disgrace to City," *Washington Post*, Jun. 20, 1899.

61. Henderson is using the term "parking" in its original sense, public space set aside for park-like uses. "Park Bills Discussed," *Washington Post*, Apr. 5, 1906.

62. Public Law 61-265, Jun. 25, 1910.

63. Francis, "BLOCK 8," 13, 23.

64. Cherkasky, Shoenfeld, and Kraft, *Mapping Segregation in Washington, DC*.

65. Roberts, oral history interview.

66. "Meridian Hill Park," Historic American Buildings Survey DC-532 (1987), 42; Schlefer, "Washington's Italianate Park on Meridian Hill," 32.

67. "Plan Unique Park on Meridian Hill," *Evening Star*, May 23, 1914.

68. "Pig in a Parlor, Term of Criticism," *Evening Star*, Jun. 23, 1916.

69. William J. Wheatley, "16th Street Park to be Beautified," *Evening Star*, Sep. 5, 1926; "Meridian Hill Park Can Be Saved, Maj. Grant Holds," *Washington Post*, Jan. 23, 1926.

70. "Meridian Hill Park Will Be Beautified," *Washington Post*, Oct. 26, 1924.

71. "Work Completed on Meridian Hill," *Evening Star*, Sep. 29, 1936: "Meridian Hill Park Is Finally Completed after 26 Years of Hard Work, Petty Strife," *Washington Post*, Oct. 3, 1936.

72. "Meridian Hill Park," 46–48; Aument, "Construction History in Architectural Conservation," 3–19.

73. Luebke, *Civic Art*, 64–74; Kohler and Carson, *Sixteenth Street Architecture*, Vol. 1, 323–35.

74. "Urge Meridian Hill Park as Site for Lincoln Memorial," *Evening Star*, Jun. 10, 1911; "A Protest from Mrs. Henderson," *Washington Herald*, Aug. 5, 1911; "Meridian Hill Site for Lincoln Memorial," *Washington Times*, Aug. 5, 1911; "Suggests Memorial Arch," *Washington Post*, Aug. 7, 1911.

75. "$100,000 Statue of Buchanan Lost to City unless Congress Soon Acts," *Washington Post*, Dec. 29, 1917.

76. "Attacks on Buchanan," *Washington Post*, Feb. 14, 1918.

77. "Statue to Dante Is Unveiled Here," *Evening Star*, Dec. 2, 1921; "Italy and France Unite under Dante," *Washington Post*, Dec. 2, 1921; "Statue of Jeanne D'Arc Unveiled with Simple but Impressive Services," *Washington Post*, Jan. 7, 1922.

78. "Meridian Hill Park Is Finally Completed."

79. "Armillary Sphere Donated to Federal City by Author," *Washington Post*, Nov. 10, 1936.

80. "A Circle Named for Hancock," *Washington Post*, Dec. 1, 1888.

81. The Hancock statue, when completed in 1896, was erected on Pennsylvania Avenue instead.

82. "The Hancock Circle," *Washington Post*, May 1, 1896.

83. "Plea for New Name," *Evening Star*, Mar. 20, 1910, 20.

84. "New Association Proposed," *Evening Star*, Nov. 21, 1903; "Plan Noble Highway," *Washington Post*, Dec. 6, 1903.

85. "Fail to Agree," *Evening Star*, Feb. 13, 1907; "Sixteenth Street's Name," *Washington Post*, Feb. 14, 1907.

86. "Would Rename 16th Street," *Washington Post*, Jan. 16, 1908; "4th of July Avenue," *Washington Post*, Sep. 1, 1907.

87. "Change of Name Favored," *Washington Post*, Jan. 26, 1908.

88. "Will Drop Old Name," *Washington Post*, Mar. 28, 1909; "Agreed on New Name," *Evening Star*, Mar. 28, 1909.

89. "Avenue of Statues," *Evening Star*, Apr. 18, 1909.

90. "Plea for New Name," *Washington Post*, Mar. 20, 1910.

91. "Feast Wins Senators," *Washington Post*, Mar. 15, 1914.

92. "The Avenue That Was," *Washington Post*, Jul. 24, 1914; "Avenue of the Presidents" (editorial), *Washington Post*, Jul. 26, 1914.

93. "Desire More Statues," *Washington Post*, Nov. 19, 1910; "Busts for Highway," *Washington Post*, Jun. 8, 1913.

94. Kohler and Carson, *Sixteenth Street Architecture*, Vol. 1, 329.

95. "Wants Trees As Memorial," *Washington Post*, Feb. 29, 1920.

96. Bates, "Remembering the Great War."

97. "Vandals Damage City Memorial to World War Dead," *Evening Star*, Oct. 28, 1929; Phil Casey, "Bronze Scavengers Deface Legion's Memorial," *Washington Post*, Jun. 9, 1966; Bob Levey, "Forgotten Men: Why Not Stop, Reflect, Repair?," *Washington Post*, May 14, 1982; "A Memorial That Deserves to Happen," *Washington Post*, May 26, 1986; John Kelly, "Living Memories of Long Ago War's Dead," *Washington Post*, May 31, 2010.

Chapter 4

1. "Washington Man Lives in a Tree to Escape World's Contamination," *Washington Times*, Feb. 17, 1907.

2. "Life in the Treetops," *National Tribune*, May 28, 1885; John Clagett Proctor, "The Story of 'Airy Castle,'" *Evening Star*, Jul. 10, 1949.

3. "Highway Extension," *Evening Star*, Dec. 18, 1897; "Real Estate Market," *Washington Post*, Mar. 5, 1899.

4. For portraits of several of these communities, see Kathryn Smith, *Washington at Home*, 273–344. For a discussion of the development of the streetcar system, see DeFerrari, *Capital Streetcars*, 76–107.

5. "Sixteenth Street Extension," *Washington Post*, Dec. 5, 1887.

6. DeFerrari, *Capital Streetcars*, 205–6.

7. Editorial, "Sixteenth Street," *Evening Star*, Mar. 22, 1904. Note that, contrary to the *Star*'s claim, the tradition of landowners donating land for municipal uses in the hopes of substantially enhancing the value of their remaining property extends back to the original landowners in the District of Columbia, who donated land to the federal government for the city of Washington.

8. "No Increase in Values," *Washington Post*, Jun. 26, 1898. Senator James McMillan, chair of the committee on the District of Columbia, had submitted the bill to the DC commissioners for their review.

9. "Real Estate Market," *Washington Post*, Mar. 5, 1899.

10. "Real Estate Market," *Washington Post*, May 18, 1902.

11. "Real Estate Market," *Washington Post*, Jan. 19, 1902.

12. Einberger, *A History of Rock Creek Park*, 74–78.

13. Editorial, *Evening Star*, Dec. 29, 1888, 4.

14. Mackintosh, *Rock Creek Park*, provides a detailed history of the creation of the park.

15. "Real Estate Market," *Washington Post*, May 18, 1902; "Bid in Their Homes," *Washington Post*, Oct. 11, 1902.

16. "Forgotten Burial Spot," *Washington Post*, Oct. 17, 1903.

17. "Sixteenth Street," *Evening Star*, Mar. 22, 1904.

18. "Bridge over Piney Branch," *Washington Post*, Jul. 13, 1905.

19. "One of the Finest," *Evening Star*, Dec. 2, 1906.

20. Myer, *Bridges and the City of Washington*, 73–74.

21. "Bridge to Be Finished," *Washington Post*, May 21, 1909.

22. "Statues for Bridge," *Washington Post*, Jun. 9, 1910. Proctor also sculpted the buffalos for the Dumbarton Bridge, which carries Q Street over Rock Creek Park.

23. "Sixteenth Street Extended Shows Rapid Development," *Evening Star*, Oct. 8, 1910.

24. "Motor Carriage Here," *Washington Post*, Apr. 3, 1897.

25. "Washington Auto Races," *Washington Post*, Oct. 18, 1903; "Auto Races at Brightwood," *Washington Post*, Oct. 28, 1903.

26. "Autos Fast in Races," *Washington Post*, Oct. 29, 1903.

27. "Light Mile of Roadway," *Washington Post*, Oct. 18, 1914.

28. Note, for example, the "heavy traffic" on Sixteenth Street extended that is mentioned in "Dim Lights Peril Life in D.C. Streets," *Evening Star*, Jan. 3, 1923.

29. "Plan Noble Highway," *Washington Post*, Dec. 6, 1903.

30. "The Future of Sixteenth Street," *Washington Post*, Nov. 16, 1904.

31. "Executive Avenue," *Washington Post*, Sep. 27, 1905; "Keep Business Away," *Washington Post*, Oct. 4, 1905; "Stores Not Wanted," *Washington Post*, Oct. 5, 1905.

32. Scott, *American City Planning since 1890*, 95–109.

33. Rothstein, *The Color of Law*, 39–57.

34. "Zone Commission Fixes Area Rules," *Washington Post*, Jul. 13, 1920.

35. Altshuler, *The Jews of Washington, D.C.*, 86–87; Solomon, *The Washington Century*, 17–20.

36. "Cafritz Will Name Committees Sunday," *Washington Post*, Sep. 20, 1923.

37. "Jewish Community Center Here Culmination of Years of Effort," *Evening Star*, Apr. 5, 1925.

38. "The Jewish Community Center" (editorial), *Washington Post*, May 5, 1925; Solomon, *The Washington Century*, 17–20.

39. "White-Robed Klan Cheered on March in Nation's Capital," *Washington Post*, Aug. 9, 1925.

40. Eugene L. Meyer, "The Center of Their Lives," *Washington Post*, Jan. 20, 1992.

41. Jackson, "Great Black Music," 24–25.

42. "Allows Bus Line Four New Routes," *Evening Star*, Aug. 4, 1921; "Buses in Capital Will Be Increased," *Washington Post*, Sep. 25, 1921.

43. "New Double-Decker Bus," *Evening Star*, Jan. 22, 1925, 2.

44. "Tress Being Pruned along 16th Street," *Evening Star*, Jul. 10, 1928.

45. Si Grogan, "Intakes & Exhausts," *Washington Post*, Jun. 27, 1923.

46. "New Signal Lights for 16th Street Ordered at Once," *Evening Star*, Jun. 19, 1925.

47. "Confusion, Comedy Attend Beginnings of Traffic Signals," *Washington Post*, Jan. 6, 1926; "Sixteenth Street Lights Are Retimed to Quicken Traffic," *Washington Post*, Feb. 9, 1926.

48. Goode, *Best Addresses*, 3–7, 27–29.

49. Advertisement, *Washington Post*, Sep. 17, 1916, R1.

50. Goode, *Best Addresses*, 25–33.

51. "Real Estate Market," *Washington Post*, Dec. 30, 1900.

52. For more details, see Goode, *Best Addresses*, 37–39.

53. "Urge Mount Pleasant Park," *Washington Post*, Jan. 7, 1904.

54. "Objects to Tall Buildings," *Washington Post*, Mar. 15, 1905.

55. Goode, *Best Addresses*, 55.

56. Peak, "Gentlewoman Who Is Landlady to the Nations."

57. "Work on New Seven-Story Apartment Building Begun," *Evening Star*, Jul. 22, 1916; "Has Many Innovations," *Washington Post*, Jul. 23, 1916.

58. Goode, *Best Addresses*, 151–57.

59. George H. Gall, "Vast Is Building Done by Wardman," *Washington Times*, Jul. 1, 1911, 4.

60. "New Apartment Rising," *Washington Post*, Mar. 26, 1916.

61. "Acquires Wardman Holding to Block Apartment Plans," *Evening Star*, Jan. 9, 1915.

62. "Dangers to City's Beauty Pointed Out by Mrs. Henderson," *Washington Post*, Jan. 17, 1926, M2.

63. Henderson, *Remarks*, 19–20.

64. "U.S. Takes Another District Building," *Washington Post*, Nov. 3, 1917. Palmer's job was to oversee the seizure, administration, and potential sale of enemy property in

the United States. In 1919 President Wilson named Palmer his attorney general. That same year an anarchist's bomb exploded on Palmer's doorstep at 2132 R Street NW, and in response he oversaw a sweeping nationwide roundup of radicals known infamously as the Palmer Raids.

65. "City Is Home Hungry," *Washington Post*, Apr. 20, 1919.

66. "Chastleton Annex Building Starts," *Evening Star*, Nov. 1, 1919.

67. Goode, *Best Addresses*, 192–95.

68. "New Hadleigh Apt to Cost $2,000,000," *Washington Times*, Aug. 9, 1919; "$2,000,000 Hotel Here," *Washington Post*, Aug. 10, 1919.

69. Goode, *Best Addresses*, 196–97.

70. "Apartment Hotel Nears Completion," *Washington Post*, Aug. 29, 1920.

71. "Bill to Limit Height of Apartment House," *Washington Post*, Sep. 5, 1919; "Would Cut Height of the Hadleigh," *Washington Post*, Nov. 2, 1919.

72. "Flu Still Spreads," *Washington Post*, Oct. 8, 1918.

73. "New Carlton Hotel at 16th and K Streets," *Washington Post*, Feb. 15, 1925.

74. "Wardman Company Anticipates Fifth Hotel Next April," *Washington Post*, Jun. 14, 1925.

75. "A Hotel's Personality," *Evening Star*, Nov. 17, 1963; Kohler and Carson, *Sixteenth Street Architecture*, Vol. 2, 129–30.

76. "Dangers to City's Beauty Pointed Out by Mrs. Henderson," *Washington Post*, Jan. 17, 1926, M2.

77. "$5,000,000 in New Apartments for Washington," *Evening Star*, Sep. 4, 1926.

78. "Hay-Adams House Nears Completion," *Evening Star*, Mar. 3, 1928.

79. Carl Bernstein, "The Washington Wardman Built," *Washington Post*, Feb. 16, 1969, 259. In 1928 Wardman decided to tear down his mansion, at Connecticut Avenue and Woodley Road NW, to make way for an expansion of the Wardman Park Hotel. He and his wife subsequently moved into the Hay-Adams.

80. "Sixteenth Street Extended Shows Rapid Development," *Evening Star*, Oct. 8, 1910.

81. "Sixteenth Street Park is Almost All Sold," *Washington Post*, Oct. 11, 1925.

82. "Sixteenth Street Extension Opened as Ritchie Speaks," *Washington Post*, May 17, 1930.

83. "Andalusian Charm Comes to Capital in Cafritz House," *Washington Post*, Jan. 23, 1927.

84. Grahek, "Clark Griffith"; Leavengood, *Clark Griffith*, 23.

85. "Demand Grows for Moderately Priced Dwellings," *Washington Post*, May 31, 1925.

86. "Clark Griffith Brings Home 5 More Children to Adopt," *Washington Post*, Nov. 24, 1925, 5.

87. "Funeral Services Held for James E. Cooper," *Evening Star*, Jan. 14, 1930, A5.

88. Kerr, *Calvin*, 334.

89. "This Morning with Shirley Povich," *Washington Post*, Mar. 13, 1939, 16.

90. Lee Poe Hart, "Motion Picture Industry from Infancy to Its Prime," *Washington Post*, Oct. 22, 1922.

91. "Harry M. Crandall Ends Life; Once Theater Magnate Here," *Evening Star*, Feb. 26, 1937.

92. "Crandall, Ex-Theater Magnate, Kills Self," *Washington Post*, Feb. 27, 1937.

93. "Street of Embassies Now Changing into Great Avenue of Churches," *Evening Star*, Apr. 1, 1924.

94. Wann, *A History of the National Baptist Memorial Church*, 17–43.

95. "President Breaks Earth for Church," *Washington Post*, Apr. 24, 1921.

96. Wann, *A History of the National Baptist Memorial Church*, 53–66.

97. "Wilson Lays Cornerstone of Presbyterian Church," *Washington Post*, Dec. 20, 1913.

98. "Shrine of Sacred Heart," *Evening Star*, Feb. 7, 1898, 10; "Sacred Heart Shrine Dedication Today," *Evening Star*, Dec. 10, 1922.

99. "Firm of Architects Marks Anniversary," *Washington Post*, Dec. 21, 1931.

100. Scott and Lee, *Buildings of the District of Columbia*, 316.

101. Benjamin Forgey, "Concrete Proof of One Man's Legacy to Washington," *Washington Post*, Mar. 31, 2001.

102. "Church Dedication Rich in Ceremonial," *Washington Herald*, Dec. 11, 1922.

103. "Cornerstone Is Laid," *Washington Post*, Feb. 14, 1913.

104. Staples, *Washington Unitarianism*, 74.

105. Scott and Lee, *Buildings of the District of Columbia*, 315.

106. "Chief Justice Taft to Attend All Souls Church Dedication," *Evening Star*, Oct. 26, 1924.

107. Scott and Lee, *Buildings of the District of Columbia*, 306–7; Kohler and Carson, *Sixteenth Street Architecture*, Vol. 2, 395–409.

108. "Tower to World Peace Dedicated by Universalists," *Evening Star*, Oct. 28, 1929.

109. Hamline merged with a nearby African American congregation to become Simpson-Hamline United Methodist Church in 1974. "1,000 Bow in Prayer at Dedication Rites of Hamline Church," *Washington Post*, Jan. 4, 1926; "Grace Lutherans Dedicate Church With Ceremonies," *Washington Post*, Mar. 19, 1928; "New St. Stephen's Church Dedicated by Bishop Freeman," *Washington Post*, Dec. 26, 1928; "Church to Occupy New Auditorium," *Evening Star*, Mar. 9, 1929. The building was purchased by the Trinity AME Zion Church in 1983.

Chapter 5

1. "Building Permits Issued in Principal Cities," in US Department of Commerce, *Statistical Abstract of the United States*, 1933, Table 775. Corresponding data is US Department of Commerce, *Statistical Abstract of the United States*, 1935, Table 810, and US Department of Commerce, *Statistical Abstract of the United States*, 1941, Table 930. A tabulation of the value of new building permits from the DC Building Permit Database yields a similarly shaped curve.

2. US Department of Commerce, *Statistical Abstract of the United States*, 1941, Table 6.

3. John Brooks Henderson Jr. to Mary Henderson, Sep. 3, 1921/22, RG 7075, Box 7, Smithsonian Libraries, Washington, DC.

4. Claudia Levy, "Jesse Shima Dies," *Washington Post*, Dec. 18, 2002.

5. "Brownstone Ghost," *Washington Post*, Jan. 19, 1949, 12.

6. "Henderson Castle Now Is Club, *Post*, Jun. 4, 1937, 20; "Meridian Hill Castle Boasts Stand-up Bar," *Washington Post*, Apr. 2, 1946, 10.

7. Miller, "Mrs. Henderson's Legacy."

8. Real estate advertisement, *Star*, Sep. 25, 1929, 40.

9. Real estate advertisement, *Washington Post*, Jul. 7, 1929, R4.

10. "Plan for Road into City from North Is Started," *Washington Post*, Jun. 29, 1927, 20; "Arts Commission Seeks to Improve City Approaches," *Washington Post*, Aug. 29, 1926, M10; "Early Completion of Maryland Road Link Seen as Near," *Washington Post*, Feb. 26, 1928, M21.

11. "East-West Highway Link Nearly Ready," *Washington Post*, Apr. 24, 1930, 2; "Sixteenth Street Extension Opened," *Washington Post*, May 17, 1930, 20.

12. "Rifle Fire Brings Down Rumrunner Car in 16th Street," *Washington Post*, Feb. 29, 1932, 14; "Rum Car Seized after Long Chase across District Line," *Evening Star*, Feb. 29, 1932, 1.

13. *Washington Post*, Feb. 29, 1932, 14.

14. "Administrative History—Success."

15. *Marjorie Webster School and Junior College Campus National Register of Historic Places Nomination Form* summarizes the history and development of the campus.

16. "Developer Exhibits Model Residence in Restricted Section," *Washington Post*, Oct. 30, 1927, 51.

17. Real estate advertisements, *Washington Post*, Jun. 6, 1926, R5, and Aug. 22, 1926, R2; "Colonial Village New Development," *Washington Post*, Nov. 28, 1930, 9.

18. "Colonial Village Is Planned in City," *Washington Post*, Apr. 5, 1931, R1.

19. Deed 1933022784, Rock Creek Park Estates Inc. to Hilda B. Eacho (Dec. 26, 1933), and Deed 1940031150, Rock Creek Park Estates Inc. to A. R. Austin (Sep. 30, 1940), both in District of Columbia Office of the Recorder of Deeds Database, are examples.

20. Compiled from District of Columbia Office of the Recorder of Deeds Database.

21. "Provide Free Sports," *Washington Post*, Nov. 6, 1906, 16; "Rock Creek Park Report," *Washington Post*, Nov. 13, 1907, 16.

22. Bushong, *Rock Creek Park Historic District Nomination*, 8–47.

23. Babin, *Links to the Past*, 253.

24. Babin, 254.

25. Bushong, *Rock Creek Park Historic District Nomination*, 7–25.

26. "Douglas Inspects Golf Course," *Washington Post*, Nov. 25, 1906; "Golf Course to Be Ideal," *Washington Post*, Sep. 1, 1907, S3; "Public Links Award to Leoffler," *Washington Post*, Dec. 10, 1932, 11.

27. "10 Muni Net Courts Available in Spring," *Washington Post*, Feb. 12, 1924, S3 8; "New Municipal Tennis Courts Ready," *Washington Post*, Jul. 20, 1924, S3; "Helen Sinclair Goes into Tennis Semifinal," *Washington Post*, Sep. 1, 1924, S2.

28. "Urge DC Men for DC Positions," *Evening Star*, Feb. 4, 1930, C10.

29. John Daly, "These Are Not the Missing Links," *Washington Post*, Aug. 31, 1930, SM5.

30. Babin, *Links to the Past*, 87.

31. "Intimates of Slain Policeman Quizzed," *Washington Post*, Sep. 13, 1931, M1.

32. "Policeman Found Dead Near Bridge; Suspect Murder" *Evening Star*, Sept 12, 1931, 1.

33. "Woman Is Sought in Morrow Death," *Evening Star*, Sept 15, 1931, 1.

34. "Death of Morrow Is Laid to Fall," *Evening Star*, Sep. 16, 1931, 1; "Morrow's Death Is Held Due to Fall," *Evening Star*, Sep. 14, 1931, 1.

35. "Widow of Morrow Asks Further Quiz," *Evening Star*, Sep. 25, 1931, 1.

36. "Death of Woman Held to Be Suicide," *Washington Post*, Oct. 13, 1931, 22.

37. "Man, 40, Out of Job, Ends Life with Gun," *Washington Post*, May 12, 1932, 22.

38. "Suicide Verdict Given for Miss Val Kovacs," *Evening Star*, Nov. 1, 1932, B-1.

39. "Man Shoots Wife and Kills Himself, Imperiling Infant," *Washington Post*, Mar. 16, 1933, 18.

40. "DC Gambler Shot Dead in Auto in 16th Street Area," *Evening Star*, Apr. 21, 1932, 1. The Court of Appeals of the District of Columbia's opinion in *Harris v. United States* (71 F.2d 532, No. 6067, May 14, 1934) recounts further details of the shooting and the trial of Charles Harris (Charles Bernstein), https://cite.case.law/f2d/71/532/.

41. "Bowie Angle Is Probed in Gang Killing," *Washington Post*, Apr. 22, 1932, 1.

42. "Suspect Returned in Henry Slaying," *Evening Star*, Jul. 18, 1932, 1.

43. Cousino, "Charles Bernstein."

44. Davol, "Shifting Mores," 49.

45. Advertisement, *Washington Post*, Sep. 24, 1928, 13.

46. Real estate advertisements, *Evening Star*, Sep. 30, 1934, G10.

47. Sarah Booth Conroy, "Sweet Sixteenth," *Washington Post*, Aug. 28, 1987.

48. Real estate advertisement, *Star*, Feb. 23, 1936, and May 17, 1936, G8.

49. "Baltimore Men Jailed for D.C. Protests," *Baltimore Afro-American*, Jan. 11, 1930, 3.

50. "Italy's Cadets Party Guests at Embassy," *Washington Post*, Jul. 16, 1931, 8.

51. "U.S. Joins Hunt for Senders of Death Parcels," *Washington Post*, Jan. 1, 1932, 1.

52. "Ethiopian Defense Body Is Formed," *Baltimore Afro-American*, Aug. 3, 1935, 3.

53. "Delegation Sees Phillips in Ethiopia," *Daily Worker*, Aug. 2, 1935, 1.

54. "Pall Covers Spanish Embassy," *Washington Post*, Sep. 11, 1936, X1.

55. "Franco Resigns Embassy Post," *Washington Post*, Sep. 10, 1936, X1.

56. "Fresh 'Battle' Disrupts Peace at Franco Sale," *Washington Post*, Sep. 23, 1936, X.

57. "Franco, Flier, Is Killed in Crash," *New York Times*, Oct. 31, 1938, 1; Edward Folliard, "De Los Rios Makes No Plans for Self," *Washington Post*, Mar. 29, 1939, 1.

58. "Workers Picket Italian Embassy," *Washington Post*, Mar. 24, 1937, 3.

59. "Film Folk Snub Mussolini's Son," *Chicago Daily Tribune*, Oct. 9, 1937, 7.

60. "Duce's Son, Heavily Guarded, Takes Tea with Roosevelt," *Washington Post*, Oct. 12, 1937, 1.

61. "Loyalist Societies Picket Italian, Spanish Embassies," *Washington Post*, Apr. 9, 1939, 9.

62. "Ghosts of Czar's Horses Gallop," *Washington Post*, Nov. 19, 1933, SM3.

63. Kohler and Carlson, *Sixteenth Street Architecture*, Vol. 1, 166.

64. "About the Town with Dudley Harmon," *Washington Post*, Nov. 27, 1938, S7.

65. US Department of Commerce, *Statistical Abstract of the United States*, 1939, Table 878; US Department of Commerce, *Statistical Abstract of the United States*, 1942, Table 958.

66. Compiled from R.L. Polk Company, *Boyd's Directory of the District of Columbia*.

67. "Louis Rouleau, D.C. Architect, Is Dead at 41," *Washington Post*, Feb. 20, 1937, 4.

68. US Department of Commerce, *Statistical Abstract of the United States*, 1947, Table 9; "Continued Gain Noted in Sales of New Houses," *Washington Post*, Dec. 15, 1940, R1.

69. Hart, "Motion Picture Industry from Infancy to Its Prime," 46.

70. "House Sales Maintain Record Pace," *Washington Post*, Nov. 23, 1941, 1.

71. "Soldiers' Home Section Shows Large Growth," *Washington Post*, May 6, 1940, 3.

72. "WPB Cites Dorchester in Priority Case," *Washington Post*, Oct. 30, 1942, B1.

73. "Plan Commission Backs 16th Street Subway," *Washington Post*, Apr. 18, 1940, 30; Howard F. Wentworth, "Second Underpass Started," *Washington Post*, Jan. 24, 1941, 4.

74. "Scott Circle Property Owners Denounce Plans for Underpass," *Washington Post*, Jul. 2, 1940, 15.

75. "Scott Circle Underpass Is Opened," *Washington Post*, Dec. 30, 1941, 21.

76. Davol, "Shifting Mores," 51.

77. Hart, "Motion Picture Industry from Infancy to Its Prime," 35.

78. Davol, "Shifting Mores," 52.

79. "U.S. Buys Meridian Hill Site," *Evening Star*, Sept 5, 1941.

80. "Women's Hotel 'Too De Luxe," *Washington Times-Herald*, Jul. 2, 1942; "Uncle Sam's Nieces Move into Hotel," *Washington Times-Herald*, Jul. 16, 1942.

81. "Meridian Hill Hotel to Reduce Rates," *Evening Star*, Aug. 9, 1942, A39.

82. Anne Hagner, "New Government Girls' Hotel," *Washington Post*, Aug. 13, 1942, 20.

83. Davol, "Shifting Mores," 52.

84. Hart, "Motion Picture Industry from Infancy to Its Prime," 153.

85. "Rooms with Board," *Evening Star*, Apr. 25, 1944, B12, May 24, 1943, B14, and Sep. 21, 1941, E15.

86. James Chinn. "New Code Urged to Curb Crowding," *Evening Star*, Apr. 18, 1941, B1.

87. "5,000 Here Pass Bier of Paderewski," *Washington Post*, Jul. 5, 1941, 11; Carolyn Bell, "Diplomatic Circling," *Washington Post*, Feb. 21, 1943, S2.

88. Hope Ridings Miller, "Capital Whirl," *Washington Post*, Nov. 21, 1941, 16; George Bookman, "President Demands Italy Recall Attaché," *Washington Post*, Apr. 4, 1941, 1.

89. "Unity Stressed at Marconi Celebration," *Washington Post*, Jul. 23, 1941, 9.

90. Anne Hagner, "Embassy Here Minors Defeat of Italians," *Washington Post*, Sep. 9, 1943, 5.

91. Waller, 126–27.

92. Hope Ridings Miller, "Here Are a Few Facts," *Washington Post*, Feb. 5, 1943, A9.

93. George Thorpe, "DC Mansions Glories Depart," *Washington Post*, Apr. 12, 1941, 15.

94. "Building Cut to Have Little Effect Here," *Washington Post*, Apr. 9, 1942, 21.

95. Hart, "Motion Picture Industry from Infancy to Its Prime," 153.

96. Kohler and Carlson, *Sixteenth Street Architecture*, Vol. 2, 125.

97. Kay Ware, "Carlton Hotel's Lounge a Cure for Headaches," *Washington Post*, Nov. 2, 1934, 10; Wirz and Striner, *Washington Deco*, 108.

98. Chanticleer, "Carlton to Open New 'El Patio' Club Tomorrow," *Washington Post*, Sep. 9, 1936, X7.

99. Chanticleer, "Card Rule Bars Vanderbilt, Jr. From El Patio," *Washington Post*, Dec. 18, 1936, X23.

100. Chanticleer, "New Night Spot Will Feature Egyptian Motif," *Washington Post*, Dec. 8, 1937, 16; Chanticleer, "New Orchestra Will Play at the Shar-Zad," *Washington Post*, Dec. 15, 1937, 28.

101. "Ringside Table with Mary Harris," *Washington Post*, Sep. 2, 1940, 12, and Sep. 9, 1940, 11.

102. Mary Harris, "News of Capital Night Clubs," *Washington Post*, Sep. 16, 1938, X16; "Make-Up Tints on Lounge Walls," *Washington Post*, Nov. 25, 1938, X13.

103. "Ringside Table with Mary Harris," *Washington Post*, Feb. 23, 1942, 8.

104. "Ringside Table with Mary Harris." *Washington Post*, Nov. 25, 1940, 6.

105. Robert H. Fetridge, "Along the Highways and Byways of Finance," *New York Times*, Jul. 24, 1949, F3.

106. "Roosevelt Hotel Is Bought by Maria Kramer," *Washington Post*, Oct. 8, 1941, 21.

107. "Ringside Table with Mary Harris," *Washington Post*, Mar. 9, 1942, 17.

108. Peiss, *Zoot Suit*, 60.

109. "Some Congressmen Like Swing," *Washington Post*, Jun. 19, 1942, 13.

110. "Ringside Table with Mary Harris," *Washington Post*, Jan. 6, 1943, B9; "Stars Arrive Today for Birthday Fete," *Washington Post*, Jan. 29, 1943, B1.

111. "Ringside Table with Mary Harris," *Washington Post*, Aug. 11, 1943, 13.

112. Lucia Giddens, "British Y.W.C.A. Aide Tells of Work in Blitz," *Washington Post*, Jun. 7, 1941, 11.

113. "How to Meet Raids Told by One Who Has," *Washington Post*, Dec. 20, 1941, 23.

114. Christine Sadler, "Defense Activities Bring Out Neighborhood Spirit in Capital," *Washington Post*, Apr. 12, 1942, B2.

115. "16th Street Heights Women to Keep Watch during Day," *Washington Post*, Jan. 6, 1942, 21.

116. "Mock Air Raid Drill," *Washington Post*, Oct. 29, 1942, B1.

117. "D.C. Air Raid Warden Service Declared One of Nation's Best," *Washington Post*, Oct. 14, 1942, B1.

118. "Cables to Parents Hint 2 Sons in Navy Were Seized at Guam," *Washington Post*, Jan. 23, 1942, 19.

119. "100 District Men among 16,000 Killed in War," *Washington Post*, Jul. 7, 1943, 11; "Harry M. Hobbins."

120. "5 Area Men Killed, 4 Others Missing," *Washington Post*, Jun. 3, 1944, 3.

121. "Bride's Father Ace in Last War," *Washington Post*, Jul. 27, 1940, 8.

122. "Bomb Attack on D.C. Forecast," *Washington Post*, Feb. 5, 1943, 1.

123. "Memorial: Frederick J. Yeager," *Princeton Alumni Weekly*, Sep. 23, 2009, https://paw .princeton.edu/memorial/frederick-j-yeager-59.

124. "Street of Embassies Now Changing into Great Avenue of Churches," *Evening Star*, Apr. 1, 1924, 13.

125. "16th Street Heights Citizens Seek Better Transportation," *Washington Post*, Nov. 16, 1940, 17.

126. "Architect Tests Gun Then Ends Life," *Evening Star*, May 16, 1932, B1.

127. "Two Workmen Hurt," *Evening Star*, Jun. 5, 1931, 1.

128. Kohler and Carson, *Sixteenth Street Architecture*, Vol. 2, 521; "Washington Chapel," Historic American Buildings Survey DC-539 (2015), 7.

129. Kohler and Carlson, *Sixteenth Street Architecture*, Vol. 2, 525.

130. "Defense Music to be Played at Washington Chapel," *Washington Post*, Sep. 7, 1941, L4.

131. "Washington Chapel," Historic American Buildings Survey DC-539 (2015), 16.

132. US Department of Commerce, *Statistical Abstract of the United States*, 1951, Table 36, 1946 and 1947 totals.

Chapter 6

1. Green, *Washington*, Vol. 2, 488–89.

2. Robert M. Buck, "New Zone for Lower 16th-st nw?" *Washington Daily News*, Jan. 16, 1947; "16th St. Would Be 'White Way,' Opponents of Rezoning Charge," *Washington Post*, Jan. 16, 1947.

3. "Banks and Office Buildings to Be Permitted on 16th St," *Washington Post*, Apr. 23, 1947.

4. "16th St Site Sold to Bakers Union," *Washington Post*, Mar. 11, 1955.

5. Sam Stavisky, "Unions Making Washington Capital of Organized Labor," *Washington Post*, Dec. 29, 1953.

6. "Ike Pays Tribute to Labor," *Washington Post*, May 1, 1955.

7. "Lafayette Closes as Hotel Occupancy in DC Declines," *Washington Post*, Jul. 16, 1971.

8. "Old Plush Apartment to Be Razed for Office, *Evening Star*, Jul. 28, 1957; "New Building Pushed by Chemical Society," *Evening Star*, Oct. 27, 1958; "Proud Luxury Building Giving Way to Wreckers' Torches, Hammers," *Washington Post*, Dec. 11, 1958.

9. "NEA Building Progresses," *Washington Post*, Oct. 24, 1955; "Education Group Buys SAR Building," *Washington Post*, Feb. 17, 1957; "NEA Building Held Symbol of Free Giving," *Evening Star*, Feb. 11, 1959.

10. "3 Aged Sisters in Court Again in 40-Year Fight to Hold Home," *Washington Post*, Jun. 9, 1944; "'Riches to Rags' Is Strange Story of 3 Aged Sisters Facing Taxes Eviction from 16th Street Home," *Evening Star*, Jun. 9, 1944.

11. Thomas Wolfe, "Gordon Hotel's End Mourned," *Washington Post*, Jul. 13, 1959, B6.

12. "D.C. Landmark Is Razed," *Washington Post*, May 23, 1967.

13. Wolf Von Eckardt, "Landmarks Unit to List Areas, Buildings to Save," *Washington Post*, Nov. 2, 1964.

14. Wolf Von Eckardt, "MPA's New Quarters: A Glass Box on Stilts," *Washington Post*, Dec. 9, 1967; "Motion Picture Association Starts Work on New Home," *Evening Star*, Dec. 9, 1967.

15. Gilmore, "District of Columbia Population History."

16. Chalmers M. Roberts, "Downtown Blight in the Nation's Capital," *Washington Post*, Jan. 27, 1952.

17. Charles Robertson and Anne Sellin, interview with the authors, Feb. 15, 2020.

18. "Georgia Douglas Johnson, Noted Poet, Author Dies," *Baltimore Afro-American*, May 28, 1966.

19. Kimberly Prothro Williams, *Strivers' Section Historic District*.

20. "Apartment Building Offered for Co-op Sale without Racial Bar," *Evening Star*, Mar. 4, 1949; DC Historic Preservation Office, "Civil Rights Tour."

21. Jacqueline Trescott, "The Once and Present Chastleton," *Washington Post*, May 3, 1977.

22. Gilbert, *Ten Blocks from the White House*, 44ff.

23. Jaffe and Sherwood, *Dream City*, 52–60; Barras, *The Last of the Black Emperors*, 123–25.

24. Barry Kalb and Woody West, "Pride's Changing Face," *Evening Star*, Nov. 26, 1967.

25. Pearlman, *Democracy's Capital*, 42; Eugene Robinson and Laura A. Kiernan, "Youth Pride Shuts Down, Cites U.S. Funds Cutoff," *Washington Post*, Aug. 12, 1981.

26. Robert L. Asher, "Nixon Labels D.C. a 'Crime Capital,' Blames Johnson," *Washington Post*, Jun. 23, 1968.

27. William Willoughby, "Area Churches Learning of Crime by Experience," *Evening Star*, May 17, 1970.

28. "War Protest in Varied Forms Marks Final Rites of Hanukah," *Evening Star*, Dec. 12, 1969.

29. Marjorie Hyer, "Communion Celebrated by Woman," *Washington Post*, Nov. 11, 1974.

30. The land was donated to a newly established corporation made up of representatives of the church and other housing groups, with the church maintaining less than 50 percent control. Betty Medsger, "Church Donates Property," *Washington Post*, Apr. 27, 1970.

31. Robert J. Lewis, "The Roosevelt: Quiet amidst Hustle and Bustle," *Evening Star*, Mar. 12, 1969.

32. Asch and Musgrove, *Chocolate City*, 366–70. A retrospective exhibit on the Pilot District Project, produced by the National Building Museum in collaboration with the Historical Society of Washington, DC, was held at the Building Museum in 2018 and 2019. See "The Pilot District Project, 1968–1973," National Building Museum, accessed Aug. 10, 2019, https://www.nbm.org/exhibition/pilot-district/.

33. Pearlman, *Democracy's Capital*, 171–76.

34. Peter Braestrup, "Pilot Police Project Seen as a Fraud," *Washington Post*, Sep. 10, 1969.

35. Louise Lague, "Police-Community Test Called Flop," *Washington Daily News*, Jul. 3, 1972.

36. Clem, *Meridian Hill Park*, 109–11.

37. Mary McLeod Bethune, "Meridian Hill Park Is Move toward Democracy in Capital," *Chicago Defender*, Jul. 9, 1949.

38. *Washington Post*, Aug. 20, 1967, A3.

39. Roberta Hornig, "Two 'Pearls' Toss Gem of a Party for 20,000," *Evening Star*, Jul. 15, 1968.

40. Hornig.

41. Clem, *Meridian Hill Park*, 120.

42. "12,000 Blacks March to Support Africa," *Washington Post*, May 28, 1972.

43. "Meridian Hill Park Lives Again," *Washington Post*, May 15, 1976.

44. John Kelly, "Where, Oh Where Is Meridian Hill Park's Armillary Sphere?," *Washington Post*, Jun. 14, 2013.

45. Linda Wheeler, "Dark Side of a Park," *Washington Post*, Aug. 30, 1981, B1.

46. Linda Wheeler, "Reclaiming Park's Lost Glamor," *Washington Post*, Mar. 29, 1990.

47. Linda Wheeler, "President Stops to Smell the Flowers," *Washington Post*, Apr. 22, 1994.

48. Olivia Cadaval, "The Latino Community: Creating an Identity in the Nation's Capital," in Cary, *Urban Odyssey*, 231–49; Asch and Musgrove, *Chocolate City*, 370–76.

49. "Barney House Location Wins Official Approval," *Washington Post*, Mar. 28, 1962.

50. Repak, *Waiting on Washington*, 63–64.

51. Ernest Holsendolph, "Bright New Junior High Is No Model School Yet," *Evening Star*, Sep. 29, 1967; Willard Clopton, Jr., "Model School Has Rocky Debut," *Washington Post*, Oct. 7, 1967.

52. See, for example, Lawrence Feinberg, "Schools Losing in War against Vandals, Decay," *Washington Post*, Feb. 6, 1977.

53. Aaron Ruvinsky, "'Project Commitment' Is Off to a Good Start," *Evening Star*, Mar. 22, 1969.

54. Elizabeth Roach, "Told to Leave, They Settled In to Win Control," *Evening Star*, Feb. 15, 1978.

55. Juan Williams, "Antioch Law School Seeks to Shed Landlord Role," *Washington Post*, Aug. 26, 1977.

56. Walterene Swanston, "Kenesaw Apartments Sold to Private Developer," *Washington Post*, Nov. 3, 1977.

57. Christopher Dickey, "'This Must Be Dream Come True,'" *Washington Post*, Jun. 9, 1978; Elizabeth Roach, "Tenants Succeed in Buying Their Building from Antioch," *Evening Star*, Jun. 9, 1978.

58. The 1980 Tenant Opportunity to Purchase Act, intended to forestall gentrification, gave DC tenants the right to purchase their building if the landlord intended to sell the property. The Kenesaw cooperative was one of the first to take advantage of the law.

59. Anne Chase, "Low-Income Tenants Buy Mt. Pleasant Building," *Washington Post*, Oct. 11, 1984. As of 2020, at least fourteen of the original cooperative owners remained in their units. See Amanda Michelle Gomez, "Replacing Decorative Balconies at This Historic Building Could Displace Low-Income Washingtonians," *Washington City Paper*, Dec. 10, 2020.

60. "Richman Towers Accepts Applications," *Washington Post*, Mar. 14, 1954.

61. "Open on 16th Street," *Washington Post*, Aug. 21, 1965, E14.

62. "Oakcrest Estate on 16th Street Is Purchased," *Evening Star*, Jun. 21, 1924.

63. Paul M. Herron, "The Luxurious Woodner Doffs Its Wraps Today," *Washington Post*, Oct. 21, 1951.

64. "Police Find $6,500 in Apartment," *Washington Post*, Jun. 26, 1953; "Two Seized in Raid on Fashionable Hotel Face Lottery Charge," *Evening Star*, Jun. 26, 1953.

65. See, for example: "FHA Basis For Woodner Loan Related," *Washington Post*, Jul. 2, 1954; "Suit Seeks to Ban Woodner as Hotel," *Washington Post*, Jul. 12, 1955; "Ian

Woodner Indicted in FHA Inquiry," *Washington Post*, Mar. 30, 1956; "Woodner Acquitted of Falsifying FHA Statement for Loan Insurance," *Washington Post*, Jan. 30, 1957; "FHA, Woodner Clash over Building's Status," *Washington Post*, Nov. 21, 1957.

66. "Harry Poretsky Area Developer and Builder," *Evening Star*, Dec. 12, 1966.

67. "Residents Fight Apartments on 16th Street," *Evening Star*, Oct. 8, 1941.

68. "District Committee Favors Purchase of 16th Street Corner," *Evening Star*, Feb. 11, 1945.

69. For a full chronology of the fight over the Crestwood Apartments, see Swerdloff, *Crestwood*, 93–94.

70. Conrad P. Harness, "Two Luxury Apartments Here to Cost $12 Million," *Washington Post*, Feb. 4, 1950.

71. Juan Williams, "Morris Pollin, Builder, District Philanthropist," *Washington Post*, Dec. 18, 1977; Jack Mann, "Abe Pollin Builds Baghdad on the Beltway," *Evening Star*, Nov. 12, 1978.

72. "$3.3 Million Apartment Started," *Washington Post*, May 13, 1956.

73. Dorothy McCardle, "16th Street Urban Evolution: Embassies for Sale or Rent," *Washington Post*, Jul. 29, 1973.

74. Katharine M. Brooks, "Looking Back at Embassy Row," *Evening Star*, Dec. 1, 1968.

75. Dorothy McCardle, "Italy Looking for a New, Well-Lighted Embassy," *Washington Post*, Apr. 19, 1970; "Italy: New Embassy," *Washington Post*, Mar. 16, 1972; "Egidio Ortona: Wild Dogs And Diplomats," *Washington Post*, Jan. 7, 1973.

76. McCardle, "Italy Looking for a New, Well-Lighted Embassy."

77. Scott and Lee, *Buildings of the District of Columbia*, 352; Francesca McKenney, "First Social Event Held at New French Embassy," *Washington Post*, Feb. 10, 1936.

78. "Divine Science School Set for Monday Opening," *Washington Post*, Oct. 12, 1946.

79. Elizabeth Maguire, "Embassy Diffuses Hospitality," *Washington Post*, Apr. 9, 1950.

80. Elizabeth Maguire, "Honduran Envoy Never Underestimates a Woman," *Washington Post*, Jul. 20, 1950.

81. "Key Compromise at the Ugandan Chancery," *Washington Post*, Apr. 12, 1979.

82. Kenneth Dole, "Gunton Temple Stays On in Flight of Churches," *Washington Post*, Feb. 23, 1957.

83. Cherkasky, *Village in the City*.

84. Paul Delaney, "Whites Ejected Again at Black Front Meeting," *Evening Star*, Aug. 2, 1968.

85. Marjorie Hyer, "Central Presbyterian Church Holds Last Worship Service," *Washington Post*, Jan. 1, 1973.

86. Normal Kahl, "Center Helps Latins Adjust to City," *Evening Star*, Jul. 17, 1971.

87. Alison Muscatine, "'Centro Wilson' Hispanic Center Is for Sale," *Evening Star*, Nov. 2, 1979.

88. William Willoughby, "Not All D.C. Mormons Want to Pull Up Stakes," *Evening Star*, Aug. 28, 1975.

89. Marjorie Hyer, "Mormons Closing City Church," *Washington Post*, Aug. 28, 1975.

90. Kohler and Carson, *Sixteenth Street Architecture*, Vol. 2, 522–43.

91. "History of All Souls."

92. For a discussion of Reeb's contributions to All Souls Church, see Staples, *Washington Unitarianism*, 147–50.

93. Rusty Hassan, "Jazz Radio in Washington, DC," in Jackson and Ruble, *DC Jazz*, 100–101.

94. Pearlman, *Democracy's Capital*, 169; Bart Barnes, "David H. Eaton, Former D.C. School Board President, Dies at 59," *Washington Post*, Oct. 22, 1992.

95. Irna Moore, "Six Churches Care for 450," *Washington Post*, May 13, 1968.

96. "New Church for Upper 16th Street," *Washington Post*, Apr. 7, 1952.

97. Marjorie Hyer, "Buddhists Pray on 16th St.," *Washington Post*, Dec. 9, 1974; O'Conor, *Stopping By*, 125–31.

98. Constance D'au Vin, "Buddhists Feel Vietnamese Impact," *Washington Post*, May 26, 1978; Marianne Bernhard, "Thousands of Area Vietnamese Celebrate Buddha's Birthday," *Washington Post*, May 12, 1979; O'Conor, *Stopping By*, 169–76.

99. O'Conor, *Stopping By*, 227–30.

100. "Ethical Society's New Building Set for Dedication, Open House Sunday," *Washington Post*, Apr. 2, 1966.

101. Haynes Johnson, "Wealthy Elite Build Class Walls within Their Own Race," *Evening Star*, May 25, 1961.

102. Neil A. Lewis, "The Shifting 'Gold Coast,'" *New York Times*, May 19, 1985.

103. LaBarbara Bowman, "Tucker Virtually Unnoticed in His 16th Street Neighborhood," *Washington Post*, Sep. 7, 1978.

104. Paul Herron, "The Disappearing Act No Longer Begins at $50,000," *Washington Post*, Mar. 6, 1955.

105. Juan Williams, "The Hallmark Neighborhood for Washington's Blacks," *Washington Post*, Nov. 21, 1982; Fitzpatrick and Goodwin, *The Guide to Black Washington*, 186–87.

106. Courtland Milloy, "Partying on Platinum Coast," *Washington Post*, Aug. 6, 1978.

107. Clarke, *History of the Nineteenth-Century Black Churches*, 113–15.

108. "Dedication Rites Slated on Sunday for Zion Baptist," *Washington Post*, Sep. 22, 1962.

109. Clarke, *History of the Nineteenth-Century Black Churches*, 91–92; Fitzpatrick and Goodwin, *The Guide to Black Washington*, 184–85.

110. LaBarbara Bowman, "Nineteenth St. Church Is Sold for $850,000," *Washington Post*, Jun. 4, 1974.

111. Janis Johnson, "Congregation Leaves Historic Church," *Washington Post*, Jan. 27, 1975.

112. Paul Delaney, "Rival Leader Tells of Efforts to Convert Black Muslims," *New York Times*, Jan. 31, 1973.

113. Paul Delaney, "Survivor Tells How 7 Moslems Died in Washington," *New York Times*, Jan. 25, 1973.

114. "Muslim Case Details Are Told," *Washington Star-News*, Jan. 25, 1973.

115. Alfred E. Lewis and Timothy S. Robinson, "Seven 'Executed' in District's Biggest Mass Murder," *Washington Post*, Jan. 19, 1973; "Slayers of 7 Hunted in Muslim 'Execution,'" *Washington Star-News*, Jan. 19, 1973.

116. Cynthia Gorney, "Reclusive Hanafis Still Mystery to Neighbors," *Washington Post*, Mar. 13, 1977.

117. Lawrence Meyer, "Trail of Clues Traced at Hanafi Trial," *Washington Post*, Mar. 7, 1974; Eugene L. Meyer, "Hanafi Slayer Sentenced to 140 Years," *Washington Post*, Jan. 7, 1975.

118. Asch and Musgrove, *Chocolate City*, 385.

119. "B'nai Israel to Lay Cornerstone Sept. 16," *Washington Post*, Sep. 8, 1951.

120. "Half of Area's Jewish Residents Now Live in Montgomery," *Washington Post*, May 18, 1969.

121. Bill Peterson, "The Jews: Migrating From D.C.," *Washington Post*, Sep. 4, 1975.

122. "Synagogue That Grew from $35 Opens Today," *Washington Post*, Sep. 25, 1921.

123. "Two Synagogue Dedications Set," *Washington Post*, Sep. 13, 1957.

124. "Tifereth Israel Group Lauded by President," *Evening Star*, Sep. 16, 1957.

125. Phil Shandler, "Congregation Asked: Was Move to Suburbia Necessary?," *Evening Star*, Sep. 13, 1969; Schiavo, "Tifereth Israel Celebrates Centennial."

126. Asch and Musgrove, *Chocolate City*, 326; Kathryn Schneider Smith, *Washington at Home*, 457, "NW Group Protests Harassment to Sell," *Washington Post*, Dec. 3, 1961.

127. "Block Plan Revealed by 'Neighbors,'" *Washington Post*, Oct. 31, 1960.

128. Asch and Musgrove, *Chocolate City*, 328.

129. Stephen S. Rosenfield, "Interracial Group Tries to Make Living Easier in Changing NW Neighborhood," *Washington Post*, Jan. 28, 1962.

130. Haynes Johnson, "Neighbors, Inc.: The Story of an Effort to Build an Integrated Community," *Evening Star*, Jan. 13, 1965.

131. Asch and Musgrove, *Chocolate City*, 329.

132. Haynes Johnson, "Neighbors, Inc."

133. Olmsted Brothers, *Rock Creek Park*, 12.

134. Alpha Corporation and Quinn Evans Architects, *Historic Structure Report*, 16–17.

135. "Sesqui Theater in Rock Creek Park to Cost $200,000," *Evening Star*, Apr. 10, 1949.

136. Alpha Corporation and Quinn Evans Architects, *Historic Structure Report*, 21.

137. "Crews Putting Final Touches on 16-Acre Amphitheater," *Evening Star*, Jul. 19, 1950.

138. Jacqueline Trescott, "Top-40 Soul after 20 Years," *Washington Star-News*, Aug. 19, 1973.

139. Jacqueline Trescott and Tom Zito, "Carter Barron's New Look," *Washington Post*, Sep. 18, 1975.

Epilogue

1. US Census Bureau, "District of Columbia," *Quickfacts*, June 1, 2018, https://www.census.gov/quickfacts/DC; US Department of Commerce, *Statistical Abstract of the United States*, 1943, Table 8.

2. Katherine Shaver, "D.C. Has the Highest 'Intensity' of Gentrification," *Washington Post*, Mar. 19, 2019, https://www.washingtonpost.com/transportation/2019/03/19/study-dc-has-had-highest-intensity-gentrification-any-us-city/.

3. "History and Explanation of Gentrification."

4. Jeff Burbank, "Venerable Envoy Is Home at Last," *Washington Post*, Mar. 28, 1985, 10.

5. Real estate advertisement, *Washington Post*, May 26, 1979, E8.

6. Burbank, "Venerable Envoy Is Home at Last."

7. J. J. McCoy, "The History Just Adds to the Mix," *Washington Post*, Jan. 15, 2000, H1.

8. Lee Hockstader, "D.C. Settlement a Milestone," *Washington Post*, Oct. 31, 1988, E1.

9. See Logan, *Historic Capital*, for a history of preservation efforts in Washington, DC.

10. Logan, *Historic Capital*, 144–52.

11. Logan, 144–52.

12. DC National Capital Planning Commission Historic Preservation Office, "Sixteenth Street Historic District" (unpublished National Register Listing Form, 1978); Joann Stevens, "D.C. Sites Added to Historic Register," *Washington Post*, Nov. 2, 1978, DC8.

13. "Homes on Castle Site Sell for Near Palatial Price," *Washington Post*, Sep. 25, 1976, D1.

14. Richard Corrigan, "9 Picket to Save Rowhouses," *Washington Post*, Oct. 3, 1965, A3.

15. Barbara Ruben, "The View from the Top," *Washington Post*, May 26, 2001, 1.

16. Sandra Fleishman, "Big Squeeze Play on 16th Street," *Washington Post*, Feb. 16, 2002, H1B.

17. Ruben Casteneda, "Community Center Finds You Can Go Home Again," *Washington Post*, Jan. 16, 1997, DC1.

18. Elizabeth Wiener, "Houses of Worship," *Washington Post*, May 21, 1992, DC1.

19. Wolf Von Eckardt, "New Church Design," *Washington Post*, Nov. 28, 1970, B1.

20. District of Columbia Historic Preservation Review Board, Historic Landmark Designation Case No. 91-05.

21. "Third Church."

22. Committee of 100 on the Federal City and DC Preservation League, *Proposed Findings of Fact*, 13.

23. District of Columbia Historic Preservation Review Board, Historic Landmark Designation Case No. 91-05.

24. Tregoning, *Mayor's Agent for Historic Preservation Order*, 2.

25. Callcott, *DC Historic Preservation Office Staff Report*.

Bibliography

Adams, Charles Francis, ed. *Memoirs of John Quincy Adams, Comprising Portions of His Diary from 1795 to 1848*. Vol. 8. Philadelphia: J.B. Lippincott, 1876.

"Administrative History—Success." Rock Creek Park District of Columbia, National Park Service. https://www.nps.gov/rocr/learn/historyculture/adhi1b.htm.

Alpha Corporation and Quinn Evans Architects. *Historic Structure Report: Carter Barron Amphitheater and Box Office*. Vol. 1. Washington, DC: National Park Service, 2018.

Altshuler, David, ed. *The Jews of Washington, D.C.: A Communal History Anthology*. Chappaqua, NY: Rossel, 1985.

Apelbaum, Laura Cohen, and Wendy Turman, eds. *Jewish Washington: Scrapbook of an American Community*. Washington, DC: Jewish Historical Society of Greater Washington, 2007.

Applewhite, E.J. *Washington Itself: An Informal Guide to the Capital of the United States*. New York: Alfred A. Knopf, 1981.

Arnebeck, Bob. *Through a Fiery Trial: Building Washington, 1790–1800*. Lanham, MD: Madison, 1991.

Asch, Chris Myers, and George Derek Musgrove. *Chocolate City: A History of Race and Democracy in the Nation's Capital*. Chapel Hill: University of North Carolina Press, 2017.

Aument, Lori. "Construction History in Architectural Conservation: The Exposed Aggregate, Reinforced Concrete of Meridian Hill Park." *Journal of the American Institute for Conservation* 42, no. 1 (Spring 2003): 3–19.

Babin, Patricia. *Links to the Past*. Washington, DC: Government Printing Office, 2018.

Baker, Jean H. *Building America: The Life of Benjamin Henry Latrobe*. New York: Oxford University Press, 2020.

Barnard, Job. "History of the Church of the New Jerusalem in the City of Washington." In *Records of the Columbia Historical Society*, Vol. 24. Washington, DC: Columbia Historical Society, 1922.

Barras, Jonetta Rose. *The Last of the Black Emperors: The Hollow Comeback of Marion Barry in the New Age of Black Leaders*. Baltimore: Bancroft, 1998.

Bates, Barbara D. "Remembering the Great War in the Washington D.C. Area through Its Memorials and Monuments." Washington, DC: Association of Oldest Inhabitants, 2018.

Batesel, Paul. *Players and Teams of the National Association, 1871–1875.* Jefferson, NC: McFarland, 2012.

Bedford, Steven McLeod. *John Russell Pope, Architect of Empire.* New York: Rizzoli International, 1998.

Bednar, Michael. *L'Enfant's Legacy: Public Open Spaces in Washington, D.C.* Baltimore: Johns Hopkins University Press, 2006.

Benson, Michael. *Ballparks of North America: A Comprehensive Historical Reference to Baseball Grounds, Yards, and Stadiums, 1845 to Present.* Jefferson, NC: McFarland, 1989.

Berg, Scott W. *Grand Avenues: The Story of the French Visionary Who Designed Washington, D.C.* New York: Pantheon, 2007.

Berk, Sally Lichtenstein. "The Richest Crop: The Rowhouses of Harry Wardman (1872–1938), Washington, D.C. Developer." M.A. Thesis, George Washington University, May 7, 1989.

Blackman, Ann. *Wild Rose: Rose O'Neale Greenhow, Civil War Spy.* New York: Random House, 2005.

Bowling, Kenneth R. *Peter Charles L'Enfant: Vision, Honor and Male Friendship in the Early American Republic.* Washington, DC: Friends of the George Washington University Libraries, 2002.

Brain, David. "Discipline and Style: The Ecole des Beaux-Arts and the Social Production of an American Architecture." *Theory and Society* 18, no. 6 (Nov. 1989): 807–68.

Brown, Glenn, ed. *Papers relating to the Improvement of the City of Washington, District of Columbia.* Washington, DC: Government Printing Office, 1901.

Brown, Letitia Woods. *Free Negroes in the District of Columbia, 1790–1846.* New York: Oxford University Press, 1972.

Brudnick, Ida A., and Paul E. Dwyer. "Salaries of Members of Congress: Recent Actions and Historical Tables." Congressional Research Service, Library of Congress, November 26, 2018. Accessed on March 25, 2021. https://fraser.stlouisfed.org/title/5996.

Bryan, Wilhemus Bogart. *A History of the National Capital, From Its Foundation through the Period of the Adoption of the Organic Act.* Vols. 1 and 2. New York: Macmillan, 1914.

Bushong, William. *Rock Creek Park Historic District Nomination.* 1991. https://planning.dc.gov/sites/default/files/dc/sites/op/publication/attachments/Rock%20Creek%20Park%20HD%20nom.pdf.

Bushong, William, Judith Helm Robinson, and Julie Mueller. *A Centennial History of the Washington Chapter, The American Institute of Architects, 1887–1987.* Washington, DC: Washington Architectural Foundation Press, 1987.

Caemmerer, H. Paul. *A Manual on the Origin and Development of Washington.* Washington, DC: US Government Printing Office, 1939.

Calbert, Madlyn W., ed. *From Strength to Strength: A History of Shiloh Baptist Church, 1863–1988.* Washington, DC: Shiloh Baptist Church, 1989.

Calkin, Homer L. *Castings from the Foundry Mold: A History of Foundry Church Washington, D.C., 1814–1964.* Nashville: Parthenon, 1968.

Callcott, Steve. *DC Historic Preservation Office Staff Report, 1108 16th Street NW.* DC HPO 14-638, Oct. 23, 2014. https://planning.dc.gov/sites/default/files/dc/sites/op /publication/attachments/Sixteenth%20Street%20HD%201108%2016th %20Street%20NW%20HPA%2014%20638.pdf.

Carpenter, Frank G. *Carp's Washington.* Edited by Frances Carpenter. New York: McGraw-Hill, 1960.

Carson, Jeffrey R., Lynda L. Smith, and J. L. Sibley Jennings Jr. *Massachusetts Avenue Architecture.* Vol. 1. Washington, DC: US Commission of Fine Arts, 1973.

———. *Massachusetts Avenue Architecture.* Vol. 2. Washington, DC: US Commission of Fine Arts, 1975.

Carter, Edward C. "Benjamin Henry Latrobe and the Growth and Development of Washington, 1798–1818." In *Records of the Columbia Historical Society,* Vol. 48, 1971–72. Washington, DC: Columbia Historical Society, 1973.

Cary, Francine Curro, ed. *Urban Odyssey: A Multicultural History of Washington, D.C.* Washington, DC: Smithsonian Institution Press, 1996.

Cater, Harold, ed. *Henry Adams and His Friends.* New York, Boston: Houghton Mifflin, 1947.

Cherkasky, Mara. *Mount Pleasant.* Charleston, SC: Arcadia, 2007.

———. *Village in the City: Mount Pleasant Heritage Trail.* Washington, DC: Cultural Tourism DC, 2006.

Clark, James. "The Horseless Age." *Missouri State Board of Agriculture Monthly Bulletin* 15–16 (1917): 26–27.

Clarke, Nina Honemond. *History of the Nineteenth-Century Black Churches in Maryland and Washington, D.C.* Silver Spring, MD: Bartleby, 1987.

Clark-Lewis, Elizabeth, ed. *First Freed: Washington, D.C., in the Emancipation Era.* Washington, DC: Howard University Press, 2002.

Clem, Fiona J. *Meridian Hill Park.* Charleston, SC: Arcadia, 2017.

Committee of 100 on the Federal City and DC Preservation League. *Proposed Findings of Fact Filed on Behalf of the DC Preservation League and the Committee of 100.* HPA 08-141, 2013. https://committeeof100.net/download/2009%20Proposed%20Findings%20 of%20Fact%20Third%20Church%20of%20Christ%20Scientist.pdf.

Conley, Rory T. *The Truth in Charity: A History of The Archdiocese of Washington.* Strasbourg, France: Éditions du Signe, 2000.

Coolidge, Charles A. "Herbert Langford Warren." *Proceedings of the American Academy of Arts and Sciences* 68, no. 13 (Dec. 1933): 689–91.

Costanzo, Adam. *George Washington's Washington: Visions for the National Capital in the Early American Republic.* Athens: University of Georgia Press, 2018.

Cousino, Meghan Barrett. "Charles Bernstein." *National Register of Exonerations.* https:// www.law.umich.edu/special/exoneration/Pages/casedetailpre1989.aspx?caseid=16.

Cromwell, John W. "The First Negro Churches in the District of Columbia." *Journal of Negro History* 7, no. 1 (Jan. 1922): 64–106.

Daniels, Jonathan. *Washington Quadrille: The Dance beside the Documents.* Garden City, NY: Doubleday, 1968.

Davol, Leslie T. "Shifting Mores: Esther Bubley's World War II Boarding House Photos." *Washington History* 10, no. 2 (Fall/Winter 1998/1999): 44–62.

DC Historic Preservation Office. "Civil Rights Tour: Housing—Equitable Realty, Opening Neighborhoods." *DC Historic Sites*. Accessed March 27, 2019. https://historicsites.dcpreservation.org/items/show/1002.

DeFerrari, John. *Capital Streetcars: Early Mass Transit in Washington, D.C.* Charleston, SC: The History Press, 2015.

Department of Highways. *Washington's Bridges: Historic and Modern.* Washington, DC: Commissioners of the District of Columbia, 1956.

District of Columbia Historic Preservation Review Board. Historic Landmark Designation Case No. 91-05: Third Church of Christ, Scientist and the Christian Science Monitor Building. December 6, 2007. http://committeeof100.net/download/historic_preservation/third_church_of_christ,_scientist/Third_Church_Landmark_Decision.pdf.

Eberlein, Harold Donaldson, and Cortlandt Van Dyke Hubbard. *Historic Houses of George-Town and Washington City.* Richmond: Dietz, 1958.

Einberger, Scott. *A History of Rock Creek Park: Wilderness and Washington, D.C.* Charleston, SC: The History Press, 2014.

Elkins, Stanley, and Eric McKitrick. *The Age of Federalism: The Early American Republic, 1788–1800.* New York: Oxford University Press, 1993.

Ellicott, Andrew. "Plan of the City of Washington in the Territory of Columbia." Perth, Scotland, 1792. Library of Congress. http://hdl.loc.gov/loc.gmd/g3850.ct004179.

Federal Writers' Project. *Washington: City and Capital.* Washington, DC: US Government Printing Office, 1937.

Field, Cynthia R., Isabelle Gournay, and Thomas P. Somma, eds. *Paris on the Potomac: The French Influence on the Architecture and Art of Washington, D.C.* Athens: Ohio University Press, 2007.

Fifty Glimpses of Washington and Its Neighborhood: Reproduced from Recent Photographs. Chicago: Rand McNally, 1896.

Fitzpatrick, Sandra, and Maria R. Goodwin. *The Guide to Black Washington: Places and Events of Historical and Cultural Significance in the Nation's Capital.* Revised ed. New York: Hippocrene Books, 2001.

Fogelsong, Richard. *Planning the Capitalist City.* Princeton: Princeton University Press, 1986.

Fogle, Jeanne. *Proximity to Power: Neighbors to the Presidents near Lafayette Square.* Washington, DC: Tour de Force, 1999.

Foote, Eunice. "Circumstances affecting the Heat of the Sun's Rays." *American Journal of Science and Arts* 22 (Nov. 1856): 382–83.

"Founding Fathers: Thomas S. Huntley." Huntley History: Local History Archives from the Huntley Area Public Library. https://lh.huntleylibrary.org/founding-fathers-thomas-s-huntley/.

Francis, Lydia. "BLOCK 8: From Emancipation to Condemnation, The Untold Story of the Residents of Meridian Hill before the Park." Undergraduate thesis, History Department, George Washington University, Washington, DC, 2017.

Friedlander, Marc. "Henry Hobson Richardson, Henry Adams, and John Hay." In *Proceedings of the Massachusetts Historical Society, Third Series, Vol. 81*, 137–66. Boston: Massachusetts Historical Society, 1969.

Garfinkle, Martin. *The Jewish Community of Washington, D.C.* Charleston, SC: Arcadia, 2005.

Gatewood, Willard B. *Aristocrats of Color: The Black Elite, 1880–1920.* Bloomington: Indiana University Press, 1990.

———. "John Francis Cook, Antebellum Black Presbyterian." *American Presbyterians* 67, no. 3 (1989): 221–29. http://www.jstor.org/stable/23330899.

Gilbert, Ben W. *Ten Blocks from the White House: Anatomy of the Washington Riots of 1968.* New York: Frederick A. Praeger, 1968.

Gillette, Howard, Jr. *Between Justice and Beauty: Race, Planning, and the Failure of Urban Policy in Washington, D.C.* Baltimore: Johns Hopkins University Press, 1995.

———, ed. *Southern City, National Ambition: The Growth of Early Washington, D.C., 1800–1860.* Washington, DC: George Washington University Center for Washington Area Studies, 1995.

Gilmore, Matthew B. "District of Columbia Population History." *Washington DC History Resources* (blog). Accessed April 2, 2020. https://matthewbgilmore.wordpress.com/district-of-columbia-population-history/.

Goode, James M. *Best Addresses: A Century of Washington's Distinguished Apartment Houses.* Washington, DC: Smithsonian Institution Press, 1988.

———. *Capital Houses: Historic Residences of Washington, D.C., and Its Environs, 1735–1965.* New York: Acanthus Press, 2015.

———. *Capital Losses: A Cultural History of Washington's Destroyed Buildings.* 2nd ed. Washington, DC: Smithsonian Books, 2003.

———. *Washington Sculpture: A Cultural History of Outdoor Sculpture in the Nation's Capital.* Baltimore: Johns Hopkins University Press, 2008.

Goodell, Robert C., and P. A. M. Taylor. "A German Immigrant in the Union Army: Selected Letters of Valentin Bechler." *Journal of American Studies* 4, no. 2 (Feb. 1971): 145–62.

Grahek, Mike. "Clark Griffith." Society for American Baseball Research. https://sabr.org/bioproj/person/clark-griffith/.

Grant, U. S. *The Papers of Ulysses S. Grant (1876).* Washington, DC: Smithsonian Institution Press, 2005.

Green, Constance McLaughlin. *The Church on Lafayette Square: A History of St. John's Church, Washington, D.C., 1815–1970.* Washington, DC: Potomac, 1970.

———. *The Secret City: A History of Race Relations in the Nation's Capital.* Princeton, NJ: Princeton University Press, 1967.

———. *Washington: A History of the Capital, 1800–1950.* Vols. 1 and 2. Princeton, NJ: Princeton University Press, 1962.

Greene, F. V., and William Bruff. *City of Washington, Statistical Maps.* Washington, DC: Commissioners, 1880. https://www.loc.gov/item/90685625/.

Grimmett, Richard F. *St. John's Church, Lafayette Square: The History and Heritage of the Church of the Presidents, Washington, DC.* Minneapolis: Mill City Press, 2009.

Gueli, Cindy. *Lipstick Brigade: The Untold True Story of Washington's World War II Government Girls.* Washington, DC: Tahoga History Press, 2015.

Guide to Washington, DC. Chicago: Rand McNally, 1904.

Gutheim, Frederick, and Antoinette J. Lee. *Worthy of the Nation: Washington, DC, from L'Enfant to the National Capital Planning Commission.* 2nd ed. Baltimore: Johns Hopkins University Press, 2006.

Hagner, Alexander B. "History and Reminiscences of St. John's Church, Washington, D.C." In *Records of the Columbia Historical Society,* Vol. 12. Washington, DC: Columbia Historical Society, 1909.

Harmon, Artemas C. "Historical Map of the City of Washington in the Year 1801–1802." Washington, DC, 1931. Library of Congress. http://hdl.loc.gov/loc.gmd/g3850.ct004387.

Harrison, Robert. *Washington during Civil War and Reconstruction: Race and Radicalism.* New York: Cambridge University Press, 2011.

"Harry M. Hobbins." Fold3. https://www.fold3.com/page/529897901-harry-m-hobbins-jr.

Henderson, Mary F. *Remarks about Management of Washington in General and Sixteenth Street in Particular.* Private printing, 1927.

———. *The Aristocracy of Health: A Study of the Physical Culture, Our Favorite Poisons, and a National and International League for the Advancement of Physical Culture.* Washington, DC: Colton, 1904.

Highsmith, Carol M., and Ted Landphair. *Embassies of Washington.* Washington, DC: Preservation Press, 1992.

Hinman, Ida. *The Washington Sketch Book: A Society Souvenir.* Washington, DC: Hartman & Cadick, 1895.

Hinton, John Howard. *The History and Topography of the United States of North America, Brought Down from the Earliest Period.* Vol. 2. 3rd ed. Boston: Samuel Walker, 1852.

"History and Explanation of Gentrification." *Gentrification.* https://sites.google.com/site/gg2wpdermotmitchell/history-and-explanation-of-gentrification.

"History of All Souls." All Souls Church Unitarian. Accessed August 5, 2019. http://www.all-souls.org/history.

Holland, Jesse J. *Black Men Built the Capitol.* Guilford, CT: Globe Pequot, 2007.

Hovey, Lonnie J. *Lafayette Square.* Charleston, SC: Arcadia, 2014.

Hutchins, Stilson, and Joseph West Moore. *The National Capital, Past and Present.* Washington, DC: Post Publishing Company, 1885.

Jackson, Kenneth T. *Crabgrass Frontier: The Suburbanization of the United States.* New York: Oxford University Press, 1985.

Jackson, Maurice. "Great Black Music and the Desegregation of Washington, D.C." *Washington History* 26, no. 1 (2014): 12–35.

Jackson, Maurice, and Blair A. Ruble, eds. *DC Jazz: Stories of Jazz Music in Washington, DC.* Washington, DC: Georgetown University Press, 2018.

Jacob, Katherine. *Testimony to Union.* Baltimore: Johns Hopkins University Press, 1998.

Jacob, Kathryn Allamong. *Capital Elites: High Society in Washington, D.C., after the Civil War.* Washington, DC: Smithsonian Institution Press, 1995.

Jaffe, Harry S., and Tom Sherwood. *Dream City: Race, Power, and the Decline of Washington, D.C.* New York: Simon and Schuster, 1994.

James, Henry. *The American Scene.* London: George Bell & Son, 1907.

Johnson, Lorenzo D. *The Churches and Pastors of Washington, D.C.* New York: M. W. Dodd, 1857.

Jones, Marvin. "Oral Histories from the Gold Coast and the Upper 16th Street Communities." *DC Digital Museum.* Accessed July 1, 2019. https://wdchumanities.org /dcdm/items/show/1741.

Jones, William Henry. *The Housing of Negroes in Washington, D.C.: A Study in Human Ecology.* Washington, DC: Howard University Press, 1929.

Junior League of Washington. *The City of Washington: An Illustrated History.* Washington, DC, 1977. Reprint, New York: Wings, 1992.

Kayser, Elmer Louis. *Bricks without Straw: The Evolution of George Washington University.* New York: Appleton-Century-Crofts, 1970.

Kerr, Jon. *Calvin: Baseball's Last Dinosaur.* Minneapolis: Wisdom Editions, 2016.

King, Julia, *George Hadfield: Architect of the Federal City.* Burlington, VT: Ashgate, 2014.

Kite, Elizabeth S. *L'Enfant and Washington, 1791–1792.* New York: Arno Press, 1970.

Kohler, Sue A., and Jeffrey R. Carson. *Massachusetts Avenue Architecture.* Vol. 2. Washington, DC: Commission of Fine Arts, 1975.

———. *Sixteenth Street Architecture.* Vol. 1. Washington, DC: Commission of Fine Arts, 1978.

———. *Sixteenth Street Architecture.* Vol. 2. Washington, DC: Commission of Fine Arts, 1988.

Kohler, Sue, and Pamela Scott, eds. *Designing the Nation's Capital: The 1901 Plan for Washington, D.C.* Washington, DC: US Commission of Fine Arts, 2006.

Kousoulas, Claudia D., and George W. Kousoulas. *Contemporary Architecture in Washington, D.C.* New York: John Wiley & Sons, 1995.

Leavengood, Ted. *Clark Griffith: The Old Fox of Washington Baseball.* Jefferson, NC: McFarland, 2014.

Leech, Margaret. *Reveille in Washington, 1860–1865.* New York: Harper & Brothers, 1941.

Leon, Carol Boyd. "The Life of American Workers in 1915." US Bureau of Labor Statistics. February 2016. https://www.bls.gov/opub/mlr/2016/article/the-life-of-american -workers-in-1915.htm.

Lessoff, Alan. *The Nation and Its City: Politics, "Corruption," and Progress in Washington, D.C., 1861–1902.* Baltimore: Johns Hopkins University Press, 1994.

Levey, Bob, and Jane Freundel. *Washington Album: A Pictorial History of the Nation's Capital.* Washington, DC: Washington Post Books, 2000.

Lewis, Arnold. *The Opulent Interiors of the Gilded Age.* New York: Dover, 2016.

Logan, Cameron. *Historic Capital: Preservation, Race, and Real Estate in Washington, D.C.* Minneapolis: University of Minnesota Press, 2017.

Logan, Mrs. John A. *Reminiscences of a Soldier's Wife.* New York: Charles Scribner's Sons, 1913.

———, ed. *Thirty Years in Washington, or Life and Scenes in Our National Capital.* Hartford, CT: A. D. Worthington, 1901.

Long, David F. *Nothing Too Daring: A Biography of Commodore David Porter, 1780–1843.* Annapolis, MD: US Naval Institute Press, 1970.

Longstreth, Richard, ed. *Housing Washington: Two Centuries of Residential Development and Planning in the National Capital Area.* Chicago: Center for American Places at Columbia College, 2010.

Luebke, Thomas E. *Civic Art: A Centennial History of the U.S. Commission of Fine Arts.* Washington, DC: US Commission of Fine Arts, 2013.

Luria, Sarah. *Capital Speculations: Writing and Building Washington, D.C.* Durham: University of New Hampshire Press, 2006.

MacGregor, Morris, J. *The Emergence of a Black Catholic Community: St. Augustine's in Washington.* Washington, DC: Catholic University of America, 1999.

Mackintosh, Barry. *Rock Creek Park: An Administrative History.* Washington, DC: National Park Service, 1985.

Maddex, Diane. *Historic Buildings of Washington, D.C.* Pittsburgh: Ober Park, 1973.

Marjorie Webster School and Junior College Campus National Register of Historic Places Nomination Form. 2013. https://planning.dc.gov/sites/default/files/dc/sites/op/publication/attachments/Marjorie%20Webster%20Junior%20College%20Historic%20District%20NR.pdf.

Marshall, Bruce T. *Unitarians and Universalists of Washington, D.C.* Charleston, SC: Arcadia, 2010.

"Mausoleum at Halicarnassus." Wikipedia. https://en.wikipedia.org/wiki/Mausoleum_at_Halicarnassus.

McKevitt, Stephen R. *Meridian Hill: A History.* Charleston, SC: The History Press, 2014.

McNeill, Leila. "This Lady Scientist Defined the Greenhouse Effect but Didn't Get the Credit, Because Sexism." *Smithsonian Magazine.* December 5, 2016. https://www.smithsonianmag.com/science-nature/lady-scientist-helped-revolutionize-climate-science-didnt-get-credit-180961291/.

Meister, Maureen. *Architecture and the Arts and Crafts Movement in Boston: Harvard's H. Langford Warren.* Hanover, NH: University Press of New England, 2003.

Miller, Hope Ridings. *Great Houses of Washington, D.C.* New York: Clarkson N. Potter, 1969.

Miller, Richard E. "Mrs. Henderson's Legacy: Roads to Diversity, Adams Morgan Heritage Trail." The Historical Marker Database. March 8, 2009. https://www.hmdb.org/marker.asp?marker=130707.

Mitchell, Henry. *Washington: Houses of the Capital.* New York: Viking, 1982.

Moeller, G. Martin, Jr. *AIA Guide to the Architecture of Washington, D.C.* 5th ed. Baltimore: Johns Hopkins University Press, 2012.

Moldow, Gloria. *Women Doctors in Gilded-Age Washington.* Champaign: University of Illinois Press, 1987.

Moore, Charles, ed. *The Improvement of the Park System of the District of Columbia.* Senate Doc. No. 166, 57th Congress. Washington, DC, 1902.

———. *Washington Past and Present.* New York: The Century Co., 1929.

Moore, Jacqueline M. *Leading the Race: The Transformation of the Black Elite in the Nation's Capital, 1880–1920.* Charlottesville: University Press of Virginia, 1999.

Moore, Joseph West. *Picturesque Washington: Pen and Pencil Sketches.* Providence: J. A. & R. A. Reid, 1887.

Morley, Jefferson. *Snow-Storm in August: Washington City, Francis Scott Key, and the Forgotten Race Riot of 1835.* New York: Nan A. Talese/Doubleday, 2012.

Moskey, Stephen T. *Larz and Isabel Anderson: Wealth and Celebrity in the Gilded Age.* Bloomington, IN: iUniverse, 2016.

Mullendore, Briana. "The Mullan Road: Stagecoaches on the Mullan Road in Montana." *Bill Youngs: An Historian's Webpage—The Mullan Road Project.* http://www.narhist.ewu .edu/mullan_road/additional_essays/stage_coaches.html. Accessed May 28, 2019.

Myer, Donald Beekman. *Bridges and the City of Washington.* Washington, DC: US Commission of Fine Arts, 1974.

National Capital Park and Planning Commission. *Washington Present and Future: A General Summary of the Comprehensive Plan for the National Capital and Its Environs.* Washington, DC, 1950.

Ochsner, Jeffrey. *H. H. Richardson: Complete Architectural Works.* Cambridge: MIT Press, 1982.

O'Conor, John C. *Stopping By: Field Visits to Selected Temples, Gurdwaras, and Centers in Metropolitan Washington, D.C.* Arlington, VA: Unitarian Universalist Church of Arlington, 1998.

O'Gorman, James F., and Henry Handel Richardson. *Living Architecture.* New York: Simon and Schuster, 1997.

O'Toole, Patricia. *The Five of Hearts: An Intimate Portrait of Henry Adams and His Friends, 1880–1918.* New York: Clarkson Potter, 1990.

Olmsted Brothers. *Rock Creek Park, A Report.* December 1918. https://www.nps.gov /parkhistory/online_books/rocr/olmsted_brothers.pdf.

Page, Arthur W., ed. *The World's Work.* Vol. 28. Garden City, NY: Doubleday Page, 1918.

Payne, Daniel A. *History of the African Methodist Episcopal Church.* Nashville: A.M.E. Sunday-School Union, 1891.

Pearlman, Lauren. *Democracy's Capital: Black Political Power in Washington, D.C., 1960s–1970s.* Chapel Hill: University of North Carolina Press, 2019.

Peiss, Kathy. *Zoot Suit: The Enigmatic Career of an Extreme Style.* Philadelphia: University of Pennsylvania Press, 2011.

Porter, David D. *Memoir of Commodore David Porter, of the United States Navy.* Albany: J. Munsell, 1875.

Proctor, John Clagett. *Proctor's Washington.* Washington, DC: private printing, 1949.

———, ed. *Washington Past and Present: A History.* Vol. 2. New York: Lewis Historical Publishing, 1930.

Prout, Jerry. "Hope, Fear, and Confusion: Coxey's Arrival in Washington." In *Washington History,* Vol. 25. Washington, DC: Historical Society of Washington, DC, 2013.

Reiff, Daniel D. *Washington Architecture, 1791–1861: Problems in Development.* Washington, DC: US Commission of Fine Arts, 1971.

Repak, Terry A. *Waiting on Washington: Central American Workers in the Nation's Capital.* Philadelphia: Temple University Press, 1995.

R.L. Polk Company. *Boyd's Directory of the District of Columbia.* Washington, DC: R. L. Polk, various years.

Roberts, Gladys Scott. Oral history interview with Mara Cherkasky, March 14, 1984. DC Public Library. http://prologuedc.com/blog/wp-content/uploads/2019/10/Gladys -Scott-Roberts-on-move-fr-Meridian-Hill.mp3.

Roberts, Kim. "The Bethel Literary and Historical Society." *Beltway Poetry Quarterly* 11, no. 2 (Spring 2010). https://washingtonart.com/beltway/bethel.html.

Robertson, Charles J. *American Louvre: A History of the Renwick Gallery Building*. Washington, DC: Smithsonian American Art Museum, 2015.

Rothstein, Richard. *The Color of Law: A Forgotten History of How Our Government Segregated America*. New York: W.W. Norton, 2017.

Savage, Kirk. *Monument Wars: Washington, D.C., the National Mall, and the Transformation of the Memorial Landscape*. Los Angeles: University of California Press, 2009.

Schiavo, Laura. "Tifereth Israel Celebrates Centennial." *Washington History* 28, no. 2 (Fall 2016): 66–67.

Schlefer, Marion King. "Washington's Italianate Park on Meridian Hill." In *Washington Renaissance: Architecture and Landscape of Meridian Hill*, by Marion King Schlefer, 29–38. Washington: Meridian International Center, 1989.

Scott, Mel. *American City Planning since 1890*. Berkeley: University of California Press, 1969.

Scott, Pamela, and Antoinette J. Lee. *Buildings of the District of Columbia*. New York: Oxford University Press, 1993.

Seale, William. *The Imperial Season: America's Capital in the Time of the First Ambassadors, 1893–1918*. Washington, DC: Smithsonian Books, 2013.

———. *To Live on Lafayette Square: Society and Politics in the President's Neighborhood*. Washington, DC: White House Historical Association, 2019.

Sefton, Douglas Peter. *District of Columbia Municipal Center National Register of Historic Places Nomination Form*. 2013. https://planning.dc.gov/sites/default/files/dc/sites/op/publication/attachments/Municipal%20Center%20Nomination.pdf.

Shackleton, Robert. *The Book of Washington*. Washington, DC: Penn, 1922.

Smith, Amanda. *Newspaper Titan: The Infamous Life and Monumental Times of Cissy Patterson*. New York: Alfred A. Knopf, 2011.

Smith, Franklin Webster. *The Aggrandizement of Washington*. Senate Doc. No. 209. 56th Congress. Washington, DC, 1900.

Smith, Kathryn Schneider, ed. *Washington at Home: An Illustrated History of Neighborhoods in the Nation's Capital*. 2nd ed. Baltimore: Johns Hopkins University Press, 2010.

Solomon, Burt. *The Washington Century: Three Families and the Shaping of the Nation's Capital*. New York: William Morrow, 2004.

Special Report of the Commissioner of Education on the Condition and Improvement of Public Schools in the District of Columbia. Washington, DC: Government Printing Office, 1871.

Staples, Lawrence C. *Washington Unitarianism: A Rich Heritage*. Washington, DC: All Souls Church, Unitarian, 1970.

Stevens, George T. *Three Years in the Sixth Corps*. 2nd ed. New York: D. Van Nostrand, 1870.

Swerdloff, David. *Crestwood: 300 Acres, 300 Years*. Washington, DC: private printing, 2013.

Tank, Holly. "Dedicated to Art: William Corcoran and the Founding of His Gallery." *Washington History* 17, no. 1 (2005): 26–51.

Tayloe, Benjamin Ogle. *Our Neighbors on La Fayette Square*. Washington, DC, 1872. Reprinted with notes by the Junior League of Washington, 1982.

Taylor, Nancy C., and Sarah Marusin. *Downtown Urban Renewal Area Landmarks, Washington, D.C.* Washington, DC: National Capital Planning Commission, 1970.

"Third Church." *DC Confidential* (blog). http://wdc-confidential.blogspot.com/2008/02 /third-church-of-christ-scientist.html.

Tregoning, Harriet. *Mayor's Agent for Historic Preservation Order: Third Church of Christ, Scientist.* Order 08-141. May 12, 2009. https://committeeof100.net/download/historic _preservation/third_church_of_christ,_scientist/2009-05-13_Mayors_Agent_ %20Decision.pdf.

Urdinola de Bianchi, Lily. *Embassy Residences in Washington, D.C.* Bogotá, Colombia: Villegas Editores, 2003.

US Department of Commerce. *Statistical Abstract of the United States.* Washington, DC: Government Printing Office, various years.

Van Rensselaer, Maria. *Henry Hobson Richardson and His Works.* 1888. Reprint, New York: Dover, 1969.

Waite, Edward, ed. *The Washington Directory and Congressional and Executive Register for 1850.* Washington, DC: Columbus Alexander, 1850. https://archive.org/details /washingtondirectoowait/page/n5/mode/2up.

Walker, Jeri E. *A Guidebook to the House of the Temple: The History, Architecture and Symbolism.* Washington, DC: Supreme Council, 33°, Scottish Rite of Freemasonry, 2015.

Wallace, Jerry L. "No Palace for Cal." *Straight Talk* (Spring 2012). https:// coolidgefoundation.org/wp-content/uploads/2014/06/CCMF_NL_spring_12_web .pdf.

Wallace, Robert, and H. Keith Melton. *Spy Sites of Washington, D.C.: A Guide to the Capital Region's Secret History.* Washington, DC: Georgetown University Press, 2017.

Wann, John L. *A History of the National Baptist Memorial Church, Washington, D.C.* Private printing, 1976.

Williams, Kim. *Lost Farms and Estates of Washington, D.C.* Charleston, SC: The History Press, 2018.

———. "Mrs. Henderson and the Making of 16th Street." Unpublished paper prepared for the National Historic Roads Conference, July 2010.

Williams, Kimberly Prothro. *Strivers' Section Historic District.* Washington, DC: DC Preservation League, 1999.

Winchcole, Dorothy. "The First Baptist Church in Washington, D.C." In *Records of the Columbia Historical Society,* vol. 57/59, 44–57. Washington, DC: Columbia Historical Society, 1957.

Winston, Chriss. *The University Club of Washington, D.C.: One Hundred Years of Fellowship.* Washington, DC: Regnery, 2004.

Wirz, Hans, and Richard Striner. *Washington Deco: Art Deco in the Nation's Capital.* Washington, DC: Smithsonian Institution Press, 1984.

Young, James Sterling. *The Washington Community, 1800–1828.* New York: Columbia University Press, 1966.

Index

About the Authors

JOHN DEFERRARI was born and raised in Washington, DC, and has a lifelong passion for local history. In addition to penning the popular *Streets of Washington* blog (www.streetsof-washington.com), DeFerrari is a trustee of the DC Preservation League and the author of three previous books: *Lost Washington, D.C.* (2011), *Historic Restaurants of Washington, D.C.: Capital Eats* (2013), and *Capital Streetcars: Early Mass Transit in Washington, D.C.* (2015).

DOUGLAS PETER SEFTON came to Washington to attend George Washington University and now considers the area his adoptive home. He has been active in historic preservation since the early 2000s and serves as a trustee of the DC Preservation League. The recipient of a master's degree in architectural history from the University of Virginia, he is the author of *Midcentury Modern Churches of Southwest Washington, D.C.* (2015).